MUSLIM POLITICS

MUSLIM POLITICS

WITH A NEW PREFACE BY THE AUTHORS

Dale F. Eickelman

and

James Piscatori

PRINCETON UNIVERSITY PRESS

PRINCETON AND OXFORD

FIRST PAPERBACK EDITION, 1996

SECOND PAPERBACK EDITION, WITH A NEW PREFACE, 2004

LIBRARY OF CONGRESS CONTROL NUMBER 2004102824

ISBN 0-691-12053-6

BRITISH LIBRARY CATALOGING-IN-PUBLICATION DATA IS AVAILABLE

THIS BOOK HAS BEEN COMPOSED IN PALATINO

PRINTED ON ACID-FREE PAPER. ∞

PUP.PRINCETON.EDU

PRINTED IN THE UNITED STATES OF AMERICA

1 3 5 7 9 10 8 6 4 2

CONTENTS

SIX

Muslim Politics: A Changing Political Geography   136

LIST OF FIGURES

PREFACE TO THE SECOND PAPERBACK EDITION

ONE HAS NEEDED tenacity and courage to speak in recent years about the prospects for public Islam and the "common good" (*al-maslaha al-ʿamma*), a term central to Islamic law and which resonates as strongly as calls to civil society in many parts of the Muslim-majority world. Colombia may still lead the world in the number of deaths directly attributable to terrorism, and Sri Lanka in the number of suicide bombers (Pape 2003), but the events of September 11, 2001, the October 2002 bombings in Bali, the May 2003 "kamikaze" attacks in Saudi Arabia and Morocco, the November 2003 attacks in Riyadh and Istanbul, and the continued bombings and violence elsewhere, including in Jerusalem and Baghdad, test the limits of civility and tolerance. Not all of these bombings are religiously inspired, but many have been, and they have often been staged to achieve maximum global attention. The use by much of the Middle East's Arabic media of the Japanese term *kamikaze*—perhaps the first Japanese word to enter the Arabic vernacular—instead of the words for "martyr" (*shahid*) or "suicide operation" (*ʿamaliyya istishhadiyya*) suggests the reticence to directly confront the issue of whether violent extremists can speak in the name of Islam. In this environment, *Islamikaze*, a term proposed by an Israeli colleague of Moroccan origin (Israeli 2003), is unlikely to catch on.

The reluctance by some state authorities and public intellectuals to directly confront religious and secular violence or to tacitly legitimize it on the grounds that it is a response to massive perceived injustices underscores the challenges that confront the emergence of more open societies in many Muslim-majority countries. Yet these challenges are being met. Thus Indonesia, the world's largest Muslim-majority country, stands out as a nation in which a political force of religious moderates deposed an autocrat in 1998 and organized open and free elections soon after (Hefner 2000).

Religious violence in the name of Islam but conducted by a tiny minority resonates globally, but also deflects attention from long-term developments that are dramatically reshaping the Muslim-majority world. The conjuncture of advancing levels of education, the greater permeability of political borders, and the rise of new communications media has contributed to the emergence of a public sphere throughout the Muslim-majority world in which large numbers of people—and not just an educated, political, and economic elite—want a say in political and religious issues.

The result has been challenges to authoritarianism, the fragmentation of religious and political authority, and increasingly open discussions of issues related to the "common good" and aspirations toward more open societies. At the same time, this trend has been uneven and often contradictory. Thus there are several strands of "Euro-Islam," many of which strongly advocate civility and full participation in the wider civil society dominated by non-Muslims; but within the Muslim-majority countries of the Middle East, as in Africa and Asia, it is often difficult to assess the strength of such voices beyond the confines of an educated and ruling elite. A major element in these debates and confrontations is the role that religious beliefs and values play in thinking about self, society, and politics.

In 1996, when *Muslim Politics* was first published, one could already recognize that the pace and ease of communications had accelerated and the ability to form transnational and global ties had intensified. In the Muslim-majority world, as elsewhere, however, no one had yet realized just how rapidly ideas, images, and practices could be projected into the global public sphere (Eickelman and Anderson 2003). The new media, satellite television, Internet websites, and new uses for older media have contributed both to the fragmentation of political and religious authority and to the projection of voices and visions—some reassuring and others apocalyptic—well beyond what was envisioned in the mid-1990s. Spokespersons legitimized by conventional systems of learning and their means of production increasingly find themselves complemented and even challenged not just by locally rooted understandings of Islam, with which they are familiar, but by rival and alternative articulations of belief and practice. Rising levels of education create audiences for articulating and justifying religious practices that erode older distinctions between "high" and "low" forms of public religious expression.

An important part of the dialogue among Muslims involves new social capital that draws on contemporary intellectual styles and uses different communication technologies to circulate messages and views about what is properly Islamic. These can range from videocassettes—used by the pre–September 11 al-Qaida organization to slickly combine CNN, BBC, and Saudi- and Russian-television video clips with their own CNN-style footage from training camps and "seminars" in Afghanistan—to the standard output of al-Jazeera Satellite Television and competing Arab satellite channels—which has profoundly captured the imagination of large numbers of Arab viewers, offering glimpses of open society and a slant on news and opinion often at variance with the standard fare of CNN, Fox, and local state media.

Prior to the coalition invasion of Iraq in 2003, one of the hottest topics of intellectual debate in the Arab world, reflected as well on al-Jazeera, was "Islam and modernity" (*al-Islam wa-al-hadatha*). Discussions of religion and modernity framed even the widely discussed 2002 (www.undp.org/rbas/ahdr/english2002.html) and 2003 (www.undp.org/rbas/ahdr/english2003.html) Arab Human Development Reports issued by the United Nations Development Program. The fact that such documents are accessible in several languages via the Internet throughout the Arab world and elsewhere also shows the rapidly changing ground rules for public discussion and debate (Gonzalez-Quijano 2003).

The new media that have proliferated since the mid-1990s offer new opportunities for propaganda but also for dialogue. Thus on February 12, 2002, an organization of 60 American intellectuals wrote an open letter, "What We're Fighting For," making the "moral case" for the war on terrorism (www.americanvalues.org/html/follow-up.html) and inviting a dialogue with Muslims. A group of 153 Saudis responded with a letter, "How Can We Coexist?" on May 7, 2002 (www.islamtoday.net). On October 23 of the same year, the American group wrote back. Of marked interest was an al-Qaida direct reply, "Letter to America," which first appeared on an al-Qaida-linked website in Saudi Arabia and which was subsequently made available in English. Although purportedly engaging the Americans in dialogue, the al-Qaida response seemed concerned mainly with the fact that Saudi Arabs were responding to the American letter. Al-Qaida was primarily interested, however, in intra-Arab dialogue (Blankenhorn 2003), seeking to legitimate an expanded Arab and Muslim constituency for itself. In other cases, new media provide a way for religious and political leaders to assert their authority and reasonableness to both followers and the curious. Thus Yusuf al-Qaradawi's website (www.qaradawi.net) appears in many different languages. With the written word, as well as downloadable audio and video clips, it also appeals to different levels of audience, as do the websites of Swiss-based Tariq Ramadan (www.tariq-ramadan.net), the London-based Islam 21 (www.islam21.net), and Hizbullah's Shaykh Fadlallah (www.bayynat.org.lb).

The greater intensity of open communications, combined with higher levels of education, also challenges and confronts local religious ideas and practices long taken for granted and understood as Islamic. It has also led to the increased scrutiny of received ideas as Muslims realize the diversity of the Muslim world and the multiple "Islamic" ways of doing things. New communication technologies play a major role in the foregrounding and questioning of local practices, so that it is not just traditional religious scholars who have a say in debates over how to be a Muslim and live a good life—although such voices remain strong and have more resilience in adapting to the modern world and novel situations than has often been realized in both the Muslim-majority world and elsewhere (Zaman 2002)—but also a much wider public (Bowen 2003; Hefner 2000).

It is also much easier than in the past to sustain contact and continued interaction between diaspora and homeland. Indeed, the greater ease of communication and contact erodes borders and boundaries that previously constituted formidable obstacles. In some contexts, this leads to a greater openness. For example, women can more directly join public discussions about their role in society and participate in public debate over such issues as family law. However in other contexts, the greater ease of communication only reinforces entrenched views and heightens fears of religious and ethnic "others."

Public debates over religion and religious symbols also take highly ironic and contradictory turns. *Muslim Politics* opens with an account of the debate in France in the early 1990s over the wearing of the headscarf, a practice—then as now—followed by only a small minority of students but seen as a threat to the wider French public. Even when, in 1994, the Minister of National Education issued a circular instructing school officials to ban distinctly religious clothing, the Conseil d'État, France's highest administrative body, resolved that the headscarf could be worn provided that it was not disruptive. The decision was left to local authorities, thus averting a possible constitutional crisis and a direct confrontation with Muslims in France. Yet the symbolism of the headscarf, in France as elsewhere, remains powerful. In the name of defending "secular" values, France's president in December 2003 called for its legal ban in state-run schools, thus imposing, in the eyes of many, the view of the state on the Muslim devout ("Religious Symbols" 2003), the very thing that the vaunted separation between church and state in most European countries was supposed to avoid. In contrast, the outright ban on religious clothing in Turkey, long rigidly enforced, is being relaxed as Turkey's public sphere—not without unease—learns to accommodate voices distinctly inspired by religious values (Çinar 2001). Religious groups and attitudes also evolve, sometimes rapidly. Just as Lebanon's Hizbullah moderated earlier positions in order to gain mainstream influence, some of Turkey's religious parties have learned, not without missteps, to embrace political secularism and secure more votes than competing secular parties (White 2002).

Unlike the mid-1990s, it is now possible to use the term "public Islam" (Salvatore and Eickelman 2004) to refer to the highly diverse invocations of Islam—the ideas and practices that religious scholars, self-ascribed religious authorities, secular intellectuals, Sufi orders, mothers, students, workers, engineers, and many others contribute to civic debate and public life. Thinking about Islam makes a difference in configuring the politics and social life of large parts of the globe, and not just for self-ascribed religious authorities. It makes a difference not only as a template for ideas and practices but also as a way of envisioning alternative political realities and, increasingly, of acting on both global and local stages, thus reconfiguring established boundaries of civil and social life.

Such practices and the resulting social spaces involve overlapping circles of communication, solidarity, and the building of bonds of identity and trust. Some of these are based on local communities. Others are geographically widespread and targeted to receptive audiences. One example is the use of e-mail among the Indonesian university students who coordinated nationwide campus protests that contributed to the downfall of President Suharto. These modern practices and new communication technologies create new, effective, and geographically more dispersed bases for effective mobilization—but they can also threaten tolerance and civil society by facilitating publicity and calls to action by extremist groups such as Indonesia's now defunct Laskar Jihad (Hefner 2003).

More so than when this book first appeared, there is a greater recognition of the role of religion in politics and public life in the Muslim-majority world, as elsewhere. Prevailing theories of modernity and modernization in the mid-twentieth century assumed that religious movements, identities, and practice had become increasingly marginal, and that only those religious intellectuals and leaders who attached themselves to the nation-state would continue to play a significant role in public life. These assertions concerning the eclipse of religion in the public life of North America and Europe were exaggerated. Casanova (1994) was one of the first to note that by the late 1970s this prevalent view was challenged by the impact of several parallel developments: the Iranian revolution, the rise of the Solidarity movement in Poland, the role of liberation theology in political movements throughout Latin America, and the return of Protestant fundamentalism as a force in American politics. In the Muslim-majority world, however, the role of religion in social and community life and its public recognition never receded, and it has changed and developed in ways often underemphasized by both Western observers and by Muslims themselves (Zaman 2002).

Muslims participate in crafting the idea of the common good in a variety of ways, and they also contribute to shaping the definitions of wider and more inclusive public goods in societies where Muslims are not a majority, as in Europe; or, as in Syria and Turkey, they are confronted with a profoundly secular elite; or, as in Iran, with an increasingly unpopular, although powerful, clerical elite. In India, Muslims live in a secular state strongly buffeted by religious extremism. Such historically known and contemporary debates argue against efforts to find a single, overarching idea of the common good shared by all Muslim societies, even if some ideologues—both those claiming to represent Islam and those attacking it—make such essentializing claims.

The first edition of *Muslim Politics* anticipated a trend in which what it meant to be Muslim and to live one's life as a Muslim would increasingly become a foregrounded matter of concern for individuals, nations, and for global society, and often a subject of intense public debate involving both Muslims and non-Muslims.

Ideas of just rule, religious or otherwise, are not fixed, even if some radicals claim so. Such notions are debated, argued, often fought about, and re-formed in practice. More so than in the past, these ideas enter domestic space through satellite television and videocassettes, making alternative social realities better understood than in the past, and increasing access to the schoolroom makes the language of religious and political authority less intimidating than before. Recognizing the contours, obstacles, and false starts of these debates, both internal to the different countries of the region and external to them, is a necessary first step to making governance less arbitrary and authoritarian.

The term "network society," first made popular by Manuel Castells (1996) and in common use for just over a decade, encapsulates the rapid spread of new communication technologies, mass education, and the increasing ease of travel—developments that have profound implications for religious belief and practice as well as political and social authority. More important than just the idea of network, however, are the styles and modes of communication that facilitate the formation of new and overlapping forms of community and association. These developments can accelerate the "scaling up" of religious and citizen networks and associations into state and trans-regional institutions. They facilitate the continuing reconstruction of religious and ethnic identities in struggles—more rapid and open than those of past eras—over ideology and authority in which shifting coalitions of elites, counter-elites, ethnic and sectarian groups, and those excluded from local authority structures compete for influence, voice, and recognition.

The advent of the "network society" also creates new possibilities for the "scaling down" of ethnic and sectarian violence—embodying transnational themes into local settings. The fluidity of possibilities of such overlapping and crisscrossing boundaries allows one to question the continuing utility of the term "diaspora" to describe Muslim communities in Europe, North America, and elsewhere. Gilles Kepel (1987) was one of the first to point out that Islam in France had become French Islam for many, indicating the growing embedding of Islamic identity in French society and the intense borrowing by example. Thus an Arabian Peninsula intellectual, Sadek Sulaiman (1998), argues that democracy is fully compatible with Islam and that the American experience of democracy, developed through fits and starts for over two centuries, is the best example available to show committed Muslims elsewhere how they can develop similar institutions in their own countries—motivated by a commitment to Islam.

Muslim Politics seeks to portray the rich diversity of political experience of Muslims in the modern world as they reassess the traditions of faith and authority. This thinking about politics involves competition and contest over both the interpretation of symbols and the control of the formal and informal institutions that produce and sustain them. Politics is thus a struggle over people's imaginations—habits of the mind, the heart, and of public space that help shape people's ideas of the common good—just as much as it is a struggle for control over groups, institutions, states, and resources.

There are signs for optimism. Over a decade ago, Olivier Roy (1994) argued that Islamic radicalism had peaked, an argument also developed by Gilles Kepel, who argues that the terrorism that we have recently witnessed "does not necessarily express the true strength of the movement to which it claims to belong" but is a last attempt to reverse the declining capacity of religious radicals who, in spite of their global networks and technical sophistication, have dramatically failed to achieve wide political mobilization (2002: 19–20). The short term will be painful, but religious liberals, although not in a majority, increasingly find a voice both in the upper reaches of the "network society" and among the vast majority of Muslims who aspire to better lives and more open societies (Browers and Kurzman 2004). *Muslim Politics* remains a timely port of entry to understanding the protagonists, shared moral codes and traditions, and ways in which the boundaries of civic debate and political life in large parts of the world are being informed by many different and contested ways of "being Muslim."

References

Blankenhorn, David. 2003. "Reading an Enemy: Analyzing al-Qaida's *Letter to America.*" www.americanvalues.org/html/reading_an_enemy.html. March 10.

Bowen, John R. 2003. *Islam, Law and Equality in Indonesia: An Anthropology of Public Reasoning.* Cambridge: Cambridge University Press.

Browers, Michaelle, and Charles Kurzman, eds. 2004. *An Islamic Reformation?* Lanham, Md.: Lexington Books.

Casanova, José. 1994. *Public Religion in the Modern World*. Chicago: University of Chicago Press.

Castells, Manuel. 1996. *The Rise of the Network Society*. Oxford: Blackwell.

Çinar, Alev. 2001. "National History as a Contested Site: The Conquest of Istanbul and Islamist Negotiations of the Nation." *Comparative Studies in Society and History* 43, no. 2 (April): 364–91.

Eickelman, Dale F., and Jon W. Anderson, eds. 2003. *New Media in the Muslim World: The Emerging Public Sphere*. 2d ed. Bloomington: Indiana University Press.

Gonzalez-Quijano, Yves. 2003. "The Birth of a Media Ecosystem: Lebanon in the Internet Age," In *New Media in the Muslim World: The Emerging Public Sphere*, 2d ed., edited by Dale F. Eickelman and Jon W. Anderson, pp. 61–79. Bloomington: Indiana University Press.

Hefner, Robert W. 2000. *Civil Islam: Muslims and Democratization in Indonesia*. Princeton: Princeton University Press.

———. 2003. "Civic Pluralism Denied? The New Media and Jihadi Violence in Indonesia." In *New Media in the Muslim World: The Emerging Public Sphere*, 2d ed., edited by Dale F. Eickelman and Jon W. Anderson, pp. 158–79. Bloomington: Indiana University Press.

Israeli, Raphael. 2003. *Islamikaze: Manifestations of Islamic Martyrology*. London: Frank Cass.

Kepel, Gilles. 1987. *Les banlieues de l'Islam*. Paris: Éditions du Seuil.

———. 2002. *Jihad: The Trail of Political Islam*. Cambridge: Harvard University Press.

Pape, Robert A. 2003. "The Strategic Logic of Suicide Terrorism." *American Political Science Review* 97, no. 3 (August): 1–19.

"Religious Symbols in France." 2003. Editorial, *New York Times*, December 20, p. 18.

Roy, Olivier. 1994. *The Failure of Political Islam*. Translated by Carol Volk. Cambridge: Harvard University Press.

Salvatore, Armando, and Dale F. Eickelman, eds. 2004. *Public Islam and the Common Good*. Leiden: Brill.

Sulaiman, Sadek J. 1998. "Democracy and *Shura*." In *Liberal Islam: A Sourcebook*, edited by Charles Kurzman, pp. 96–98. New York: Oxford University Press.

White, Jenny B. 2002. *Islamist Mobilization in Turkey: A Study in Vernacular Politics*. Seattle: University of Washington Press.

Zaman, Muhammad Qasim. 2002. *The Ulama in Contemporary Islam: Custodians of Change*. Princeton: Princeton University Press.

PREFACE

THIS IS A BOOK about how to think about "Muslim politics." A vast amount of literature exists on Islam and politics, and from different perspectives we ourselves have contributed to it. Drawing on that literature, we seek to clarify the meanings of such concepts as tradition, authority, ethnicity, protest, and symbolic space that are inescapably part of the professional inheritance of our disciplines—anthropology and political science—but which often recede into the background of ethnographic or political case studies.

It is thus not a book about the Islamic revival, nor is it a handbook to the politics of individual Muslim societies, much less to the politics of the Middle East. Rather, this book is intended to pose questions about the nature of one kind of politics—similar to but not synonymous with what Michael Mann (1986) calls "ideological politics"—in a variety of regional settings. In the elaboration of such a broadly comparative essay, conventional wisdom will inevitably appear suspect; and fixed, paradigmatic ways of thinking, misleading if not also dangerous.

The term "Muslim politics" is not meant to imply a concentration on self-ascribed religious authorities. The traditionally educated scholars (*ulama*) clearly play a role, but so, too, do lay intellectuals, mothers, government leaders, and musicians. They are the protagonists of the Muslim political drama, not merely because they share normative codes but because they invoke the symbols of those codes to reconfigure the boundaries of civic debate and public life. It is these symbolic politics that account for why political actions and choices are recognizably Muslim, and in this sense "Islam" makes a difference in configuring the politics of a broad swathe of the world.

Yet doctrine, it will be apparent, is of secondary importance. Muslim politics is not predetermined by a template of ideas; it is influenced by a number of factors, which, while including scripturally defined precepts, also include national identities, economic circumstances, and social status. The politics we seek to elucidate possesses a similar profile and parallel functions among both Sunnis and Shi'a, and it follows that the presumption of an engrained sectarian divergence obscures the workings of complex, but common, processes.

Also unhelpful are the customary dichotomies of social analysis—public and private, internal and external, high and low politics. Our intention is not to subvert common sense but to indicate the ways in which such unnuanced sets of contrasting markers deter awareness of the constant interpenetration of social and political networks in the Muslim world. The multiple roles of women may be hidden under the rubric "private," much as transnational concerns over the condition of a Muslim minority may be minimized in viewing the matter as "internal" to one society.

Much of what follows will appear familiar, and in the recognition of the similarity of form and process that Muslim politics shares with other religious traditions, Islam's putative uniqueness may be diminished. Islam is neither especially religio-political, nor particularly hostile to ethnic and cultural variations. It is neither unprecedentedly revolutionary, nor abnormally resistant to nationalism. Such demystification of Islam will simultaneously afford—for both academics and policymakers—more subtle understandings of Muslim politics and less alarmist views of an "Islamic threat."

Any book that draws upon materials in Arabic, Bangla, Malay, Persian, Turkish, and Urdu, among other languages, poses considerable problems of transliteration, especially as we must incorporate colloquial as well as literary usages. With as much consistency as possible, we use the system for consonants adopted by the *International Journal of Middle East Studies* for Arabic, Persian, and Turkish. Diacritics are omitted, but we use ʿ to represent the ʿayn, as in daʿwa, and ʾ to represent the hamza, as in Qurʾan. We drop the terminal hamza from words such as ʿulama. The plural of words in languages that have "broken" plurals is formed by adding an "s" to the singular, except in cases such as ʿulama, in which the transliterated plural form has become standard. When persons or writers are known to have a preferred spelling of their name in a European language, we generally use this form.

We are grateful to a number of people who have helped us with the preparation and production of this book. Christine Eickelman, Deborah Hodges, and Moorhead Wright commented on all or parts of the manuscript. Tamara Chalabi, Sophie Claudet, Jeneen DiBenedetto, Jane Langdell, and Riva Richmond were our assistants at various points in the past several years and facilitated our research and the preparation of the manuscript. Nancy Fenton provided efficient cartographic assistance, and Lesley Yorke copyedited the manuscript with unusual care and sensitivity. Brigadier Malcolm Dennison, Her Majesty's Lord Lieutenant of Orkney, offered us an exceptional working environment on several occasions, access to an impressive personal library, and steady encouragement.

We are also happy to acknowledge the generosity of the Claire Gar- ber Goodman Fund for the Anthropological Study of Human Culture at Dartmouth College. This grant made it possible for coauthors to bridge the distance between New England and Wales. The Vice-Princi- pal's Research Fund of the University of Wales, Aberystwyth, pro- vided further travel assistance.

MUSLIM POLITICS

1

WHAT IS MUSLIM POLITICS?

Controlling Symbols

I N FRANCE in 1989, a controversy erupted over female students
wearing the traditional Muslim headscarf in public schools. Five
girls who insisted on wearing them were barred from attending
classes. "By nature," the school principal argued, "the scarf was a sign
of proselytism and exercised pressure on other Moslem girls who did
not wear scarves" (Cody 1989; David 1992). By law, public schooling
in France has been secular since 1905, yet the families of the girls argued that their beliefs made the practice of "Islamic" dress obligatory.
After nationwide public controversy, the Conseil d'État (Council of
State), the country's highest administrative body, resolved that headscarves could be worn as long as there was no pressure exercised on
other students to do so. Each school could decide whether the wearing
of the headscarf was disruptive. But the government was so concerned
about the larger question of Muslim integration into French life that—
in part as a result of this incident—it formally, though perhaps only
outwardly, adjusted state policy by creating pertinent public agencies.
In 1989, it formed the Conseil de Réflexion sur l'Islam en France (Ad-
visory Council on Islam in France), and in March 1990 it created a separate committee to combat racism.[1]

Many French saw the wearing of the headscarf as a direct challenge
to French national values, and so the controversy continued to sim-
mer. In November 1993, eight months after a change of government,
the principal of a primary school in the eastern French town of Nantua
suspended four Muslim girls of Turkish and Moroccan origin for
wearing headscarves. The local Turkish *imam*, who had only arrived
from Germany two weeks previously and did not speak French, declared that "God's law takes precedence over French law" (Guigon
1993). The Ministry of the Interior deported the *imam*, and *Le Monde*
reported that the "silent majority" of moderate Turks in Nantua and
neighboring towns, where they constituted 25 percent of the population, were "pleased" with the expulsion because it would ease local
tensions (Guigon 1993). On September 10, 1994, the French Minister of
National Education, François Bayrou, sharpened the controversy in
a circular instructing school officials to ban distinctly religious clothing (Bayrou 1994). By early November, however, the vice-president of
the Conseil d'État responded that the September circular from the

Minister of Education had no legal force, so that school directors could continue, as the Conseil advised in 1989, "to make their own decisions" ("Express politique" 1994).[2] According to one poll, 86 percent of French were against authorizing wearing of the headscarf at schools. Nonetheless, the Conseil d'État upheld the right of students to do so. In late 1993, a conservative government, antagonistic to the idea of multiculturalism and concerned about integration of Muslims into French life, encouraged school authorities to adopt restrictive dress codes that would ban the headscarf in schools.

Similarly in Egypt, veiling has taken on political significance. Although Egypt is a state with a Muslim majority that has led Muslim opinion worldwide, in the late 1980s, the Egyptian authorities came to regard veiling as an act of defiance against the largely secular ideology that they wished to promote. Accordingly, they barred Muslim women with veils or headscarves from university precincts. In the mid-1990s, officials at some Egyptian universities continued to ban female students and professors from wearing *niqab*, which covers all of a woman's body, including her face. Defending use of the veil, some religious leaders answered that forcing women to unveil weakens them and leads to immorality ('Isa 1992; see also, Hedges 1993). It is worth recalling that Egyptian women were legally obliged to unveil in 1923, although the law has rarely been enforced (Guindi 1981; Ayubi 1991:241).

Both the French and Egyptian examples illustrate "Muslim politics." Veiling is not inherently a political act, but, rather it becomes one when it is transformed into a public symbol. A dialectical relationship between individuals and the government assures this production. Women don the veil for a variety of reasons and in spite of the government's desires, and the government's responses to the veiling further ensure that it is no longer a private, inconsequential act. A symbol has been created and now is integral to the identity and aspirations of groups of like-minded individuals as well as to the self-defined mission of the authorities. These examples, then, are *political* in part because they involve challenges to the limits of state authority but also because they involve a contest over people's understandings of and wishes for social order. The examples are *Muslim* because they relate to a widely shared, although not doctrinally defined, tradition of ideas and practice. As we shall see throughout this book, the forms of political contest and discourse as well as the meanings of traditions vary widely, but a constant across the Muslim world is the invocation of ideas and symbols, which Muslims in different contexts identify as "Islamic," in support of their organized claims and counterclaims.

Muslims everywhere, both in Muslim majority countries and elsewhere, are so increasingly aware of their global presence that individuals and groups in Europe, North America, Russia, and elsewhere have a heightened consciousness of forming part of a world community and use this awareness to amplify their voice and political strength (see fig. 1). At times some Muslims resort to violence to advance their goals, as the November 1979 attack on the Grand Mosque in Mecca and the 1981 assassination of Egypt's President Sadat indicate. Such groups in Egypt and Algeria, in particular, have continued to threaten state officials, intellectuals, journalists, and foreigners with kidnapping or assassination in the hope of forcing governments to make strategic concessions. Yet other Muslim groups in such countries as Jordan, Egypt, Pakistan, and Malaysia call for democratization, thus indicating that Muslims can use existing political systems to reflect their political views and pressure governments to reform.

Rulers, for their part, routinely invoke Islamic imagery and ideas to legitimize their rule and to defend themselves against Muslim critics. At the time of the French invasion of Egypt in 1798, Napoleon attempted to use Islamic symbolism to win indigenous support for his rule. Although the effort was unsuccessful in the end, it was not for lack of enthusiasm. His proclamation to the people of Egypt began with the standard Muslim invocation of "God, the Merciful, the Compassionate," and he went on to say: "I worship God (may He be exalted) far more than the Mamlukes do, and respect His Prophet and Glorious Quran . . . [T]he French also are sincere Muslims" (cited in Hourani 1970:30). Nearly two centuries later, shortly after the August 1990 Iraqi invasion of Kuwait, King Hussein (b. 1935, r. 1953–) addressed the Jordanian parliament. After describing U.S. plans to break up Iraq into spheres of influence, he told the deputies that "if they wanted to honor him they should call him Sharif Hussein," a title which stressed both his descent from the Prophet and his great-grandfather's commitment to Arab unity and protection of Islam's holy places (Layne 1994:26–27, 37).

Imagining Politics

Muslim politics involves the competition and contest over both the interpretation of symbols and control of the institutions, formal and informal, that produce and sustain them. The interpretation of symbols is played out against the background of an underlying framework that, while subject to contextualized nuances, is common to Muslims throughout the world. Evolving doctrinal considerations, it should be noted, are only one factor among many that contribute to the creation

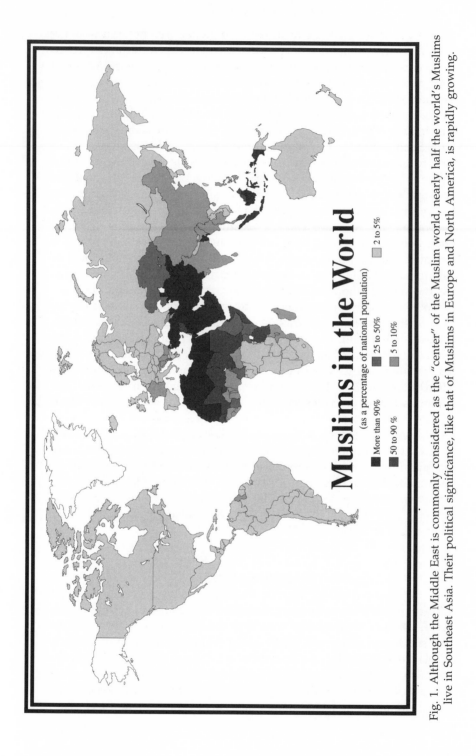

Muslims in the World

(as a percentage of national population)

■ More than 90%   ■ 25 to 50%   ■ 2 to 5%
■ 50 to 90 %   ■ 5 to 10%

Fig. 1. Although the Middle East is commonly considered as the "center" of the Muslim world, nearly half the world's Muslims live in Southeast Asia. Their political significance, like that of Muslims in Europe and North America, is rapidly growing.

of this framework. A political system, whether in the Muslim world or elsewhere, inevitably involves the management of competing, even clashing, interests. Indeed, the authoritative allocation of resources and the demarcation of boundaries are integral to the political process, but are not the whole of it. "Who gets what, when and how" (Lasswell [1935] 1965:3) and the division between political and nonpolitical spheres of activity are only part of the larger equation. They make sense only when the dichotomizations common to political analysis— "high" and "low" politics, "public" and "private"—are qualified by a recognition of the interpenetrating networks that evolve in the social and political life of Muslims (compare Mann 1986:1–33). For example, as Chapter 4 will argue, because the family is so valued in the Muslim world, it is not surprising that, even among those not in the elite, economic and social relations are often organized around it. The religious and moral meanings invested in the family also provide a standard by which individuals may assess whether their governments and other social groups fit into the larger moral, and Islamic, order.

There is a tendency to put the struggle for power at the heart of politics (Morgenthau 1961:27, 39). Political scientists have long conceptualized power in this way, but a major tradition in anthropology has also seen the "command of organized force" or, in "stateless" societies, "a distribution of the command of force" as central to politics (Fortes and Evans-Pritchard 1940:14–15; compare Caton 1987). But politics, including in the Muslim world, is not simply concerned with established authority compelling obedience. As other theorists have argued, politics may have as much, if not more, to do with bargaining among several forces or contending groups as with compulsion. Gibbins (1989: 5–6) points out that conservative philosophers such as Wittgenstein and Oakeshott conceptualize politics, at least implicitly, as public negotiation over the rules and discourse that morally bind the community together.

Even game and collective goods theories, influenced by the contributions of both strategists and economists, appear at first to reaffirm the need for a coercive political apparatus, but in the end, they place structured, high-stakes negotiation at the core of politics. Without the restraining and punitive hand of the state, they argue that individuals or groups are likely to remain "free riders," concerned only with their own self-interest. Coercion is thus necessary to induce cooperation. Yet, what passes for coercion is really an urgent attempt by political authorities to persuade the citizen to forego selfishness, with the promise that everyone else will be required to make a similar sacrifice (Stein 1990:32–36).[3] Although game and collective goods theories can be faulted for placing too great an emphasis on the rationality of members of society, they illuminate how political authorities must cajole and bargain, as well as suppress and punish.

Societies, whether European industrial democracies, Third World developing countries, or bedouin tribal communities, are comprised of an often complex balance of forces. These forces may take the form of political parties and labor unions, or of military and professional associations, ethnic and religious minorities, and prominent families. While it is true that the highest decision-making body—a parliament, oligarchic elite, ruling junta, or tribal council—often imposes its will and enforces decisions on subordinates, the use of force may sometimes be counterproductive, risking greater instability than is already present. For the sake of collective order, authorities must often mediate differences among various groups in society. They may even find themselves in the position of needing to negotiate social, economic, or political policy with ostensibly subordinate groups (see Soysal 1994).

The French response to the headscarf dispute indicates the shortcomings of assuming that politics can be reduced to the use of legitimate force or the allocation of material "interests." Had the government in 1989 defined the wearing of the headscarf as a challenge to the legal principle of secular education, it would have run the risk of precipitating a major domestic crisis. Muslims constitute over 5 percent (some 4 million persons) of France's population (Chirac 1995; also see Kepel 1987:13). They do not constitute a cohesive political bloc, and the majority of French Muslims did not support demands for the wearing of the headscarf at school. However, the demands of a vocal minority precipitated a political problem for the majority of Muslims in France as well as for the state. Some Muslims saw this debate as the catalyst for the vigorous enforcement of French immigration policies that followed. French policymakers, moreover, saw their response to the headscarf issue as potentially threatening France's relations with some Muslim states: A ban could have affected adversely France's international relations. At home, the government's response brought about a confrontation with a significant number of French Muslims, and it may have intensified debates, fostered by right-wing nationalists such as Jean-Marie Le Pen, as to whether Muslims can be fully integrated into French society.

The fact that the succeeding French government took a more confrontational approach in 1993 does not mean that the fear of adverse reaction, at home and abroad, was without substance. Rather, Muslim protest, including violent protest, at what are regarded as officially tolerated inequities and injustices has not been absent in France, and all governments have had to recognize the limits of confrontation. In Turkey, Indonesia, Britain, and Germany, authorities have reacted very differently to the politically and religiously charged issue of wearing headscarves or veils. In each of these cases, the outcome has usually been a face-saving compromise and an absence of "definitive" rulings to forestall direct challenges to the limits of state authority. In all cases, the headscarf issue exemplifies the struggle to control and interpret symbols integral to Muslim politics.

Political interests, whether of the state or other groups, can never be defined as solely material. As Max Weber points out, socially defined values play an important role in formulating the identities and goals of individuals and collectivities: "As a separate structure, a political community can be said to exist only if, and in so far as, a community constitutes more than an 'economic group'; or, in other words, in so far as it possesses value systems ordering matters other than the directly economic disposition of goods and services" (Weber 1968:902). These values, constitutive of a political community, are expressed in symbolic forms.

Symbols are signs that point to values, and often—although not always—these symbols are expressed in language. Sometimes they are expressed in images as well as language. The interconnection of values, symbols, and languages has a powerful effect: "Jointly shared symbolic expressions which are articulated through languages are the means of socialization and create a social bond between individuals and groups, since the roles and social relations available in society are transmitted through language" (Pekonen 1989:132).

The idea of politics as centered on power relations and "interests" alone clearly does not take account of cooperative relations among individuals in a society or between societies that are based on what they think is right, just, or religiously ordained (Cerny 1990: 17–18). Kyösti Pekonen's definition of politics as "a struggle about people's imaginations" (Pekonen 1989:132) is a corrective to some conventional thinking. More broadly, politics can be conceived as competition and struggle over the meanings of symbols (for example, Geertz 1973:193–233) and control of the institutions that define and articulate social values. As Immanuel Wallerstein argues, power resides not only in the possession of economic resources but also "in the control of cultural institutions" (Wallerstein 1983:34). Politics as Leviathan is thus transformed into politics as symbol maker.

In this regard, David Easton's (1965:50) definition of politics as "the authoritative allocation of values" is unhelpful because the qualifier "authoritative" overstates the extent to which a consensus on values exists, and "allocation" overstates the degree to which consensus is maintained from above. Clive Kessler's analysis of politics in Malaysia illustrates how values are not simply allocated and how state control of symbolic power is not always unchallenged. Values and symbols acquire focal political significance in ways that are not always predictable: "The symbolic is not a residual dimension of purportedly real politics; still less is it an insubstantial screen upon which real issues are cast in pale and passive form. The symbolic is real politics, articulated in a special and often most powerful way" (Kessler 1978:244–45).

Symbolism in politics may reduce spatial separations or emphasize temporal connections. In September 1993, Palestinians in Khartoum who were connected with Hamas (Harakat al-Muqawama al-Islamiyya), the Palestine-based Islamic resistance movement, protested against the accord between the Palestine Liberation Organization (PLO) and Israel over the Gaza strip and Jericho. Their protest, in a main public square, centered around a scale model of Jerusalem's Dome of the Rock. This symbolism affirmed that any agreement had to take into account the views of Palestinians in the diaspora, such as themselves, and had to be based on the liberation of all Palestinian land, including Jerusalem (BBC SWB ME/1796 MED/6, September 17, 1993). On December 16, 1994, the seventh anniversary of the founding of Hamas, members of the group in Gaza, which several months earlier had kidnapped an Israeli soldier, reenacted before a crowd of thousands the Israeli raid in which the hostage was killed. The public performance, which dramatized the threat of further action, visibly reaffirmed the continuity of the struggle.

The cult that is rapidly developing around the tomb of Ayatullah Khomeini in Iran illustrates how symbolic politics "become real." After Khomeini's death on June 3, 1989, Iranians and other Shi'i Muslims began to regard his tomb at the Behesht-e Zahra cemetery south of Tehran as a place of pilgrimage (*ziyara*) nearly equal in importance to the tombs of the twelve Shi'i Imams. According to the Islamic Republic News Agency ("Frenzy of Grief", 1990), "more than eight million" pilgrims from South Asia, the Soviet Union, and Iran assembled at the cemetery in 1990 on the first anniversary of the Ayatullah's death. In addition to the traditional expressions of mourning, pilgrims shouted political slogans such as "Death to America" (*marg bar Amrika*). They also used the occasion to acclaim Khomeini's successor, Ayatullah 'Ali Khamene'i (b. 1940), the "guide" (*mawlay*) of the revolution .

Visits to the tomb had become so popular by the second anniversary of Khomeini's death that the occasion was transformed into a national political rally.[4] Iran's president, 'Ali Akbar Hashemi Rafsanjani (b. 1934), invoked Khomeini's calls for Islamic unity and warned Iranians that the achievements of the revolution would be endangered if they became politically divided. Ayatullah Khamene'i, for his part, addressed foreign-policy aspects of the Islamic movement (BBC SWB, ME/1090/A10, June 5, 1991, and ME/1091/A4, June 6, 1991). He indicated that he was in ill health but "could not stop myself from being with you on such a day and in such a gathering." In September 1993, Ayatollah Khomeini's son, Ahmad, used the occasion of a Revolutionary Guards ceremony at his father's tomb to denounce the "shameful treachery" of the Israeli-PLO accord (BBC SWB ME/1796 MED/18, September 17, 1993). The tomb has been invested with such central political significance that, contrary to what might have seemed appropriate in light of the late Khomeini's asceticism, green Italian marble now adorns it.[5]

As this example suggests, the symbolic component of politics is especially significant because it can be used as an instrument of persuasion as well as coercion. Bargaining models of politics suggest that persuasion, rather than force, is increasingly considered to be the basis of politics. Steven C. Caton makes this point in the context of Middle Eastern tribal settings: "[W]hen one examines the ethnographic record to determine what it is that Middle Eastern tribesmen are doing in political acts, one finds that they are talking to each other probably more than they are fighting . . . with the consequent or attendant belief that the basis of power is *persuasion* rather than the exercise of force" (1987:89; emphasis in original).

The Language of Politics

In the case of Muslim societies, like others, persuasion is largely an act of speech, and the symbolic and persuasive dimension to politics has become virtually synonymous with the politics of language. It is now commonplace to argue that language is a social and political practice, and that the way we use language is intimately related to how we construct communal identities and promote and defend our aspirations (for example, Shapiro 1984:8; Habermas 1981:397). Never neutral in itself, language may be used to affirm or reaffirm hierarchies of power. In the world of psychiatric care, for example, psychiatrists grow "angry," but patients become "aggressive"; nurses "daydream," but the hospitalized "withdraw" (Edelman 1984:49). Language may also be used to subvert existing hierarchies, as when Margaret Thatcher, both in opposition and in office, undermined the postwar social welfare consensus in Britain by identifying "freedom" and "efficiency" with the free market; the public sector was "tyrannical" and "inefficient" (Kellner 1988). Finally, language can take on unintended meanings, leading to unforeseen consequences. For example, the concept of "people's democracies" in the former Eastern bloc was a thinly disguised attempt to endow a form of legitimacy on dynastic and one-party tyrannies. Yet, as conditions changed, the concept had the ironic effect of legitimizing the revolutionaries who brought down the old order.

In the case of the Muslim world, rulers such as Sadat in Egypt and Hassan II (b. 1929, r. 1961–) in Morocco have legitimized the existing political hierarchy by referring to themselves as "the President-Believer" (al-ra'is al-mu'min) and the "commander of the faithful" (amir al-mu'minin) respectively. Conversely, critics of those in power can help to delegitimize established authorities by denouncing them as "infidel" (kafir) or "ignorant [of Islam]" (jahil). Muslim activist groups in Egypt, for instance, have pronounced Egypt the "land of unbelief" (dar al-kufr) because of the "un-Islamic" ways of the government and society. Finally, as noted above, language can evade the control of those who use it and take on unanticipated connotations. When, for example, the Kuwaiti royal family sought to validate its rule by endorsing the tribal and Islamic idea of "consultation" (shura), it encouraged expectations of participatory politics. Yet the dissolution of the National Assembly in 1976 and 1986 and the postponement of elections in the immediate wake of the 1990–91 Gulf crisis frustrated these expectations and cast the regime in a harsh and critical light.

It is not an exaggeration to say, as have several scholars (for example, Vatin 1982:221–50), that "Islam" constitutes the language of politics in the Muslim world. Although multiple interpretations can exist, Islam is a relatively stable type of expression and thus constitutes a discursive but culturally specific genre of politics (Bakhtin 1981:47; compare Bayart 1991:64). As the examples cited above indicate, the Islamic vocabulary contains words of undoubted political resonance, and a review of their historical development helps to explain their durable attraction (for example, Lewis 1988). Yet it would be misleading to conclude that the political language of Islam is simply composed of terms used in a predictable manner or to see these terms as possessing uniform relevance to political and social action. Rather, Islamic political language requires a broader conceptualization.

If, as we have just indicated, Islam may be thought to constitute the language of politics, there is also a "politics of language" in the Islamic world that must be taken into account (Piscatori 1990:771–74). This added perspective points to the variable usage of language, suggesting that the utility of Islamic terminology to both rulers and opponents is enhanced in times of upheaval and stress. It also depicts an Islamic language that is more than simply a vocabulary. In addition to socially defined words, this language is made up of both symbols and media-tors—those who modify and rework the symbols in specific circum-stances and for particular purposes (compare Habermas 1981:54, 70–72, 95–96; Derrida 1974). ʿAli Shariʿati (1933–77) captures this point:

> The language of religion, and particularly the language of the Semitic religions, in whose prophets we believe, is a symbolical language. By this we mean a language which expresses meaning through images and sym-bols—the most excellent and exalted of all the languages that men have ever evolved. . . . A simple and straightforward language, one deprived of all symbol and image, may be easier for purposes of instruction, but it has no permanence. (Shariʿati 1979:71)

The mediators of the language of Muslim politics include traditional, *madrasa*-educated religious intellectuals and the increasingly promi-nent "new" religious intellectuals who have emerged from modern state or secular schooling, as is the case for most Muslim activists, or who have had experience with both styles of education. Shariʿati him-self exemplifies the mixing of educational styles.[6]

Saddam Hussein's invocation of Islamic symbolism and terminol-ogy in the Gulf crisis of 1990–91 is instructive. As leader of the Arab Baʿth Socialist Party, with its commitment to secularism and Arab so-cialism and its policy of repression of Islamic groups in Iraq, Saddam would have been expected to frame his appeals for support in the lan-guage of anti-imperialism rather than Islam. Yet he pointedly referred to the "infidels" of the West arrayed against him and called for *jihad* (holy war) to combat them. His audience was aware of his poor Islamic credentials, and there is little evidence to suggest that the invocation of such concepts automatically aroused sympathy or instinctively rallied support for him.

In fact, there was considerable feeling in much of the Muslim world that Saddam was, at best, an opportunist and, at worst, a hypocrite. However, when Western troops went to Saudi Arabia, Saddam found a receptive audience for his anti-Western and anti-Saudi rhetoric. Words such as *jihad* do not automatically engender social and political action, but they acquire specific meanings in the context in which they are applied. The context in this case was that "infidel" troops on Ara-bian soil had exposed the Saudi monarch, the "Servant of the Two Holy Places" (*khadim al-haramayn*), to the charge that he was consort-ing with the infidels and, by extension, with their "natural" allies, the Israelis. The linkages among the House of Saʿud, the United States, and Israel are graphically represented in figure 2, the cover of *Saffah al-Saʿudiyya* [The bloodletter of Saudi Arabia] (al-Nafiʿ 1993), a multi-

Fig. 2. Anti-Saudi caricatures, often sponsored by Iranian and Iraqi groups, were common prior to the 1990–91 Gulf war, but they proliferated thereafter. This is the cover of a 1993 anti-Saudi book.

colored representation of a bloody dagger, with an American flag on its handle, suspended over a map of Saudi Arabia and the Arabian peninsula. A benignly smiling King Fahd (b. 1920, r. 1982–) hovers over the map, sporting a Star of David in his *'iqal*, the rope-like band that holds his headcloth (*ghutra*) in place.

Saddam received a sympathetic hearing when he asked why his troops should withdraw from Arab land when the Israelis continued to occupy Palestine, including Jerusalem. It was seen partly as a matter of justice, but Muslim interest in Jerusalem was also at work. Islamic tradition holds that the Prophet Muhammad was transported to Jerusalem in a "night journey" (al-isra'), and in a second journey (mi'raj), he ascended to heaven where, at the throne of Allah, he learned the proper manner of prayer. The al-Aqsa mosque, mentioned in the Qur'an (17:1), and the Dome of the Rock commemorate this special relationship between the Prophet and Jerusalem. After Mecca and Medina, it is the third holiest city of Islam, and Palestine has become one of Islam's holy lands.

Saddam was able to draw a link between the Israeli occupation of Palestine and the supposed Western occupation of Saudi Arabia, the land containing the holy cities of Mecca and Medina where the Prophet lived and died: "Oh, Arabs, oh, Muslims and believers every-where, this is your day to rise and defend Mecca, which is captured by the spears of the Americans and the Zionists. . . . Keep the foreigner away from your holy shrines" (cited in Brinkley 1990:14). The call fell on receptive ears, partly because of the unpopularity of the oil-rich Gulf monarchies, which, to many less wealthy Muslims, appeared corrupt and arrogant. The Muslim Brotherhood in Jordan, which was agitating for greater influence in the Jordanian political system, in February 1991 called on Muslims "to purge the holy land of Palestine and Najd and Hijaz [provinces of Saudi Arabia] from the Zionists and imperialists" (Milton-Edwards 1991b:98).

The rhyming slogans used in Moroccan street demonstrations, moreover, revealed popular sentiment against Saudi Arabia and the perceived linkage between Saudi Arabia and Israel. Referring to the Saudi monarch and his guardianship of the Ka'ba, the shrine in Mecca that is the focal point of the hajj (pilgrimage), one crowd chant was "Fahd, Fahd, ya humar, ba'ti l-Ka'ba bil-dular" [Fahd, Fahd, O donkey, you sold the Ka'ba for a dollar]. Another slogan, invoking Iraqi missile names that possessed religious and historical resonance, affirmed that Jews and the Saudi dynasty were the common enemy: "Al-'Abbas li-l-yahud, wa-l-Husayn li-s-Sa'ud" [The 'Abbas (missile) to the Jews, and the Husayn to the (house of) Sa'ud]. Even among Muslims in China, some believed that the dispatch of Western troops was the latest sign of the Saudi regime's un-Islamic character (Gladney 1994b:686).

When Saddam said that the Saudis, by allowing Western troops on their soil, were effectively in league with the Israelis, he drew together powerfully related symbols of Muslim politics: the sanctity of the two Muslim holy lands of Arabia and Palestine and Saddam, the new Saladin, as the restorer of Islamic rule over these sacred places.[7] Many Muslims responded to Iraqi rhetoric in part because the direct intru-sion of Western forces to Arabia seemed threatening to Islam. They also responded because their affiliation with institutions and groups, such as the Muslim Brotherhood and other voluntary religious associations, helped to articulate and heighten the potency of the symbolism at a time when their governments were often constrained to adopt ambiguously pro-Western positions.

As the second Gulf War suggests, Muslim politics becomes incomprehensible if the symbolism and shared assumptions of Muslims are disregarded. There is an implicit consciousness of common notions—an underlying framework of language, ideas, and values which, while not always self-evident or explicitly expressed, becomes apparent when the shared assumptions are violated or attacked. A striking feature of the Rushdie affair, in which Ayatullah Khomeini condemned a British novelist to death in 1989 for having written a "blasphemous" novel, was the near unanimity of outrage at the perceived defamation of the Prophet among Muslims of widely varying backgrounds and political opinion. Similarly, as we have pointed out, state authorities in Algeria, Indonesia, Turkey, China, Egypt, France, the Soviet Union, and elsewhere have inadvertently stimulated Muslim self-consciousness by disregarding sensitivity on issues such as marriage rites and the use of headscarves in public.

Doctrine and Political Action

Doctrine plays a part in such reactions but is not decisive by itself. When we say that politics is "Muslim," we do not mean to imply that doctrine invariably motivates action. Indeed, there are two reasons why the relationship between doctrine and practice is more complicated. First, the permanence of doctrine itself is a conceptual fiction. Established religious hierarchies, wishing to promote their own interests as "defenders of the faith," suggest that divinely inspired or sanctioned principles are by nature fixed and universally applicable. However, like all religious traditions, Islamic principles must be constantly reinterpreted. The result is a flexibility of ideas and divergence over time and space. As Brinkley Messick says of the distinction between the divinely ordained *shariʿa* and interpretations of it: "In this gap between divine plan and human understanding [lies] the perennially fertile space of critique, the locus of an entire politics located in the idiom of the shariʿa" (1993:17).

The Islamic notion of *zakat* (almsgiving) is an example. There is little agreement other than using it for humanitarian or charitable purposes: The Qurʾan encourages Muslims to spend their *mal* (wealth) "out of love for Him, for your kin, for the needy, for the wayfarer, for those who ask, and for the ransom of slaves" (2:177). Some Muslims argue that it is a voluntary act of faith; others argue that it is obligatory. Some contend that it is to be collected by the central government, as in Pakistan, where it was instituted along with the Islamic punishments of flogging and the amputation of limbs to bolster the regime's legitimacy through its commitment to "Islamization" (Novossyolov 1993). Islamic associations such as the Muslim Brotherhood in Egypt sometimes levy *zakat* on their members (Mitchell 1969:275). An indication of the degree to which doctrine is malleable is the specific political use of *zakat* in a resolution of the Organization of the Islamic Conference (1981:699). It endorses the collection of *zakat* to support the work of the Palestine Liberation Organization, rather than, for example, to support Palestinian widows, orphans, and refugees as might be expected. In the West Bank, Hamas receives money from *zakat* committees to support its poorer members and social welfare activities. The expenditures strengthen support for the movement (Milton-Edwards 1991a:278).

Similarly, doctrine proves to be flexible in the case of *waqf*s (pious endowments). The protests of some *ʿulama* notwithstanding, the Pakistani state, like many governments elsewhere, has appropriated to itself the administration of the endowments, thereby enhancing its identification with Islam. It effectively creates a state monopoly over the doctrine and its interpretation (Malik 1990).

Doctrinal change, like all change, is complex and is often tied to rearrangements in political structures (see Cerny 1990:4). Moreover, actors always have alternative political visions available and the need to articulate them. An important component, therefore, of understanding politics is the recognition of the ways in which these different, oppositional visions alter or replace currently dominant and authoritative ones. Assertions that credos, beliefs, or traditions are timeless and immemorial should not obscure the fact that they are subject to constant modification and change.

The second reason why the relationship between doctrine and practice is complex is that doctrinal prescriptions are but one factor in motivating social action (see Eickelman and Piscatori 1990:6–15). As traditional Muslim theorists maintain, ideas such as *zakat* and *jihad* play a role in inspiring social and political conduct. However, considerations such as family, ethnicity, class, gender, and bureaucratic access can be equally important. Doctrine enjoins the pilgrimage to Mecca on all believers able to do so, but believers are just as likely to fulfill this obligation because of the opportunity to improve their social status, commercial possibilities, or, in the case of Saddam Hussein, political influence.

Setting Boundaries

In the process of articulating symbolic politics, various forces seek to draw lines between public and private, government and civil society, obligatory and forbidden, moral and immoral. The drawing of boundaries is part of the political process, whether it involves the demarcation of decision-making units in society and the enforceable rules for resolving jurisdictional disputes among them (compare Deutsch 1966:254–55), or demarcation of areas open to state control over the production of dominant values and those that are not. Indeed, a political system has often been thought to reflect a relatively stable and hierarchical consensus on boundary setting, but in fact challenges to this consensus and the desire to shift boundaries have always been present (Eisenstadt 1986:30–31). Immigration, for example, is a political question because it involves drawing lines around "the club" of a society or nation-state, with membership in the club a necessary component of political success. Yet, as the Muslim migration to western Europe and the rise of neofascist movements there indicate, these lines are increasingly contested because of the growing mobility of peoples and the diminished social welfare capabilities of governments.

While conservatives and neoconservatives find support for their views on limiting immigration in demarcational politics, liberals also view politics as the drawing of necessary boundaries between areas of activity, for instance, separating military from civil authority. The blurring of lines produces uncertainty and opportunities for abuse of power, whereas boundary setting is a guarantee of liberty: The state "has a special influence, for it is the agent of separation and the defender . . . of the social map. It is not so much a night watchman protecting individuals from coercion and physical assault as it is the builder and guardian of the walls, protecting churches, universities, families, and so on from tyrannical interference" (Walzer 1984:327; compare Walzer 1983).

Boundary setting is important, though not exclusively so, in Muslim politics. Political scientists have often focused on the state's role in setting down markers, but an examination of Muslim politics indicates that this "top-down" view is distorting. Boundaries can also be set by religious authorities, Islamist protest movements, and kin groups, among others. For instance, the religious authorities (ʿulama) in Egypt vigorously protested against President Sadat's effort in 1979 to liberalize family law and women's marital rights because they saw this as an intrusion on their authority. Similarly, Indonesia's usually compliant ʿulama, who have accepted pançasila, the secular national ideology, reacted strongly to the government's attempt to implement a marriage law that would have departed significantly from Islamic family law. In the early 1990s, Muslim activist groups in Algeria were locked in a struggle with the socialist and secular government over the limits of state control of society: Should the government build state-run schools and mosques, or should it distribute the funds to various Muslim associations so they could build and maintain their own institutions?

In revolutionary Iran, disputes over boundaries have been endemic. The Majlis-i Shura-ye Islami (National Assembly) and Council of Guardians have competed with each other to set the legislative agenda, and each has warily regarded the power of the supreme *faqih* (literally "jurisprudent," or leader of the revolution). The issue of land reform has proven particularly contentious. Leading Shi'i clerics, themselves often landowners, have tended to uphold the sanctity of private property, while younger *mullahs* and radical groups have agitated for large-scale expropriation and redistribution of lands. A land reform measure, which was approved by the Revolutionary Council in April 1980 and which required the breakup of a large number of estates, met with a fierce opposition. As a result, Ayatullah Khomeini halted the redistribution of these lands in October 1980. Cognizant of the depth of this dispute, the then-speaker of the Majlis, Hashemi Rafsanjani, himself a supporter of land reform because he felt that it would stabilize the social order, sought Ayatullah Khomeini's guidance in October 1981. Preferring ambiguity to favoring one faction over another in this dispute, Khomeini failed to intervene decisively. Two bills were introduced, both purportedly representing his intentions. Although an Agrarian Reform Law favorable to landlords was finally approved in December 1982, even this was rejected in January 1983 by the Council of Guardians, which is composed of senior religious scholars and which unanimously ruled that the proposed law violated "the principles of the sharia" (Schirazi 1993:204; see also, Baktiari in press).

Pressed again by Rafsanjani in early 1983, Ayatullah Khomeini suggested that if the Majlis wished to impress upon the Council of Guardians the urgency of reform measures, it should approve them by a two-thirds majority. The parliament proceeded to pass laws on privately owned urban land and landlord-tenant relations by such a majority, but not before it had taken some of the Council's reservations into consideration. For its part, the Council "continued to regard itself as the final authority on questions of Islamic law—a position upheld by the constitution, affirmed repeatedly by Khomeini himself, and conceded on several occasions by the speaker of parliament (Bakhash 1985:19; see also, Bakhash 1990). A land redistribution bill was narrowly approved in October 1986, and the fact that it was allowed to stand indicates a relative shift in favor of factions that were demanding greater and faster change (Baktiari in press). But this dispute, as with others over banking, taxation, and cultural issues, remained unresolved, and the Ayatullah was eventually impelled to create a new institution, the High Council for the Discernment of Interests, which was ostensibly to act as his eyes and ears and resolve disagreements over fundamental issues that would endanger the revolution (Schirazi 1993:171–232).

The Council did not end the legislative confusion, however. As a letter to Khomeini signed by more than ninety Majlis deputies in late 1988 makes clear, there was ambiguity concerning its proper place in the system. The Majlis feared that the Council was becoming a rival legislative body that would "cause the proliferation of numerous contradictions in the laws of the country," thereby stimulating systemic instability. Khomeini's response was characteristically Delphic: telling the deputies they were "absolutely right," but noting that because of the prolonged war with Iraq (September 1980–August 1988), "the interests of Islam and the system [had] necessitated that the blind knots of law be speedily unraveled for the benefit of the people and Islam" (Foreign Broadcast Information Service [FBIS], NES-88–237, December 9, 1988, pp. 42–43). That Khomeini did not provide concrete guidance for the future only guaranteed that much of Iranian politics would center on the definition of institutional boundaries.

Muslim politics, like politics everywhere, thus involves a contest over the extent of state control—locating the boundaries of legitimate state and nonstate activity or what has been unhelpfully termed the "public" and "private." But, as Chapter 3 will argue, boundaries are also negotiated between and among nonstate actors, such as those between the religious scholars and mystical (Sufi) shaykhs. Moreover, as Chapter 4 will suggest, the boundaries between public and private are constantly shifting; family concerns can also have a "public" dimension. A notable consequence of this more diffuse process of boundary setting, in which various individuals and groups compete to represent the claims of Muslims, is the fragmentation of authority that we will discuss in Chapter 5.

The need to place Muslim politics into multiple and shifting contexts thus becomes apparent. Like power, symbolism and language—integral components of politics—"must be located within a nexus of social and cultural relationships" (Grillo 1989:21). This need for contextualization applies to all politics, and in this respect, Muslim politics is not unique. As we have argued, neither can it be said to be unique because of any singular determination of doctrine.

The distinctiveness of Muslim politics may be said to lie rather in the specific, if evolving, values, symbols, ideas, and traditions that constitute "Islam." These include notions of social justice and communal solidarity that have been inspired by the founding texts of Islam such as the Qur'an and the sayings (*hadiths*) of the Prophet. They may also include a sense of obligation to authority that has been informed as much by social practice as by Qur'anic injunction, the practices of mystical orders (*tariqas*), and the established schools (*madhhabs*) of Islamic law. Such ideas and values, as expressed through symbols and language, constitute an image of the ideal Muslim society. Precisely because the symbolism and the language are inherently flexible and even ambiguous, one Muslim's image can be another's "counter-image" (Kessler 1990:15). Just as those not habituated to the marketplace may have a moral ambivalence toward the "unapologetic jockeying" for material advantage that occurs in it (Geertz 1979:221), many Muslims—as the adherents of other religions regard their own faith—may prefer to think of Islam as fixed in form and content, yet implicitly, even if grudgingly, accept that its interpretations change over time. Increasingly, in the venture of Islam, Muslim politics constitutes the field on which an intricate pattern of cooperation and contest over form, practice, and interpretation takes place.

2

THE INVENTION OF TRADITION

IN MUSLIM POLITICS

FROM THE MID-1950s the conventional wisdom was that Middle Eastern societies faced a stark choice—"Mecca or mechanization" (Lerner 1964:405; see also, Berger 1964, 1970:719–20, 724–27)—a phrase that epitomized modernization theory as applied to Middle Eastern and Muslim societies. The concepts underlying the phrase also governed "real world" political decisions. The late Shah of Iran was only one of many leaders of Muslim societies who tried to delegitimize the role of Islam in politics by identifying religion with the past and backwardness. Ayatullah Khomeini (1902–89) provided a measure of how other Muslim leaders reject this dichotomization:

> The claim that Islam is against modern (technical) innovations is the same claim made by the deposed Mohammad Riza Pahlevi that these people [Islamic revolutionaries] want to travel with four-legged animals, and this is nothing but an idiotic accusation. For, if by manifestations of civilization it is meant technical innovations, new products, new inventions, and advanced industrial techniques which aid in the progress of mankind, then never has Islam, or any other monotheist religion, opposed their adoption. On the contrary, Islam and the Holy Qur'an emphasize science and industry. (Khomeini [1983] n.d.:22)[1]

This unhesitant affirmation of Islam's compatibility with modernization seems even more striking, given the Western media's depiction of the Ayatullah in particular and the Iranian revolution in general as reactionary and even "medieval." The idea that Islam is a hindrance to the process of development also owes its currency to the persistence of modernization theory.

The "Modernization" of Muslim Societies

There have been various manifestations of modernization theory, the single most important social theory to influence both academic and policy approaches to the Third World from the 1950s to the late 1970s.

So pervasive was the impact of its early or "classical" formulation that it fashioned the aid and development policies of the industrialized Western states and such international institutions as the World Bank and International Monetary Fund. Common to all variations of this theory was the assumption that complex economic structure and political development proceed in tandem. In one influential formulation, "The forces of technological change and cultural diffusion are driving political systems in certain directions, which seem discernible and susceptible to analysis in terms of increasing levels of development" (Almond and Powell 1966:301).

Economic specialization, it was argued, leads to political institutionalization; and the displacement of traditional, usually landed, elites by urban middle classes leads to the emergence of centralized commercial, bureaucratic, and educational structures. According to this formulation of modernization theory, superstition wanes and religion recedes from a role in public life. The religious establishment comes to be seen as resistant to change. As the civic order becomes secularized, "rational" conduct becomes the norm, and this leads to greater political participation or, at the least, political stability.[2]

The secular bias of modernization theory had its specific echo in analyses of the Islamic world. In the early 1960s, modernization theorists saw the Muslim world as facing an unpalatable choice: either a "neo-Islamic totalitarianism" intent on "resurrecting the past," or a "reformist Islam" that would open "the sluice gates and [be] swamped by the deluge" (Halpern 1963:129). This intensely negative view of the possibilities of evolution in Muslim societies betrayed an inherent preference for such militantly secularizing reformers as Turkey's Mustafa Kemal Atatürk (1881–1938) and the Pahlavi shahs of Iran, Reza Shah (1878–1944) and his son, Muhammad Reza Shah (1919–80). In the 1970s, assumptions about Islam's role in the development process continued to be similarly unnuanced: "In an industrializing nation, the gap between political and religious authority ... becomes progressively greater," whereas "Islamic influence and control are strongest when maintaining the status quo in a backward community" (Bill and Leiden 1979:69).[3]

The inherent defects of modernization theory have been well documented (for example, Higgott 1983; Binder 1986), and its limitations have become equally apparent in analyses of the Muslim world (Binder 1988:76–84; Hudson 1980:5–10). The fundamental difficulty with the theory lay in the sharp contrast between two artificial constructs, "modernity" and "tradition," and the consequent misunderstanding of the entrenched social functions of tradition. As Black observes, "If one thinks of modernization as the integration or the reintegration of societies on the basis of new principles, one must also think of it as involving the disintegration of traditional societies (1966:27)." "Modernity" was seen as an "enlargement of human freedoms" and an "enhancement of the range of choices" as people began to "take charge" of themselves (Madan 1987:748). Tradition is thus devalued as implying contrary values. It is also seen as so inimical to modernization that its displacement often gives rise to violence and a political instability, "strewn with wrecks and skeletons" (Black 1966:27–28, 164–65). Since the 1980s, several modernization theorists have come to accept that positing a sharp division between tradition and modernity oversimplifies a complex process of interaction in which religion and tradition coexist with economic development and the needs of a modern society (for example, Weiner and Huntington 1987).

In many ways, Marxist-Leninist theories of development and modernization theories evolved similarly. Just as the 1979 Iranian revolution helped to trigger a rethinking of modernization theory in the West, it had similar repercussions in the Soviet Union, where scholars and policymakers worked largely in isolation from their Western counterparts.[4] The Islamic revolution in Iran and the rise of Islamic political activism as a force in world politics could not be explained by conventional Soviet frameworks. Soviet thinking was conditioned by the Marxist-Leninist assumptions that religion belonged to an ideational superstructure that was destined to disappear with the social and economic formations that supported it. As Mikhail Piotrovsky of the Hermitage, St. Petersburg, commented in 1990, "Twenty years ago we considered religious beliefs to be dying. Now we are reaping the harvest of this neglect" (cited in Eickelman and Pasha 1991:632).

Many Marxian (those broadly influenced by Marxist traditions), socialist, and leftist writers, however, persist in seeing politics in the Middle East and elsewhere as governed by a "neopatriarchal" petit bourgeoisie defined by and supportive of traditional values. The neopatriarchal elite, in such a view, stands in contrast to a bourgeois elite intent on modernization and a proletarian elite committed to revolution (Sharabi 1988:8–9). The problem is thought to lie with cultural schizophrenia, yet the oversimplified dichotomization of tradition and modernity is again evident:

> The neopatriarchal ruling classes and states of the Middle East are Janus-faced because they look both backwards and forwards, towards tradition and modernity. They are dualistic because they are neither totally developmentalist nor completely pre-capitalist and pre-industrial. This is why no Middle Eastern country has produced manufactures on the level of

South Korea, Brazil, Mexico, the Philippines or Thailand . . . and why there is so much oscillation and vacillation in the region, especially over the woman question. (Moghadam 1991:206)

Hisham Sharabi presents a subtle discussion of patriarchal and neopatriarchal societies, which develop in several stages and which consist of a number of types of social formation. Neopatriarchy is a "dependent, nonmodern socioeconomic structure" that "represents the quintessentially underdeveloped society" (Sharabi 1988:6–7). Although he argues that neopatriarchy will not be replaced "all at once" by "development" or "modernization," he implicitly affirms a dichotomous approach. He refers to modernity as "a break with traditional (mythical) ways of understanding reality in favor of new (scientific) modes of thought" (1988:10), and he concludes with the hope that Arab society will "overcome its innermost disease, patriarchy, and . . . become modern. . . . The coming of modernity, secular democracy, and libertarian socialism" would displace "the neopatriarchical status quo" (1988:155).

In contrast to the assumptions of early modernization theory and Marxist-inspired theories, tradition is often a profound vehicle for evolutionary and revolutionary change. In contemporary European usage, tradition implies procedures handed down from the past, not amenable to conscious modification, and resistant to "modernity." In the view of one Western scholar writing in the early 1960s, tradition does little to help the Muslim to "cope with the modern world that threatens his undoing." In fact, "to be traditional . . . is to remain unrelated to modern political choices" (Halpern 1963:114–15). As we have indicated, many Middle Easterners, especially those educated in the West or influenced by Western values, also accept this pejorative notion of tradition. To them, the label "traditional" (taqlidi) implies being chained to the past and unwilling to participate in debates concerning the reform of existing social and political institutions.

Yet, as newer modernization studies have argued (So 1990:85–87), tradition need not be construed in negative terms only. Traditional family and religious networks may in fact facilitate development, and social and political changes are often made possible because they are cast in terms of the traditional framework (see Findley 1992:149). "Entrepreneurial familism" and nepotism, for example, have contributed to Hong Kong's economic success (Wong 1988:170–71). Although it has been argued that Islam does not aid the process of modernization (Bill and Leiden 1984:67), to construct a claim that changes are Islamic is to render them legitimate and acceptable. By defending changes as in keeping with the "essence" of Islam, reformers deflate criticism that their changes run counter to the basic values of society. Likewise, by tying reforms to the fundamental responsibility of Muslims to obey God and those in authority, as enjoined in the Qur'an (for example, 4:59), they encourage the belief that innovative regulations are obligatory.

Emendations and additions to a purportedly invariant and complete Islamic law (*shari'a*) have occurred throughout Islamic history, particularly since the mid–nineteenth century. Muslim jurists have rigorously maintained the pious fiction that there can be no change in divinely revealed law, even as they have exercised their independent judgment (*ijtihad*) to create a kind of de facto legislation.[5] For instance, the nineteenth-century Ottoman reforms—the Tanzimat of 1839–76—including the Commercial Code of 1850, gave the Ottomans criminal and commercial regulations similar to those found in Europe. The *Majalla* of 1870, the codification of laws inspired by one of the main Islamic legal traditions, the Hanafi school of law, provided for the greater degree of regularity required in complex economic transactions, including trade with non-Muslim powers. In the twentieth century, laws governing *awqaf* (religious endowments), which were promulgated in Egypt (1946), Lebanon (1947), and Syria (1949), attempted to remedy the situation created by endowments that put productive land out of use and that could be designed, under the pretext of religious philanthropy, to deprive an individual's heirs of property to which they would normally be entitled.

Even in such a reputedly conservative country as Saudi Arabia, legal reforms routinely occur, often made possible by an invocation of the "public interest" (*maslaha 'amma*) as an overriding Islamic concern. To give but one example, the Social Insurance Law of 1970 is a notable departure from the classical laws of inheritance in the case of a deceased worker: Inheritors of his governmentally guaranteed insurance would now be principally his wife and children and not simply—as might be expected—male agnatic relatives (see Piscatori 1986:122–24).

So common has this social legislation become in Saudi Arabia that King Fahd opened the Jurisprudence Academy of the Organization of the Islamic Conference with a ringing defense of *ijtihad* as a means to find new solutions to the problems of the age:

> Such *Ijtihad* must be validated by the Ulema ['*ulama*, men of learning] after due research in and consideration of old and new jurisprudence. In this regard, the call for the establishment of [this academy] reflects an imperative need at this stage of development of the Muslim Ummah [*umma*, Islamic community]. Indeed, it provides the truly Islamic response to questions raised by the challenges of modern life. This requires

the pooling of efforts by jurists, scholars, sages and thinkers throughout the Muslim World with a view to seeking answers to the questions posed by the challenges of our time, based on the reality of our tolerant Shariah. (Fahd 1983:5)

In so arguing, Fahd has subtly blended a reaffirmation of the need for independent reasoning with an endorsement of the role played by Muslim intellectuals and thinkers who do not belong to the cadre of traditionally educated religious authorities.

If the invocation of the traditional framework facilitates incremental change, even revolutionary action is often justified by appeal to precedent. The Sudanese Mahdi, Muhammad Ahmad (1844–85), gained considerable popular support by asserting that his strategy and daily round of activities corresponded on a day-to-day basis with what the Prophet Muhammad did in seventh-century Arabia. Such claims of an exact replication of the past are extreme, and contemporary political conduct relies on more subtle invocations of past values and practice.

A more recent case in point is the development of constitutionalism in Iran. At the time of the Constitutional Revolution (1905–11), Shaykh Fadlallah Nuri (1842–1909) objected to the idea of a written constitution, in part because it presumed to guarantee equality, which could not exist between the free man and the slave, husband and wife, Muslim and infidel, the healthy and ill. He also found the idea of a constitution unacceptable because it provided for a legislative body, which would infringe on divinely revealed law (Nuri 1982: 292–96). For him, a written constitution fell outside the acceptable Islamic framework.

Ayatullah Khomeini, although he expressed admiration for Shaykh Nuri, was nevertheless instrumental in formulating the 1979 constitution of the Islamic Republic. Notions of the limitations on the powers of government and of the central role of the people, such as expressed by Mehdi Bazargan (1905–95; r. 1979), his first prime minister, would have been known to him: "[T]he Holy Book affirms that any kind of government or vicegerency should stem from the people, and that they themselves should, having chosen and stated their preference for the kind of government in question, be the motivating force behind its enforcement and control" (Bazargan 1979:30).[6]

The preamble of the constitution, incorporating the idea that Muslims form a community based on submission to the will of God, says that the government "is a crystallization of political idealism based on religious community and concord which provide its organization—which through the process of ideological transformation turns its path toward the final goal (movement toward God)." Although the authors of the constitution thus directly affirm its Islamic credentials, they combine ideas of submission and participation. On the one hand, "the purpose of sovereignty is to make people grow toward the divine order," while on the other, the constitution provides for "participation . . . in order to perfect every person."

The substantive clauses of the constitution display the coexistence of these two contrasting notions of sovereignty. They affirm the traditional concept of the absolute sovereignty of Allah (Principles 2 and 56), while accommodating the very different idea of popular sovereignty in conceding the people's right to determine their own "destiny" (Principle 3:8) and allowing for occasional referenda (Principle 59) and a popularly elected assembly (Principle 62) (Iran 1980).[7]

The Blurring of Tradition and Modernity

Muslims and non-Muslims alike tend to take at face value the ideological claim by some Muslims that the key elements of Islamic tradition are fixed. Indeed, the idea of tradition is profoundly conditioned by the central role played by both founding texts and Prophetic example. Just as Muslims consider the Qur'an, the direct word of God, to be immutable, the *hadith* (sayings) and actions of the Prophet Muhammad are regarded as a template for action in the present.

All traditions are created, however, through shared practice, and they can be profoundly and consciously modified and manipulated under the guise of a return to a more legitimate earlier practice. Of even more significance, changed economic and political conditions can profoundly alter the meaning and significance of ideas, movements, social and personal identities, and institutional arrangements, without the proponents of these ideas being fully aware of the nature of the change. From Indonesia to Morocco, communities and regions assume that there is an Islamically defined continuity to their ways of doing things.

Politics, as we have shown, is intimately connected with the process of symbolic production. But, because symbols are general and ambiguous rather than specific, they simultaneously provide a link with the past and room for change (Scarritt 1972: 29). The effects of what might be called "postmodernization" can be mitigated by both this rootedness and flexibility. Since values take on symbolic form, the parameters of the culture appear to remain intact while the renewal and transformation of values are in fact taking place. Thus, the constancy of traditions and shared myths is affirmed, even while changes of belief and value are underway and traditions are reinvented (Barthes

1957:41–46; Samuel and Thompson 1990:14). In the case of the United States, for example, the reassuring mythology of the Constitution holds that it is amended only rarely. In practice, however, it is reinterpreted almost daily by myriad judicial, administrative, and legislative decisions.

In the case of Islam as well, there is scope for change, and several Islamic traditions can be found. Since the late 1970s, the Iranian Shiʿa, for whom dialogue and debate at all levels of religious awareness have always played a major role, have become conspicuously multinational. Even within Iran, the multiple languages of the Shiʿa—Persian, Azeri, Kurdish, and Arabic (both as the first acquired language for some Iranians and as a prerequisite for higher religious studies)—encourage awareness of multiple perspectives of ethics, politics, and interpretations of the past. The pilgrimage to Mecca; visits to the shrines of Shiʿi martyrs; and the rituals of birth, marriage, circumcision, and death, in exile or abroad, all give rise to a reinterpreted sense of history and what is "essential" to belief and practice (Fischer and Abedi 1990).

The sense of history and the past is never politically neutral. Edward Shils (1981:185) distinguishes between the pasts of occurred events and the "much more plastic" perceived past. Actually, because the line between occurred and perceived pasts depends upon the construction, dissemination, and acceptance of authoritative historical narratives, the past of occurred events exists mostly as a pool of resources which can be drawn upon in traditional and modern settings to sanction present practice. In effect, the line between occurred and perceived events is inherently blurred because the process of creating tradition is both conscious and explicit, and unconscious and implicit.

The invention of tradition is the "process of formalization and ritualization, characterized by reference to the past" (Hobsbawm 1983:4–5). Invented traditions can emerge from the shared practices of extended families, neighborhoods, and tribes; they can develop more formally (as in court etiquette or merchant guilds); or they can be bureaucratically initiated and codified. Less attention has been given to a critical awareness of how such traditions—claims as to what is "really" Islamic, for example—are affected by political and economic circumstances and changing modes of transmission. Modes of transmission encompass oral, unwritten traditions passed on by local authorities as well as traditions learned from state-controlled television and official texts such as schoolbooks.

The invention of tradition occurs in all times and places, but, as Hobsbawm indicates, "We should expect it to occur more frequently when a rapid transformation of society weakens or destroys" older social patterns or produces "new ones to which they were not applicable

(1983:5)." In contrast to the assumptions of both nineteenth-century liberal thought and mid–twentieth-century modernization theory, he points out that traditions are formalized in "modern" as well as "traditional" societies, again reminding us that the sharp contrast between traditional and modern is misleading.

From Caliphate to Islamic State

Nowhere does the tendency to justify present innovation by past practice show more clearly than in recent arguments on the nature of the Islamic state. This debate did not occur in a vacuum: It crystallized in the early twentieth century as Muslims sought an alternative to the doctrine of the caliphate in the declining Ottoman Empire (Enayat 1982:69).

The Ottoman caliphate, which had its origins in the late fourteenth century, was formally abolished by republican Turkey in 1924. At the height of Ottoman power in the sixteenth and seventeenth centuries, the title and the concept of caliphate were not greatly stressed. But when invoked, the caliphs' claim to authority rested on their assertion that, by the will of God, they were the most effective defenders of Islam. In succeeding to the caliphate (*khilafa*), they had thus assumed all the powers of Muhammad except prophecy.

In the eighteenth and nineteenth centuries, as the Empire declined under increasing internal pressure and external challenges from the West, the Ottomans reinvented the caliphal tradition. In the eighteenth century, a legend developed that the last ʿAbbasid caliph in Cairo had transferred the office of caliph to the Ottomans in the early sixteenth century, thus legitimizing an unbroken succession from the time of the Prophet (Inalcik 1970:320–23). "There were obvious political reasons why Ottoman sultans of the age of decline reformulated and appropriated the classical theory of the caliphate" (Inalcik 1970:320).

The idea of the Islamic state in the twentieth century emerged as a similar reinvention of tradition. The most common word for state in Arabic, *dawla*, appeared as early as the mid–eighth century, when it referred to the dynastic rule of the ʿAbbasids (Lewis 1988:36; Ayalon 1987:81–82). In the twentieth century, the term was transformed into *al-dawla al-islamiyya* (the Islamic state), to which Muslims aspire. Like the earlier theory of the caliphate, justification for the Islamic state centers on upholding the *shariʿa* (Islamic law).

Arab Muslim intellectuals played a major role in this process. The concept of the Islamic state was promoted as the functional equivalent of the caliphate. Abu-l-Hasan al-Mawardi's (991–1058) treatise on the caliphate, *Kitab al-ahkam al-sultaniyya* [The principles of government]

(1960), is regarded as the archetypal Sunni treatment of the subject. He argues that a caliph is necessary to uphold the *shariʿa* and implement its principles; he used this argument to sustain the authority of ʿAbbasid rule in the face of attacks by local warlords in Iraq and Egypt who also claimed to be "rightful" rulers of the entire Islamic world (Watt 1968:101–2) (see fig. 3).

The Egyptian reformer, Rashid Rida (1865–1935), was an important link between classical theories of the caliphate, such as al-Mawardi's, and twentieth-century notions of the Islamic state. Rida, harkening back to the "golden age" of Islamic governance and drawing on a well-established point of view in Muslim historiography, distinguished between the ideal caliphate of the first four successors to the Prophet Muhammad and the actual caliphate, which was obliged to compromise with tyrants and became tyrannical itself. Rida (1934:57–65) argued that the men of learning (ʿulama), who were charged with the responsibility for maintaining the *shariʿa*, became corrupted through compromise with temporal authority (*sulta*) and consequently often lent themselves to the support of tyrants.

Rida recognized the impossibility of reviving the caliphate as the sole source of spiritual authority, but he saw the transfer of its function to the Islamic state as a practical alternative. The terms he used to describe the Islamic state, including "the government of the caliphate" (*hukumat al-khilafa*) and the "Islamic caliphate" (*al-khilafa al-Islamiyya*), stress the linkages between the theory of the caliphate and that of the Islamic state (Enayat 1982:77). In retrospect, Rida's thought was ambiguous and paradoxical; Rosenthal goes so far as to consider his basic position "utopian and romantic" (1965:83–85). Nonetheless, he delineated the issues common to later proponents of the Islamic state and formulated the "tradition" that this state incorporates notions of popular sovereignty and human legislation (Enayat 1982:77).[8]

Olivier Roy characterizes as "inanity" the attempt to concretize the "illusion" of the Islamic state. He bases this judgment on the intellectual bankruptcy of contemporary Islamists in facing the challenges of modern societies. He argues that they have no solutions to the dominant problems of the day—"misery, rootlessness, the crisis of values and identities, the collapse of educational systems, North-South antagonism, and the problem of the integration of immigrants in host societies" (1992:43).

Nonetheless, the invention of the tradition of the Islamic state is profoundly affecting the political processes of Muslim societies everywhere and qualifying public policy debates in them. In Egypt, critics of the regime, who range from the relatively accommodationist Muslim Brotherhood to the more uncompromising network of "Islamic Associ-

Fig. 3. The caliphate, like control over the holy places of the Arabian peninsula, implies a geographical center and territorial cohesiveness to the Muslim world. This vision is increasingly displaced by a multiplicity of political centers. Indeed, a Mecca-centric view of the world distorts the contest over Muslim politics that includes what was once thought of as "peripheral" China, Indonesia, and America.

ations" (Jamaᶜat Islamiyya), have wondered how Egypt could presume to be Islamic if the *shariᶜa* remained only a source of law rather than its principal or sole source. The dominant Islamic group of Algeria, the Front Islamique du Salut (the Islamic Salvation Front [FIS]), participated in the December 1991 parliamentary elections and called for the transformation of the Popular and Democratic Republic of Algeria—to give the country its full formal name—to an Islamic state. The success of FIS in the first round of elections prompted the resignation of the president and precipitated a political crisis that brought the intervention of a military intensely hostile to the demands of FIS and similar groups. In the Central Asian republic of Tajikistan, the Islamic

Renaissance Party, which has branches in other Central Asian republics and in Russia, became so popular after the collapse of the Soviet Union that many were concerned that Tajikistan would become the region's first Islamic republic (Rashid 1991b).

The concept of the Islamic state has become so central to Muslim discourse that it has shaped the symbolic politics of Nigeria and Indonesia. In Nigeria, the government's application in 1986 for full membership in the Organization of the Islamic Conference (OIC), the intergovernmental organization of Muslim states, precipitated riots and political protests. Muslim activists supported the application to the OIC in the hope that it would encourage the Islamization of Nigeria's Muslim population, while Christian leaders feared that membership in the OIC would imply movement toward an Islamic state and the undermining of Nigeria's secular pluralism (Gambari 1990:307–10). Similar sensitivities about the development of an Islamic state have been present in Indonesia and are the result of a long history of dispute over the nature of the state in a multisectarian society with a preponderant Muslim majority (estimated at 90 percent). Although the government is officially committed to secularism and pluralism, as represented in the official ideology, the *pançasila* (the "five principles"), demands for an Islamic state fueled the Dar-ul Islam revolt in West Java (1948–62) and have remained high on the political agenda (Horikoshi 1975).

The Islamic "Golden Age"

In the view of its Muslim advocates, the Islamic state is justified by reference to the early years of Islam. They argue that the Islamic state first became an issue with the death of the Prophet. In the Prophet's lifetime, writes one modernist, "sanctions were entirely moral, and [bore] no relation to conventional methods of state coercion" (el-Affendi 1991:21). In this view, allegiance to the Islamic state was voluntary during the Prophet's lifetime. After his death, however, "a coercive political authority seemed indispensable." Although the issue of leadership was resolved with "reasonable unanimity," other issues soon led to civil war and the collapse of the "idealist state" (1991: 22–26).

Contemporary Muslims regard the period of the Prophet's first four successors, the "rightly guided caliphs" (*al-khulafa al-rashidun*), as one in which there was little divergence between ideals and reality. Of these four, however, only the first, Abu Bakr (r. 632–34), died a natural death. 'Umar ibn al-Khattab (r. 634–44) was assassinated by a Christian slave of the governor of Basra. The third, 'Uthman ibn

ʿAffan (r. 644–56), was killed and his house pillaged by rebels who regarded his rule as tyrannical. And the last of the four, ʿAli ibn Abi Talib (r. 656–61), the Prophet's son-in-law, was killed on his way to the mosque at a time when the Islamic community was increasingly rent by dissension.

The invocation of a golden age is especially prevalent in the thinking of Muslims whose principal aim is to certify Islam's compatibility with the universal "goods" promised by the modern age: science, democracy, social justice, and human rights. These intellectuals, whether they call themselves modernist reformers or religious activists, have found invocation of the golden age a useful instrument with which to argue the need for reform within Muslim societies. In effect, even if the era of the rightly guided caliphs had not been preeminent in its moral instructiveness, they would have had to invent such a paradigm in order to highlight the present state of affairs and provide an unimpeachable standard by which to judge and condemn it. The early community of the Prophet and his four immediate successors was invested with the moral qualities so conspicuously missing in the subsequent centuries when *bidaʿ* (unworthy innovations) set in. This degradation was thought to be especially evident during Umayyad (661–750) and ʿAbbasid (750–1258) rule.

The school of thought that emerged in the late nineteenth century and became known as the Salafiyya (from *salaf*, the ancestors of Islam) illustrates this tendency to find inspiration in the early Muslim community. One of its most important exponents, Muhammad ʿAbduh (1849–1905), argued, for example, that Muslim neglect of the common good in legal matters and rulers' emphasis on obedience above justice engendered intellectual confusion, legal stagnation, political corruption, and the decline of Islam (ʿAbduh [1925] 1978:104–23). Muslim activists continue to echo this refrain in the late twentieth century.

Sadiq al-Mahdi (b. 1936; r. 1966–67, 1986–87, 1988–89), a former prime minister of Sudan and great-grandson of the Sudanese *mahdi* who led the nineteenth-century revolt against the British (1881–98), finds the age of the rightly guided caliphs exemplary because of their direct contact with the Prophet and the purity of the early community's faith. On the basis of his interpretation of the early Muslim community, al-Mahdi argues that "Islam produced political principles such as freedom, justice, equality, [and] the necessity of government for the people." The modern democratic order has evolved to resemble these ideas, but Muslims must seek to recapture today the essence of their own tradition "produced fifteen centuries ago" (al-Mahdi 1990:197).

Al-Mahdi's argument reminds us that political theory in the Muslim world is most concretely expressed through the representation of historical tradition. The formalization of the "golden age" tradition thus functions to provide both a powerful indictment of the waywardness of modern Muslim societies and a blueprint for action. Tradition acts, in effect, both to legitimize criticism of the status quo and to facilitate revolutionary as well as incremental changes.

The "Call" (Da'wa) to Islam

The transformation that is occurring in the concept and practice of *da'wa* indicates how the reworking of basic Islamic concepts involves not only state elites and intellectuals but also the masses. Change is initiated from the apex of society, as it were, but also from the base. *Da'wa* is mentioned in the Qur'an (14:46) as God's "call" to human society to find in Islam the true religion. The term has developed over the centuries into an explicit ideology of proselytism. Never dissociated from the political and social contexts of Muslims, *da'wa* has been used to propagate the specific claims of dynasties such as the 'Abbasids and sects such as the Isma'ilis. Under the latter, in fact, the term became virtually synonymous with propaganda, and Isma'ili missionaries (*du'a*) of the Cairo-based Fatimid dynasty (969–1171) became accomplished at recruiting followers to both a religious doctrine and political affiliation. Education was central to all conceptualizations of *da'wa*. Whether formally at court, as with the Fatimids (Canard 1965:169), or in informal circles of scholars, Muslims as well as non-Muslims acquired through missionary work an understanding of the living faith—how to recite the Qur'an, apply the *shari'a*, and conduct the affairs of everyday life in an Islamic spirit.

Today this tradition of *da'wa* has begun to be reformulated in a subtle but important way. Education remains central, and even the pattern of politicization has recurred. For example, one of the main Shi'i groups in Iraq opposed to the rule of Saddam Hussein (b.1937) bears the name Hizb al-Da'wa al-Islamiyya (Islamic Call party), and one of the chief instruments for the dissemination of Libyan religious and political ideas is the Jam'iyyat al-Da'wa al-Islamiyya (Islamic Call Society). Yet the tradition of *da'wa* is also being redefined to include the idea of social welfare activism—free medical clinics, soup kitchens for the poor, subsidized housing, and other forms of mutual assistance which often substitute for ineffective or nonexistent government services. The explicit linkage with the "prior" tradition is the assertion that Muslims, obliged to follow God's call, must respond to the

Qur'anic duty to create balance (*mizan*) and justice ('adl, qist) in the affairs of men (16:90 and 58:25). Since Islam involves a total way of life, Muslims would abdicate their responsibility if they failed to redress social injustices and economic inequalities.

The influential Lebanese Shi'i religious figure, Musa al-Sadr (1928–disappeared 1978), promoted a new kind of Shi'i activism that included, among other things, the establishment of a vocational training center in Tyre, al-Mu'assa, which is still in operation (Ajami 1986:111). Hizbullah, the "party of God," has also developed an extensive social welfare system in Lebanon that involves educational, agricultural, medical, and housing assistance. In Beirut's Bir al-'Abid quarter, it has run a supermarket cooperative, selling produce below retail costs (see Chipaux 1988; also see Piscatori 1989:30), but, more importantly, it also provides scholarships, runs health clinics, and subsidizes housing for the needy. In the United States, the American Muslim Council (1992) emphasizes the need to develop "social service institutions," and the Jama'at Nasr al-Islam (Society for the Victory of Islam) in northern Nigeria operates health clinics and an "aid group" that functions much like the Red Cross. In Jordan, the Islamic Hospital in Amman is highly valued. In Malaysia, ABIM (Angkatan Belia Islam Malaysia), the Muslim Youth Movement of Malaysia, talks of the need for "Islamic outreach," and Darul Arqam has operated a public health clinic as well as farms and factories for the production of *halal* ("permitted") food, toothpaste, and soap (Anwar 1987:37). Such social welfare activities strengthen the communitarian basis of Islamic groups at the same time as they serve the groups' power-seeking strategies.

Ashfaq Ahmad, a member of the Islamic Society of Papua New Guinea, has captured the deliberateness with which this reformulation of *da'wa* tradition is occurring:

> Da'wah work must be supplemented with the social, cultural, and economic development of the country. A substantial amount of funds should be allocated to be spent in these countries for health, education, and better living conditions for the people living there in the form of grants, aids or loans. . . . The spirit of service and brotherhood should inculcate and permeate all the activities of development, so that people may appreciate the difference between this work and colonialism. (1981: 29).

Those who carry out these practices of *da'wa*—missionaries, health workers, educators, and engineers—may not consciously intend to transform tradition, but their activities contribute as much to the process of transformation as the formal discourse of Muslim intellectuals.

The Objectification of Muslim Consciousness

As we have seen, tradition is a subtle and elastic concept. It sometimes refers to the unwritten shared understandings of small-scale, relatively isolated communities, which change as they are passed from generation to generation, although these changes are hard to perceive because of the lack of fixed records of "the way things were." Tradition can also refer to the shared understandings of extended family groups or households. The concept also encompasses major elements of world religious traditions, such as the four recognized Sunni "schools" (*madhhabs*) of Islamic jurisprudence. All these senses of tradition are subject to considerable flexibility as they are sustained and recreated in various social and historical contexts, ranging from the intimacies of family life to the conduct of state affairs. Notwithstanding the powerful metaphor of the great Muslim thinker Abu Hamid Muhammad al-Ghazali (1058–1111; n.d.:14) that the "glass" of traditional faith, once broken, cannot be mended, the view of tradition that we have presented suggests that the substance and form of tradition are flexible and subject to reinvention.

Rather than conceive of tradition and modernity as sharply dichotomous, broad-banded distinctions, it is useful to narrow our focus to the processes by which many aspects of social and political life become subject to conscious reflection, discussion, and debate. A concrete example will illustrate this point. In a provincial capital of the Sultanate of Oman in 1979, one of the authors slept in the guest room (*sabla*) of a major tribal leader. An hour before sunrise, the other guests, all Omanis, rose to perform their ablutions for their morning prayers. The author fell back asleep and failed to respond to a later "wake up" call. The tribal leader was summoned and asked the author whether he was sick. The author explained later that he prayed in a different way and so did not proceed to ablutions and prayers. He subsequently learned from a young Omani that it was taken for granted that the author, an Arabic-speaker who was aware of local etiquette, would follow all local practices. Omani Ibadis of the northern interior knew of course of other Muslim and non-Muslim traditions, but they were marginal to their social and moral imagination.

In the same community several years later, a much more conscious sense of tradition had begun to emerge, inspired by the growing cohort of young Omanis who had received a secondary or postsecondary school education and who, with the increasing ease of transportation and the expansion of networks of youth met through schooling, military service, and employment, began to question what it meant to be a Muslim. As one of Oman's first generation of village schoolteachers observed of the northern Oman interior, "People here do not know Islam; they pray and sacrifice, but they do not know why" (interview, Nizwa region, March 9, 1988).

Before the mid-1970s, such a consciously critical statement would have been almost incomprehensible in most of the towns and villages of Oman. It would not have occurred to most people that their practice of the faith could be brought into question. By the late 1980s, however, such questioning had become common, and what we call "objectification" had reached into all parts of the Muslim world.

Objectification is the process by which basic questions come to the fore in the consciousness of large numbers of believers: "What is my religion?" "Why is it important to my life?" and "How do my beliefs guide my conduct?" Objectification does not presuppose the notion that religion is a uniform or monolithic entity (although it is precisely that for some thinkers). These explicit, widely shared, and "objective" questions are modern queries that increasingly shape the discourse and practice of Muslims in all social classes, even as some legitimize their actions and beliefs by asserting that they advocate a return to purportedly authentic traditions. Objectification is thus transclass, and religion has become a self-contained system that its believers can describe, characterize, and distinguish from other belief systems.

Since Iran's Islamic revolution, many of Tehran's Friday sermons illustrate this tendency to present Islam as an abstract system of ideas that can be distinguished from other such systems. In these sermons, leading religious authorities explain policies, problems, and events of the week to much wider audiences than those of the Shah's time, despite the state's control over mass communications. In a sermon in June 1991, Ayatullah Muhammad Yazdi, head of the Iranian judiciary, reiterated a common theme in warning his listeners against "American-style Islam." This he defined as a "monopoly in certain types of individual worship and slogans, having nothing to do with political issues, not discussing world events, possessing some simple rituals and disregarding others. . . . One should be very careful [because] the danger of an American-style Islam, that is, one that says that the government has nothing to do with Islam, is far greater than that of weapons" (BBC SWB, ME/1106/A1–2, June 24, 1991).

Ayatullah Yazdi's characterization of "American-style Islam" illustrates the "objectification" of the Islamic tradition. So, however, does the "politicized" Islam which he implicitly advocates as more "authentic." Because these sermons often refer to published sources and provide arguments that invoke recognizable authorities, the implication is that the audience is familiar with texts and the principles of citation. Not all in the audience can follow such arguments in detail, but they recognize the forms of authority. This form of argument may be even more important for religious leaders not primarily identified with traditional learning. For example, Siddiq Fadhil, one of the leaders of ABIM in Malaysia, "is not readily accepted as an ʿalim (religious scholar) by the older generation of Malays and those from the rural areas, [but] his regular and deliberate resort to quotations from the Qurʾan and Sunnah in his speeches has tended to promote his image as a leader in the eyes of many Muslims" (Mutalib 1990:76)

The process we call objectification is not unique to Islam. Hefner (1985:246–65; 1987) describes it in ethnographic detail as it occurs among both Hindus and Muslims in the Tengger highlands of eastern Java, and Madan (1987) describes the implications of objectification for religion and politics in India.[9] Wilfred Cantwell Smith (1963:85), however, argues that Muslims are more likely than participants of other religious traditions to present Islam "as an organized and systematized entity." From this perspective, "being Muslim" acquires more political significance in the modern world than participation in other religious traditions because of the self-conscious identification of believers with their religious tradition.

In assessing the implications of this heightened self-consciousness—of the systematization and explicitness of religious tradition—for political conduct, our primary focus is on how, in the late twentieth century and in certain contexts, Islam has become objectified in the consciousness of many Muslims. Three facets of objectification are noteworthy. First, distinctive to the modern era is that discourse and debate about Muslim tradition involves people on a mass scale. It also necessarily involves an awareness of other Muslim and non-Muslim traditions. Just as the sixteenth-century Christian Reformation has been aptly called "the daughter of printing" because printing made possible a broader dissemination of ideas, mass education and mass communication in the modern world facilitate an awareness of the new and unconventional. In changing the style and scale of possible discourse, they reconfigure the nature of religious thought and action and encourage debate over meaning.

Mass education and mass communication are important in all contemporary world religions. However, the full effects of mass education, especially higher education, are just beginning to be felt in much of the Muslim world. In the Middle East, for example, mass education is a relatively recent phenomenon. In Egypt, mass primary education began in earnest only after the 1952 revolution. It was another fifteen to twenty years before large numbers of students completed the advanced cycles of state-sponsored education. The timing of educational expansion varies for other parts of the Muslim world. Major educational expansion in Morocco, for instance, began in the late 1950s; it began in the early 1970s for Arabian peninsula countries such as Oman and Yemen. In Oman, a mere 32 students completed the complete cycle of secondary education by 1975–76, although this number had risen to 13,500 by 1987–88. Only in the late 1980s did a critical mass of people with postsecondary education, capable of sustaining an expanded internal market for newspapers, periodicals, and books, begin to emerge.[10]

A complementary measure of change is book production on a larger scale. As of 1982, the Arab world produced 40 books per million inhabitants, far below the world average of 162 titles per million. Although more recent figures are unavailable, there are signs that this gap is rapidly closing (Sabat 1989:18). In countries such as Morocco, a demand for "quality" books in Arabic has developed since the mid-1980s (Albin 1990).

At the same time, however, the most rapid growth for the printed word is in what Gonzalez-Quijano (1994) calls "Islamic books," inexpensive, attractively printed texts, accessible to a readership that lacks the literary skills of the educated cadres of an earlier era. The written form often evokes the breezy style of colloquial diction. The covers take advantage of modern printing technologies and, as a result, are both readily accessible and eye-catching. In one example, a Saudi pamphlet has a curious cover that shows a bright red ball plunging into a well in an otherwise parched desert (fig. 4). The text explains that democracy, which is "creeping" (*tatasarrub*) into the Muslim world, is incompatible with Islam because Islam offers governance by the Creator (*al-khaliq*), as understood by a properly instructed religious elite, whereas democracy, a non-Arabic term, necessarily implies rule by the created (*al-makhluqin*), in which unbelievers and the ignorant have an equal say in governance and usurp God's rule (al-Sharif 1992/1412:16–18). In many parts of the Muslim world, including North Africa, this style of argument is regarded with amusement by many, but it also offers an accessible style of argument for many recent beneficiaries of mass education.

In Ilorin, Nigeria, there has been a proliferation of Islamic educational institutions, helping to stimulate a market for Arabic publications. The formal educational sector consists of Western-style schools, encouraged by the British colonialists; modern style Arabic-language schools in which Islamic and modern subjects are taught; and "traditional" schools devoted to Islamic learning. These are not mutually exclusive forms of education, for students are typically exposed to more

Fig. 4. Unoriginal in argument, Muhammad Shakir al-
Sharif's *The Truth about Democracy* (1992) nonetheless
addresses a theme that concerns many religiously
minded Muslims. Its low price and wide distribution
give it a significant audience.

than one kind of school. In the late 1970s and 1980s, possibly 75 percent of students in the formal educational sector—involving increasing
numbers of girls—were enrolled in Islamic schools. Arabic has thus
emerged as a popular educational and literary medium. Of particular
importance has been the influence of *shaykh*s such as Adam al-Iluri
(1916–92), who, with his influential school near Lagos and his Arabic
writings, stimulated both awareness and discussion of Arabic publications among the public (Reichmuth1993).

Like modern mass communications, mass higher education and
publishing contribute to objectification by inculcating pervasive "habits of thought" (Bourdieu 1988, 1989). They do so by transforming reli-

gious beliefs into a conscious system, broadening the scope of religious authority, and redrawing the boundaries of political community. The objectification of Islam means that religious beliefs and practices are increasingly *seen* as systems (*minhaj*) to be distinguished from nonreligious ones. When activist thinkers such as Sayyid Qutb (1906–66) write of Islam as a *minhaj*, they imply more than "system" or "program," the translations commonly given. The term can also imply that something has been made open, manifest, and clear. For Qutb, as for other activists, it is not sufficient simply to "be" Muslim and to follow Muslim practices. One must reflect upon Islam and articulate it. When activists declare that they are engaged in the "Islamization" of their society, the sense of thinking of religious beliefs as an objective system becomes explicit. Thus "the Muslims" (*al-muslimun*) is a term used by Moroccans since the 1980s to refer to activists who say that they wish society to live exclusively by Islamic precepts. Irony is far from absent in the term, since all but about 20,000 of Morocco's 26 million citizens are Muslim.

Another indication of the systematization of Islam is the growing popularity of catechisms among Muslims. For example, the influential Egyptian preacher Muhammad Shaʿrawi (n.d.) has compiled a catechism-like primer of thirty pages on questions involving women's acts of faith, social relations, and the Islamic laws that regulate them. Similarly, Aʿusht (ca. 1982) provides the Ibadiyya of Algeria, Zanzibar, and Oman with a description of the "essential" tenets of Ibadi doctrine, history, and principles. One use of such tracts is to explain doctrinal tenets to other Muslims. Omani students in the United States are provided with pamphlets in English (such as "Who Are the Ibadhis?") for this purpose (al-Khalili 1988; see also, Eickelman 1989b:4–5). Such catechisms assume that their users are familiar with the subject headings and indexes that format the information.

In the case of the Nurculuk movement, which began in Turkey early in this century and today has followers in Germany, California, and elsewhere, the teachings of its founder, Saïd Nurcî (1873–1960)—originally written and passed on by hand because of Turkish government hostility—have been collected in pamphlets with titles such as *The Miracles of Muhammad* (1985a), *Belief and Man* (1985b), and *Resurrection and the Hereafter* (1985c). These pamphlets have "the function of explaining, in accordance with the understanding of the age, the truths of the Qur'an" (1985d). Nurcî insists that books, not people, "have waged a battle against unbelief" (Nurcî in Mardin 1989:4). As these pamphlets demonstrate, the formalized textual transmission of ideas is especially valued as a way to advance approved understandings of Islam. Other examples of this genre include Hamidullah (1959), intended as a "correspondence course on Islam" and available in several languages, and Soymen (1979), available in Turkish and English as a "manual" for Muslims. Pilgrimage manuals, another popular literary form throughout the Muslim world, similarly indicate a growing systematization of the ways in which belief is expressed (see Metcalf 1990).

A second facet of objectification is that authoritative religious discourse, once the monopoly of religious scholars who have mastered recognized religious texts, is replaced by direct and broader access to the printed word: More and more Muslims take it upon themselves to interpret the textual sources, classical or modern, of Islam. This transformation was implicitly recognized in King Fahd's statement, cited earlier, that points to the broad spectrum of permissible interpreters of Islamic law in the modern period. Hasan al-Turabi (b. 1930), Sorbonne-educated leader of the Muslim Brothers in the Sudan and a former attorney-general, has made the point more forcefully: "Because all knowledge is divine and religious, a chemist, an engineer, an economist, or a jurist are all ʿulamaʾ" (1983:245). Turabi is implicitly building on an Islamic tradition that affirms the authority over the faithful of those who possess religious knowledge (ʿilm). One saying (hadith) of the Prophet found in al-Tirmidhi's compilation is that "the superiority of the learned man over the worshipper (al-ʿabid) is like the superiority of the full moon over the stars" or like the Prophet's authority over the least of his followers (cited in Asad [1961] 1980:86–87).

Although the possession of religious knowledge continues to have similar political consequences, religious activists in Egypt, the West Bank, Central Asia, Indonesia, and elsewhere are more likely to be the products of mass higher education than of such traditional educational institutions as the madrasa, or mosque school. Indeed, Muslim activist discourse, like that of Morocco's Abd Assalam Yassine (b. 1928), assumes a familiarity with the language of Marxist and other "Western" discourses against which it confidently reacts (1981). Likewise, Sayyid Qutb's book, Maʿalim fi-l-tariq [Signposts] (1981), written by a nontraditional intellectual and said to be the most widely read book among younger Muslims worldwide, would never have had the impact it has had without the spread of mass education and the access to analytical and exegetical texts that education provides.

Third, and finally, following directly from our point concerning the implications of direct access to the printed word, objectification reconfigures the symbolic production of Muslim politics. An objectified Islam has come to seem so natural and the impact of Islam on mass politics so clear that the question of who speaks for an objectified Islam becomes central to Muslim politics. Whereas the ʿulama and the state have often made mutually beneficial accommodations to each other, the relationships between them and the newer Muslim leaders have become unpredictable. Who could have predicted in 1990 that a forty-year-old mechanic in Tajikistan, Muhammad Sharif Hikmat Zade, would become the leader, two years later, of a transnational political movement in Central Asia and Russia, the Islamic Renaissance party?

In effect, the state, the ʿulama, and the "new" religious intellectuals all compete to gain ascendancy as the arbiters of Islamic practice. The political implications of this process were evident in nineteenth-century India, where the multiplication of printed texts, at first controlled by the ʿulama, "struck right at the heart of person-to-person transmission of knowledge; it struck right at the heart of Islamic authority" (Robinson 1993:239). Print at first enabled the ʿulama to expand their influence in public affairs because they sponsored and controlled religious publications. Yet the ironic consequence of printing was to reduce the authority of the ʿulama in the long run because of the rapidly increasing number of educated persons and the shift to more accessible vernacular languages (Robinson 1993:245). Similarly, the educational reforms that unfolded in the Tanzimat period in the Ottoman Empire brought about profound changes in the content and methods of transmission of knowledge. Education had previously been tied to the Islamic sciences and was transmitted from person to person. Textbooks, dictionaries, manuals, and encyclopedias supplemented, if they did not displace, the direct authority of the teacher. The results of this process became apparent in the 1890s, with the first generation to emerge from the reformed schools of the Tanzimat:

> Speculation and projection of information culled from books opened up a Pandora's box roughly similar to that which had informed early modern criticism of the text of the Bible in Europe. But even more was afoot: young officials preparing plans for new institutions were now propelled into a realm of abstract possibilities which was beginning to seem much more real than the conglomerate of rickety frame houses, crumbling public buildings and venal officials from which they started. (Mardin 1989:120)

In the last third of the twentieth century, this process of educational and social change has been intensified by mass higher education and mass communications and has created "Islamists," that is, Muslims whose consciousness has been objectified in the ways we have described and who are committed to implementing their vision of Islam as a corrective to current "un-Islamic" practices. This commitment implies a certain measure of protest, demonstrated in a variety of ways, against the prevailing political and social status quo and establishments. The term "Islamists" (al-islamiyyun) is used by Muslim activists, such as Lebanon's Muhammad Husayn Fadlallah (b. 1935), to refer to adherents of "the Islamic movement" (*al-haraka al-Islamiyya*) (for example Fadlallah 1990:238–40), and Tunisia's Rashid al-Ghannouchi (b. 1942), for whom it contextually implies ideologically motivated Muslims (al-Ghannouchi 1992:47).[11] Islamist authority to remake the world derives from a self-confident appropriation of what they believe to be "tradition." The rules of the game—whether or not they were ever unambiguous—are thus certainly complex and uncertain now. The stakes are high, and it is to this Muslim competition over what we call sacred authority that we now turn.

3

SACRED AUTHORITY

IN CONTEMPORARY MUSLIM SOCIETIES

The Linkage of Religion and Politics

MOST DISCUSSIONS of Islam and politics assume that "Islam" makes no distinction between the religious and political realms. Western scholarship—and, to a significant extent, Muslim scholarship—emphasizes the inseparability of the two by comparing Muslim with Christian political thought. Although the metaphor changed in early and medieval Christian writings, the idea of a separation of powers remained constant: God's and Caesar's due, the pope's and emperor's swords, the ecclesiastical sun and imperial moon. In Islamic thought, in contrast, the frame of reference has been the indivisibility of the whole: *din wa-dawla*, "religion and state."

This view of indivisibility finds support in more than forty references in the Qur'an to the need to obey "God, His Prophet, and those of authority among you" (for instance, 4:59). It also builds on the example of the Prophet, at once a spiritual leader and the head of a political community. As we have discussed, the defense of the institution of the caliphate was also predicated on the belief that religious and political power needed to be combined in one office, thereby allowing the *shari'a* to be implemented and the community of Muslims protected.

A careful reading of the historical record indicates that politics and religion became separable not long after the death of the Prophet and the establishment of dynastic rule. It has been argued that the bifurcation of the legal system over time, with *shari'a* courts operating alongside the *diwan al-mazalim* (board of grievances), "came close to the notion of a division between secular and religious courts"; the institutions represented two different authorities, that of God and the ruler (Coulson 1964:128–29). Some date the separation of functions and institutions to the Turkish Seljuk dynasty, which took virtual control in the 'Abbasid capital of Baghdad in the mid–eleventh century (Lewis 1979:169–70) or to the Buwayhid intervention in Baghdad in 945, which "terminated the Abbasid caliphs' dual role as the temporal and spiritual leader of the Islamic nation" (Ahmed 1985:18). Others argue that this functional separation had taken place by the ninth century, with the establishment of schools of law and the emergence of an inter- preting class—the ʿulama—who possessed semiautonomous sources of financial and political support.

Lapidus (1975:383) argues that opposition was particularly signifi- cant to the rule of the Caliph al-Maʾmun (813–33), who insisted that all Muslims adhere to the Muʿtazali theological movement. Opposition centered around the Hanbali school of law, which qualified caliphal claims to absolute power by emphasizing the availability of the Qurʾan and Prophetic traditions (hadith) to every believer. Although the Han- balis remained loyal to the ʿAbbasid state, they devalued the caliph's presumption of a monopoly on the basis of religious legitimacy. "The growth of religious loyalty to hadith and the long struggle over doc- trine and authority had crystallized a conception of the umma of Mus- lims as a community founded upon loyalty to religious principles. . . . Henceforth, the Caliphate was no longer the sole identifying symbol or the sole organizing institution, even for those Muslims who had been most closely identified with it" (Lapidus 1975:383). While the ʿulama continued to cooperate with the political authorities, the religious sphere acquired its own identity, institutions, and discourse. In effect, a religious establishment emerged as a complement—and sometimes as a rival—to the political establishment.

Many Arab historians perceive a major division between the rule of the rightly-guided caliphs and that of their successors (see, for exam- ple, Ibn Khaldun 1967:1:418–23). Mulk (royal authority, or kingship), implying dynastic rule, came to be seen as a deviation from the purity of the caliphate. This view implicitly acknowledges that a cleavage be- tween religion and political rule began when the Umayyad dynasty came to power in 661. In the case of Muhammad's first four successors, "No mention was made of royal authority, because royal authority was suspected of being worthless, and because at that time it was the prerogative of unbelievers and enemies of Islam" (Ibn Khaldun 1967:1:418).

One can argue that the division of spiritual and temporal powers occurred even earlier—on the death of the Prophet in 632. The caliph- ate was merely a temporal institution since religious succession to Muhammad, the "seal of the Prophets," was impossible. The caliph held political and military powers, and while it was true that he could serve as an Imam during prayers and deliver the khutba or sermon, other Muslims were also able to do so. "The caliph's relation to reli- gion was merely that of a guardian. He defended the faith just as any European emperor was supposed to do, suppressed heresies, warred against unbelievers, and extended the boundaries of Dar al-Islam (the abode of Islam), in the performance of all of which he employed the power of his secular arm" (Hitti 1953:185).

In the Shi'i world, the Imamate—the institutional apex of authority—is assumed to possess both religious and political powers. But the view that the Imamate is ineluctably a religio-political office developed only gradually, largely in response to repeated failures to exercise power. Despite the common insistence that the Imams descended in an unbroken line from 'Ali and Husayn, it is likely that at least two Imams were not recognized as having this status in their lifetimes. Moreover, although they aspired to rule, in fact they failed to capture the caliphate. Political failure inspired maximal religious justification, and there was a growing recognition that the spiritual powers of the Imamate were more important than its temporal rule.

In the Ithna 'Ashari ("Twelver") tradition, the dominant Shi'i tradition, hopes of Shi'i rule were decisively abandoned by the death of the eleventh Imam, al-Hasan al-'Askari (845–73), and his position accordingly acquired superhuman, divinely appointed qualities in the late ninth and tenth centuries. The Imamate emerged as the "proof" (hujja) for mankind in the ninth century and it was soon considered immune from sin, and, only slightly later, from error as well (Halm 1991:29, 45–46). A full-blown rationale for Imamate authority thus developed over time and was applied retroactively.

Following the occultation (ghayba) of the last Imam in 941, the question of who represents him intensely complicated the Shi'i theory of religio-political rule. The 'ulama positioned themselves as the heirs and defenders of the Imamate, but political rule largely came to be viewed as illegitimate in the absence of the Imam. The state was thus essentially an invalid institution as long as the Imam was not himself present to rule. Not until the advent of the Islamic revolution, which, as we have seen in Chapter 2, redefined the nature of the Islamic state, were the 'ulama anything more than the guardians of the religious traditions, the moral critics of the regime, or, perhaps more often, the legitimizers of secular rule.

Politicizing Religion

As common as the concept of din wa-dawla is, there are significant variations in its interpretation. Ayatullah Khomeini felt so strongly that the 'ulama had abdicated their responsibilities in the shah's period that he constantly inveighed against apoliticism and disinterest. Opposition to the Saudi monarchy, which has espoused the need for acquiescence to prevailing political authority, strengthened the Ayatullah's antipathy toward those who would not engage fully in the political fray. As Khomeini wrote in his will: "As for [those] who consider Islam separate from government and politics, it must be said to these ignoramuses that the Holy Qur'an and the Sunnah of the Prophet contain more rules regarding government and politics than in other matters" (Khomeini [1983] n.d.:22).

Although Khomeini had pronounced views, his thinking evolved throughout his lifetime and ended in what many regard as an extraordinary, even heterodox, position. His 1941 book, *Kashf al-asrar* [The discovery of secrets], juxtaposed virtuous Islamic government with the sorry state that obtained in nominally Muslim societies but conceded that "bad government is better than no government" (cited in Fischer 1980:152). Although some kings were morally corrupt, the institution of kingship is permissible. Moreover, "we do not say that government should be in the hands of the *faqih* [jurist]; rather we say that government must be run in accordance with God's law . . . and it is not feasible except with the supervision of the religious leaders" (cited in Fischer 1980:152).

Khomeini's opposition to the shah intensified after the reforms in property ownership, education, and women's rights during the White Revolution of 1961–63 angered a significant portion of the ʿulama. He emerged as the indisputable leader of the June 1963 uprising against the reforms and, as a consequence, was sent into exile. While in the Shiʿi shrine city of Najaf in Iraq, and partly as a result of his interaction with two politically active scholars, Musa al-Sadr and Muhammad Baqir al-Sadr (d. 1980), among others, Khomeini began to formulate a more assertive theory of Islamic government that put the *fuqaha* (sing., *faqih*) at the center of power. Revising the ideas of Shaykh Murtada Ansari (d. 1864) on the limited *wilaya* (guardianship) of the ʿulama, Khomeini (cited in Enayat 1983:163) argued that "*wilaya* consists of government and administration of the state and the implementation of the laws of the sacred path." But this responsibility cannot be entrusted to kings. Islamic government requires a governor who knows the *shariʿa*—the sole law—and is just. The Shiʿi Imams possessed these qualities, and since their occultation, *wilaya* has fallen collectively to the *fuqaha*. The inexorable logic of this approach, of course, casts the most learned and just of the jurists in the position of supreme power. "Guardianship of the jurist" (*vilayat-i faqih*) thus becomes the imperative of Islamic government, and the obligation to obey it is essential.

Toward the end of his life, Khomeini's theory became even more extensive. Faced with a constitutional deadlock in which the majority of the Majlis, or national assembly, and the supervisory Council of Guardians could not agree on certain legislation, he was asked by

President ʿAli Khameneʾi to comment on the president's interpretation of the limitations on the power of the supreme *faqih*. Khomeini asserted that Khameneʾi had been wrong to say that the government could exercise power "only within the bounds of divine statutes." Because the need for Islamic government is absolute, it—and, by extension, the ruler—possesses nearly absolute power.

> I should state that the government which is a part of the absolute vice-regency of the Prophet of God ... is one of the primary injunctions of Islam and has priority over all other secondary injunctions, even prayers, fasting and hajj. ... The ruler can close down mosques if need be, or can even demolish a mosque which is a source of harm. ... The government is empowered to unilaterally revoke any Shariʿah agreements which it has concluded with the people when those agreements are contrary to the interests of the country or of Islam. It can also prevent any devotional or non-devotional affair if it is opposed to the interests of Islam and for so long as it is so. The government can prevent hajj, which is one of the important divine obligations, on a temporary basis, in cases when it is contrary to the interests of the Islamic country. (BBC SWB 0043, A/7, January 8, 1988)

Doubtless with an eye to the critics of the Majlis who had formulated their criticism in Islamic terms, Speaker Hashemi Rafsanjani seized on the Ayatullah's pronouncement: "It is an immense injustice to Islam if it cannot demonstrate its power on essential issues of the state" (BBC SWB 0043, A/8, January 8, 1988). Suitably chastened, President Khameneʾi now noted the Ayatullah's wisdom in creating a thirteen-member assembly, the High Council for the Discernment of Interests, to break the legislative impasse. Because Khomeini had delegated his powers of supreme *faqih* to this new body, it could determine the interests of the state: "And what it deems to be the interests of the regime is then an Islamic and religious decree. Why? Because the preservation of the regime depends on it, or the preservation of social welfare depends on it, or the preservation of security and order depends on it" (BBC SWB 0087, A/3, February 29, 1988).

Inverting the commonly held assumption that the purpose of the Islamic state is to preserve and protect the *shariʿa*, Khomeini thus declared that the regime is empowered to curtail provisions of the *shariʿa* in order to protect the regime. President Khameneʾi baldly summarized the argument: "The preservation of the Islamic regime is a theological order, the preservation of the Islamic Republic is a tenet of jurisprudence" (BBC SWB 0087, A/3, February 29, 1988). Another leading religious figure, Ayatullah Niʾmatullah Salihi-Najafabadi, contributes to the doctrinal controversy by arguing that the *vilayat-i faqih* is based on a social contract between the people and the *faqih* and incorporates the principle of majority rule (Moussavi 1992).

Prior to the Islamic revolution, the highest recognized level of religious leadership was the *marjaʿ-i taqlid* ("source of emulation"). Ayatullah Muhammad ʿAli Araki, the last of the generally recognized *marjaʿ*s, died in December 1994, following the deaths of Ayatullah Abuʾl-Qasim al-Khuʾi in mid-1992 and Ayatullah Muhammad Reza Golpayegani in late 1993. The cumulative effect of these deaths was to throw the Shiʿi world into confusion over how to choose a successor or successors. Consistent with the maximalist view of the Islamic state that the Iranians have promoted since 1988, elements within the Iranian government appeared to nominate the supreme leader of the revolution, Ayatullah Khameneʾi, to this position. Others suggested that his erudition was not of sufficient distinction to merit this status, and the followers of Ayatullah Khuʾi have suggested that while the Iranian government has a special place in the deliberative process, the traditional colleges of Shiʿi learning, particuarly Najaf, must not be marginalized ("The Future of the Marjaʿiyya" 1994). These reevaluations of the powers of the *faqih*, Islamic government, and the *marjaʿ-i taqlid* indicate once again that doctrine is never fixed and that it may evolve in surprising directions—directions that many would regard as heretical.

Functional Division of Religion and Politics

By way of distinct contrast, others believe that too great an involvement with politics may mislead or corrupt the believers. For example, the Tablighi Jamaʿat, a significant movement of reform that originated in South Asia but now has worldwide influence, believes that the separation of religion and politics is necessary in the short term. It implicitly criticizes the quest for political power in which other Muslim groups, such as the Muslim Brotherhood, are engaged. As God's vicegerent (*khalifa*), men are given the earth to govern but are not worthy to do so until they can govern themselves. In effect, therefore, they must eschew politics until they prove themselves worthy of being political (generally, see Masud 1995).

Taking this further, some argue that Islam is only ritual and that politics must be separated from religion. An early example of this was seen in the military opposition to the ʿAbbasid caliph al-Nasir (1180–1225). The military leaders argued:

> If the caliph is the Imam, then his constant occupation must be prayer, since prayer is the foundation of the faith and the best of deeds. His preeminence in this respect and the fact that he serves as an example for

the people is sufficient for him. This is the true sovereignty; the influence of the caliph in the affairs of government is senseless; they should be entrusted to sultans (recorded by the Persian historian Ravandi [al-Rawandi], cited in Lewis 1988:47–48).

Reflecting the obvious desire to ward off religiously based opposition, contemporary leaders, including Jordan's King Hussein and the Algerian government, prefer to emphasize the spiritual nature of Islam and caution against mixing religion and politics. In Malaysia, Prime Minister Tun Hussein bin Onn (1922–90, r. 1976–81) warned against allowing "religion to be made a political tool" (Mutalib 1990: 147). In announcing the creation of a Ministry of Religious Affairs in March 1992, Tunisian president Ben ʿAli (b. 1936; r. 1987–) spoke of religion as "an element of unity and amity" that must remain "above political considerations" as it guides all Tunisians to "do good deeds and to shun evil, sin, and transgression" (BBC SWB 1322, A/11, March 6, 1992). Explicitly adopting a tenet of Christian political thought, King Hassan of Morocco denounced Islamic "fundamentalism" (al-usuliyya) as "religious deviation" (al-shudhudh al-dini) and spoke disparagingly of its adherents, who have placed themselves outside Islam by their political manipulation of religion: "We should resort to what the Christians say: render unto God that which is God's and unto Caesar (Hiraql) that which is Caesar's" (Hassan II 1993:8).

Unlike Hassan II, Iraq's President Saddam Hussein does not bear the title amir al-muʾminin (commander of the faithful), but his views on mixing religion and politics are similar:

> For the sake of religion, we should not name ourselves clergymen or mix religion and the state's performance of its duties. . . . If we in Iraq were to use politics in a religious framework, we would become a team within a certain religion or teams within religions and sects. Then we would be dividing the Iraqi people. The same thing would happen in Egypt. Therefore, we must first separate religion from politics and then avoid being sectarian. (FBIS, NES-87-127, July 2, 1987, p. K4)

Although the political expedience of this line of thought is obvious, some writers have invested the separation of religion and politics with doctrinal significance. ʿAli ʿAbd al-Raziq (1888–1966), a shaykh of al-Azhar mosque-university in Cairo, ignited an explosive controversy in 1925 when his book, al-Islam wa-usul al-hukm (Islam and the roots of government) suggested that the religious and administrative powers of the Prophet were separate. Muhammad's governance of the Muslim community at Medina was not part of his Prophetic mission, and his successors, the caliphs, succeeded only to temporal power.

Although ʿAbd al-Raziq was made to stand trial before his colleagues (Henderson 1925; Egypt 1925) and was ultimately removed from his teaching position, this line of argument has persisted. The Pakistani writer Qamaruddin Khan, for example, has proposed that the political theory of Islam does not arise from the Qurʾan but from circumstances and that the state is neither divinely sanctioned nor strictly necessary as a social institution. The Muslim "constitution" is flexible and should not have become the rigid and intellectually indefensible institution it has become as a means to defend the political status quo in Muslim societies. Khan argues that Muslims need to understand that there is nothing preordained about the intimate admixture of religion and politics:

> The claim that Islam is a harmonious blend of religion and politics is a modern slogan, of which no trace can be found in the past history of Islam. The very term, "Islamic State," was never used in the theory or practice of Muslim political science, before the twentieth century. Also if the first thirty years of Islam were excepted, the historical conduct of Muslim states could hardly be distinguished from that of other states in world history. (1982:74)

The modernist Fazlur Rahman believes that the injection of politics into the religious sphere has been deleterious. He argues that Islamic precepts should govern politics, but what has occurred instead is the exploitation of Islamic concepts and organizations by political groups and elites. The result has been "sheer demagoguery" rather than morally inspired politics. "The slogan 'in Islam religion and politics are inseparable' is employed to dupe the common man into accepting that, instead of politics or the state serving the long-range objectives of Islam, Islam should come to serve the immediate and myopic objectives of party politics" (1982:140).

The Indonesian intellectual Nurcholish Madjid (b. 1939) has argued that Islam does not require an Islamic state (*negara Islam*) and that "secularization" (*sekularisasi*)—the process of distinguishing the divinely ordained from what has been devised by humans—is essential. In his early writings, he argued that any separation of religion and state would unacceptably mean that "God has no right to administer worldly affairs" (cited in Hassan 1982:24) and would thus be a deviation from the principle of *tawhid* (the oneness of God). But since 1970 his thinking, influenced by the ideas of Harvey Cox and Robert Bellah, has evolved, with *tawhid* becoming the very reason for secularization: "Islam itself, if examined truthfully, was begun with a process of secularization. Indeed, the principle of Tauhid represents the starting point for a much larger secularization" (cited in Hefner 1993:6; see also Hassan 1982:92–93). While Madjid acknowledges that many understand "secularism" when they read "secularization" and that such misunderstandings are to be regretted (Madjid 1995), he is committed to the view that the Muslim community will benefit from an unambiguous distinction between matters which are transcendental and those which are temporal. In so desacralizing human activities, the *umma* will be liberated of the hold of traditionalism and will be open to progress and a future based on rationality and the modern sciences.

Nasr Hamid Abu Zayd, an Egyptian professor denied tenure at the University of Cairo for his supposedly un-Islamic views, has elaborated a sophisticated indictment of the deleterious political ramifications of ascribing to oneself the definitive right to interpret sacred texts. In *Naqd al-khitab al-dini* (A critique of religious discourse), he argues, despite obvious differences between the official religious establishment and oppositional Islamists, that their religious discourse is remarkably similar in its claim to represent holy writ. In invoking textual authority to justify what in effect is their interpretative license, their reasoning becomes circular and closed, denying others a similar right to interpretation. Al-Azhar ʿulama thus proclaim the Islamists of al-Jamaʿat al-Islamiyya (the Islamic Associations) as beyond the pale of orthodoxy, and the Islamists similarly anathematize both the ʿulama and the secular elite, thereby polarizing and subverting the political life of society (Abu Zayd 1992).

Muhammad Saʿid al-Ashmawi, a prominent Egyptian judge and writer, argues that many of the past failures of Islamic history have been due to the very mixture (*khilt*) of religion and politics. An examination of the bases of Islamic law in his view reveals that the Qurʾan contains relatively few direct legal commands, and the attempts of the "fundamentalists" to prescribe action in every sphere, justified as required by the *shariʿa*, is self-aggrandizing. This presumptuousness inevitably leads to distortions of Islam and limitations on individual liberties. The first sentence of his *al-Islam al-siyasi* (Political Islam) emphatically throws down the challenge to dogmatic Islamists and is daring in its certitude: "Allah intended that Islam be a religion, [whereas] people (*al-nas*) understood it to mean politics" (al-Ashmawi 1987:7; see also al-Ashmawi 1990).

The Libyan leader, Muʿammar al-Qadhdhafi (b. 1942, r. 1969–) incurred the wrath of many Muslims in Libya and throughout the world and such groups as the Muslim Brotherhood for his revision of the Muslim calendar, his radical criticism of the tradition of the Prophet (*sunna*), and his harsh treatment of the ʿulama (Davis 1987:56). He has not been adverse to manipulating Islamic traditions and discourse to justify his policies and extend his own influence. Yet, he has also endorsed the view that religion and state are separate realms which, when combined, become dangerous: "Prophecy has nothing to do with politics or the state. . . . [W]hen we deal with politics the supernatural becomes irrelevant. . . . [T]he political factor and all that is related to it is a subjective problem facing the human communities on this planet—a problem they have the right to resolve the way they deem fit" (al-Qadhdhafi 1985).

In Indonesia, the Nahdatul Ulama ("the Revival of the 'Ulama") party (NU) eschewed a direct political role from its inception in 1926. It preferred to emphasize the social welfare duties of Muslims. Although it joined other Muslim groups in 1973 to form the United Development party, NU—which has some thirty million followers— returned to its apolitical stance when it chose Abdurraham Wahid (b. 1940) its leader in 1984. Committed to the idea of a pluralist, democratic, and nonsectarian Indonesia, Wahid has vigorously argued that religion and politics are separate, and that Islam does not incorporate any notion of state: "Islam should be implemented as social ethics and mores, not laws. We have to protect the national view, not the Islam view" (cited in Schwarz 1992a; also see Schwarz 1992b; Wahid 1995). This apolitical stand appeared to be reinforced at NU's twentyninth national conference in December 1994, when Wahid was reelected as leader.

An extension of this argument, although it is held by a minority, holds that religious thought, by its very nature, is obscurantist. Religious scholars, in particular, take upon themselves the role of defending tradition, but in fact they utilize it as a means to power and control. Sadiq al-'Azm, a Syrian philosopher who has written on Immanuel Kant, has trenchantly criticized the prevailing ideological straightjackets and deceptions of the modern age, whether these be Arab nationalism (1968) or religion (1982). In his view, "fundamentalism"— Christian or Islamic—is based on a "principled rigidity" (1993b:91), and while it is possible that fundamentalists will adapt to the needs of the modern world, this will mark the triumph of secular reason: "In the longer run the resulting socio-historical secular reality will inevitably burst through the mystical shell of Islam" (1993b:97). Although the manner of argumentation is markedly different, Aziz al-Azmeh, a professor of Arab and Islamic Studies at the University of Exeter, similarly undermines the assumption of an indivisibility of religion and politics. Rather than making secularism the antithesis of Islam, he questions the dichotomy and points to the possibility of an "Islamic secularism" (1993).

It is evident that Muslims hold a variety of opinions on the relationship between religion and politics. Yet, despite both the intellectual diversity and the early history of Islam, the assumption of "Caesero-papism," the indivisibility of the two realms, persists in the study of Islam. This is the case for some Western writers (for example, Endress 1988:32; Watt 1980:29) and for Muslim writers who advocate particular interpretations of Islam. The view that Islam is indistinguishably religious and political is found in the writings of Khurshid Ahmad (1976:36–37), Muhammad Asad (1980:2–6), Muhammad Husayn Fadlallah (1986:258–62), Rashid al-Ghannouchi (1993:51), Abu-l Aʿla al-Mawdudi (1976:17–18; 1986:68–69), and Hasan al-Turabi (1983: 241–42; 1987).

The presupposition of the union of religion and politics, *din wa-dawla*, is unhelpful for three reasons, however. First, it exaggerates the uniqueness of Muslim politics. Religion is obviously central to the political life of peoples around the world, not simply to Muslims. The Moral Majority in the United States, "base ecclesiastical communities" and advocates of liberation theology in Latin America, Archbishop Desmond Tutu in South Africa, Pope John Paul II in Poland and eastern Europe, Sikh activists in India, Buddhist monks in Burma or Vietnam—these are a few of the practitioners of "religious politics" at work throughout the world who sometimes assert the indivisibility of religion and politics. Indeed, issues such as abortion, racism, political and economic refuge, and nuclear war have prompted religious groups to take a direct stand on policy issues and to seek to inject divine injunctions into all levels of the political process. In this regard, although the issues have not always been the same, the Muslim political process is not radically different from that of other societies.

Second, the emphasis on *din wa-dawla* inadvertently perpetuates "Orientalist" assumptions that Muslim politics, unlike other politics, are not guided by rational, interest-based calculations. Part of the reason lies in the general preference in the social sciences for the rational actor, which, as discussed in Chapter 2, tends to make religion a nonrational—if not an emotional and irrational—factor. But an Orientalist scholarship that emphasizes differences between "East" and "West" and often projects stereotypes has not been averse to accepting nonrational religion as the defining characteristic of Muslim political and social life. In effect, therefore, because of the omnipresence of religion, Muslims are thought to be passionate, uncontrollable, intransigent, and impossible to negotiate with. As Yehoshafat Harkabi, a former chief of Israeli military intelligence, has observed, "Islam doesn't recognize coexistence as a basic doctrine. Coexistence goes against Islam's sense of world order" (cited in Gelb 1992).

Third, the *din wa-dawla* assumption contributes to the view that Muslim politics is a seamless web, indistinguishable in its parts because of the natural and mutual interpenetration of religion and politics. Because Islam is thought to incorporate all aspects of life and because everything is thus assumed to be political, political structures are underestimated. Like all political communities, Muslim societies have distinguishable, though overlapping, structures. The mosque, *madrasa* (Islamic school), and *majlis al-shura* (consultative assembly), as well as the bureaucracy charged with regulating religious matters and professional associations, such as women's lawyers' groups, are institutions with shared but identifiable functions related to one set of religious beliefs and practices. They are the components of "sacred authority."

Authority and the Interpretation of Symbols

Consistent with the argument developed in Chapter 1, our criticism of the *din wa-dawla* argument is built on a view of politics as the contest over the interpretation of symbols and as the setting of and negotiation over boundaries between spheres of social activity and institutions. Standard assumptions that religion and politics are inseparable or that religion and politics must be separated tell us little about how religious politics function. The key to understanding the intricate and intersecting relationships between religion and politics lies, rather, in the nature of authority.

"Sacred authority" as a concept may appear to reaffirm the indivisibility of religion and politics—the conventional wisdom that has been questioned in this discussion. But our use of the term makes two fundamental assumptions:

1. Sacred authority is one *kind* of authority among others. It is not predicated on the indivisibility of religion and politics because not all authority is based on religion. Indeed, we are talking about a specific type of authority, one which remains distinct from authority based on control of, say, the military (leading to what some call the "praetorian state") or the intelligence and security apparatuses—what has in the Middle East been called the *mukhabarat* (security police) state (see, for example, Wenner 1993:179). Our analysis, by way of contrast, is not exclusively preoccupied with the "Islamic state," nor does it assume that religious authority is all-encompassing.

2. Sacred authority does not, by the same token, assume that religion and politics are completely independent spheres of activity. They are separable spheres that intersect and overlap according to context. The interaction occurs when groups or states vie to manipulate religious language and symbolism to induce or compel obedience to their wishes.

To have authority, like power, is "to be able to make a difference to the world" (Lukes 1986:5), but the two cannot be simply equivalent to each other. Whether authority is based on "the institutionalization of the normative order" (Parsons [1963] 1986:113) or "respect" (Arendt [1969] 1986:65), crucial to its meaning is its recognition as legitimate, whereas this recognition is not essential in the case of power. To answer the basic question of why does authority exist, the complex relationship between the carriers and followers of authority must be considered, and three interconnected levels of analysis are apparent—ideological, locational, and functional:

• *Ideological.* Without wishing to predicate the argument on an abstract and unverifiable state of nature, as is common in political philosophy, we recognize that authority is invested in individuals and institutions because they are thought to incorporate and exemplify the moral order. In part, authorities are given authority because they appear to embody cherished values and represent the symbolic reference points of society, including sacred texts (Eickelman 1985:58–71; Messick 1993). Yet it is also clear that deference or acquiescence, the voluntary investiture of authority, is only part of the story. Those bearing authority transform themselves over time into "natural" leaders and, through the manipulation of the symbols of society and the invocation of tradition, they make claims of obedience and obligation on others. Authority inheres in those who are considered to have justifiable control over a society's symbolic production, and with enhanced and routinized elaboration of this control, leaders can compel obedience but usually prefer to encourage it (compare Mann 1986:22–24).

• *Locational.* In the case of the Muslim world, where values and symbols revolve around people's engrained belief in a transcendent yet immediate presence, the institutionalization of sacred authority entails multiple individuals and groups which hope to speak for the divine presence. These may be religious scholars, Islamist movements, the religious bureaucracy of the state, Sufi *shaykhs*, or traditional leaders such as village headmen or healers. Because symbols are ambiguous by nature and subject to widely differing interpretation, they are manipulable by these contenders for authority—thus promoting the fragmentation of authority. As elsewhere, the contention in Muslim societies over control or "appropriation" of symbols is intense, and authority is in part defined by one's position relative to competitors.

• *Functional.* Authorities also derive their prestige and influence from the performance of a number of functions. Endowed with symbolic capital, they are looked to for guidance and thus are expected to delimit and defend the "proper" place of Islamic discourse and practice. However, the logic of their role is somewhat circular. They draw boundaries because they have authority, and doing so further confirms their authority. Moreover, given the multiple centers of power in a society—whether expressly concerned with Islamic matters or not—authorities are esteemed because they mediate among the various poles. Illustrative of this are the *'ulama*, who help to break through bureaucratic obfuscation and rigidity to secure housing or other social benefits for their "clients."

The bearers of sacred authority, including but not limited to the *'ulama*, may not only serve as go-betweens but also represent specific social and economic interests. Sufi *shaykhs* in the African countryside often represent the interests of the peasantry, for instance, and the *'ulama* in countries such as Iran, Syria, and Saudi Arabia often defend the interests of the bazaar or *suq* merchants, while Islamist groups may represent the interests of disenchanted and relatively nonmobile middle-class professionals. But values and interests are not radically divorced from each other, and, of course, values can be interests and interests can be valued. Interests are doubtless important in any political order, including the Islamic world, but they do not remain value-free or detached from the larger understandings that the political order engenders.

The interconnection of these ideas is evident even in societies where Muslims are a minority. In the Ningxia Hui Autonomous Region of Northwest China, local authorities guardedly tolerate the new emphasis among Hui Muslims on performing "correct" Islamic rituals, often spearheaded by Sufi orders such as the Khufiyya. They see this emphasis on ritual as socially and politically conservative. Yet they fear that the next stage of this religious revitalization may be "fanaticism." Hui Muslims do not differentiate between their ethnic and religious identities, whereas state authorities seek to maintain a sharp distinction between them out of fear that religious activities may contribute to political destabilization. This dispute between state authorities and community religious leaders over the exclusion of the "religious" from the "political" domains is clearly expressed in the words of a local Communist party official in Yinchuan: "The Hui are allowed to maintain their ethnic customs that are influenced by Islamic traditions, but religion and ethnicity are two separate matters and should not be confused" (Gladney 1992a:97; see also Gladney 1991:132). In effect, state and local Sufi leaders contest the limits of sacred authority.

The case of Mayotte, a village of the Comoros Islands in East Africa, suggests that boundary questions are just as relevant to societies that have experienced less revolutionary change. Michael Lambek demonstrates that local religious officials (*fundis*) derive their immense authority from their knowledge of Islamic texts and a reputation for personal integrity. Yet they do not possess automatic political authority. Villagers appear willing to accord a senior religious man great respect and to follow his prescriptions in personal affairs and ritual, but they consider his intervention in a village dispute improper. The "partial disconnection of religion and politics" is the result. "Villagers believe that the *fundis* create and uphold the morality of the community by being *fundis*; once they engage in partisan politics they threaten the very nature of morality itself" (Lambek 1990:34).

Fundis see it differently, however, believing that the moral universe encompasses land or tax disputes and even the programs of political parties. This disagreement over where morality ends and politics begins—or, to put the point somewhat differently, over what constitutes the nature of morality in a Muslim society and who creates and controls it—is intensely political.

Contesting Sacred Authority: Saudi Arabia

The Muslim politics of Saudi Arabia has also invoked questions about the changing nature of sacred authority there. At one level of interpretation, Saudi Arabia appears to be a near-perfect example of the indivisibility of religion and politics. In the mid–eighteenth century, Muhammad al-Saʿud (r. 1745–65) was a local prince (*amir*) and Muhammad ibn ʿAbd al-Wahhab (1703–87) a zealous but unsuccessful puritanical reformer until they concluded a mutually advantageous alliance. The alliance propelled the Saudis to control of most of the Arabian peninsula and solidified "Wahhabism" as a major reform movement in modern Muslim history.[1] In the present period, the symbiotic relationship continues between the political and religious establishments: The monarchy needs the cooperation and approbation of the ʿulama to enhance its legitimacy, while the ʿulama need royal support and patronage to maintain their privileges and, to a lesser extent, to wield influence over policy making.

On another level of interpretation, a subtle contest over boundaries has taken place between the ruling family and religious officials. The monarchical elite has often circumvented the ʿulama by relying on royal decrees (*nizams*), rather than *fatawa*, to make administrative, economic, and social changes. Although religious judges (*qadis*) retain substantial latitude in the judicial system, the king has often invoked his sovereign prerogative to mitigate the impact of *shariʿa* court decisions.

The ʿulama, for their part, have focused opposition on certain policies to force the regime to cede ground. For example, the Saudi government issued a decree in November 1950 that imposed an income tax on everyone in the kingdom, both Saudis and non-Saudis. The purpose was to increase the revenues of the state, primarily from the profits of the Arabian American Oil Company, but the *ulama* objected to a tax on Saudi citizens because it would detract from the Muslim obligation to give alms (*zakat*). As a consequence, the revised royal decree of June 1951 deleted the income tax obligation on Saudis (CEDEFS 1967).[2]

In March 1992, King Fahd announced a series of administrative changes, which, because of their sweeping and unparalleled character, amounted to a constitutional package for the kingdom. Several of his predecessors had proclaimed their intention to reform the system by creating a consultative assembly, but they proved reluctant to command it (Piscatori 1983a:68–69). The regime appeared to have weathered the shocks of Nasserist pan-Arabism in the late 1950s and early 1960s, the rapid increase in oil-generated wealth in the 1970s, the Iranian revolution and the siege of the Grand Mosque in Mecca in the late 1970s, and the Iran-Iraq war in the 1980s. But the climate turned unfavorable early in the 1990s, partly as a result of the cumulative effects of rapid economic growth and the expansion of the educational system and partly as a result of the direct threat to the regime posed by the 1990 Iraqi invasion of Kuwait.

This invasion brought matters within Saudi Arabia to the boiling point. Middle-class elements regarded a regime that required hundreds of thousands of foreign troops to defend it as weak and narrowly based, while religious elements viewed it as tainted by intimate association with infidels. Both elements have pressed for reforms in a number of publicly circulated petitions or "advice" (*nasihas*). For example, a letter signed by forty-three merchants and professionals in December 1990 demanded greater accountability and called on the king to create consultative assemblies on both the national and local levels, to allow women greater freedom, and to curb the power of the "religious police" (*al-mutawwaʿun*).

A petition signed by eighteen Saudi religious leaders on May 18, 1991, called for the creation of a consultative council (*majlis al-shura*). Their concern was both to enhance the Islamic bases of the political system and to limit the influence of the more secular-minded among the middle classes. The religious scholars suggested, for example, that the assembly's members be selected on the basis of their "competence"—presumably in Islamic matters—and not on the basis of their social status or gender. They also called for the Islamization of the economy, media, military, and foreign policy (Haeri 1991). Reflecting the regime's unease, senior *ulama* denounced the public manner in which the demands were made; advice, they said, should not be divisive, and gratitude is owed the rulers for the stability and prosperity they have provided (BBC SWB, ME/1090, A/6–7, June 5, 1991).

Concerned about the general disquiet, the king maneuvered between the various factions when he promulgated the systemic reforms of 1992. His speech to the nation was a ringing reaffirmation of the religious nature of the state: The kingdom had been founded "on a clear programme of politics" that could be summarized by "belief and shari'a" (Fahd 1992). In the Basic Law of Governance (al-nizam al-asasi), the government was also careful to reiterate the Islamic basis of the state. According to the text of this law (Saudi Arabia 1992), it does not constitute a constitution (dustur) because only the Qur'an and the sunna of the Prophet are the true constitution of a Muslim society (Article 1). The political system is a monarchy (Article 5), but government "derives its authority (sultathu) from the Book of God Almighty and the sunna of His Prophet"(Article 7). Moreover, "the state protects the credo of Islam; it implements its shari'a; it orders people to do right and avoid evil; it fulfills the duty of the call (da'wa) to God" (Article 23).

These provisions appeal to the religiously inclined elements of society, but the regime was also aware that many Saudis were irritated at the entrenched position of the 'ulama. As a result, the Basic Law of Governance incorporates provisions that qualify their traditional position in Saudi society. It requires that fatawa be based on the Qur'an and the sunna (Article 45) and that shari'a court decisions be similarly based on the principal sources of Islam as well as on "statutes issued by the ruler [waly al-amr]" that are consistent with those sources (Article 48). Perhaps the most important provisions, however, limit the de facto powers of the religious police. "No one shall be arrested, imprisoned or have their actions restricted except in accordance with the provisions of the law" (Article 36), and, more importantly, "The home is sacrosanct [hurmatan] and shall not be entered without the permisssion of the owner or be searched except in cases specified by statute (al-nizam)" (Article 37).

The Saudi regime therefore walks a tightrope between competing claimants on the system. Despite the all-encompassing rhetoric in the Basic Law of Governance about the Islamic nature of the state, the regime has endeavored to delineate boundaries between its authority and those of the religious leaders and, to a lesser extent, the educated professional classes. Yet problems persist. In September 1992, over one hundred Saudi professionals and 'ulama signed a memorandum bluntly calling for an end to corruption in royal and governmental circles and termination of the alliance with the United States. On May 3, 1993, a human rights group was formed in Riyadh by four university professors, a civil servant, and two lawyers; it was supported by a small number of *ulama*. Careful to invoke the traditional framework of *shari‘a* in its name—Lajnat al-Difa‘ ‘an al-Huquq al-Shar‘iyya (Committe for the Defense of Legitimate Rights)—and calling for greater implementation of Islamic law (*shari‘a*), the committee was openly critical of the Saudi goverment (see, for example, "Lajnat al-Difa‘ ‘an al-huquq al-shar‘iyya" 1993; *New Saudi Rights* 1993.

One religious scholar in the group, Shaykh ‘Abd Allah ibn ‘Abd al-Rahman al-Jibrin, had joined other *ulama* in July 1992 in criticizing the regime for allowing torture and other abuses, in violation of Islamic law. The Minister of the Interior, Prince Nayf ibn ‘Abd al-‘Aziz, insisted that "governed by our Muslim beliefs, we in the Kingdom respect human rights more than any other state or society in the world" (BBC SWB 1690, A/9, May 17, 1993). Yet this assurance did not prevent the group's proscription or the continued arrests of critics and dissidents. On May 12, 1993, the government secured a *fatwa* from the twenty-one members of the Hay’at Kubar al-‘Ulama (Council of Grand ‘Ulama), saying that the formation of the committee was unjustified because the kingdom, by God's grace, was already ruled by Islamic law and that Saudis were able to redress grievances through the *shari‘a* courts and other bodies ("Lajnat al-Difa‘ ‘an al-huquq al-shar‘iyya" 1993:7; see also, Walker 1993). In September 1994, 110 critics of the regime—including two religious scholars, Salman al-‘Uda and Safar al-Hawali—were arrested. One year earlier the king had asked the Council of Grand ‘Ulama to investigate and confront the dissident *ulama*, but they had refused to recant their views. According to the regime, it was necessary to act before civil disorder (*fitna*) became entrenched, and the government resolved to act against those who interfered with the "destiny of the country" (*muqaddarat al-bilad*) and the "sanctities" (*muqaddasat*) of Muslims ("al-Sa‘udiyya" 1994:4). Therefore, since the second Gulf war, the contest over the state's hitherto relatively unchallenged monopoly on sacred authority has become intense.

Images in the Contest over Authority

In a less subtle way than the Saudis, Saddam Hussein has appropriated the symbols of Islam to bolster his rule. During the Iran-Iraq war, he ordered the construction of a massive new monument to celebrate Iraq's inevitable victory over the Iranians and Saddam's heroic leadership (see fig. 5). The monument depicts two giant hands holding crossed blades that represent the sword of Qadisiyya, symbolic of the battle in 637 in which Arab Muslim forces defeated Iran and brought it into the Islamic realm. The official invitation to the monument's ded-

Fig. 5. The Qadisiyya Monument, Baghdad.

ication in August 1989 left no doubt as to the connection between the divinely inspired leadership of seventh-century Muslims and that of Saddam Hussein which the monument is meant to suggest: "The ground bursts open and from it springs the arm that represents power and determination, carrying the sword of Qadisiyya. It is the arm of the Leader-President, Saddam Hussein himself (God preserve and watch over him) enlarged forty times" (al-Khalil 1991:2).

Faced with signficant Shi'i opposition to his secular and repressive rule, Saddam has also invoked specifically Shi'i symbolism to legitimize his position, despite his 1987 pronouncement, cited earlier in this chapter, that religion and politics should remain separate. Although he hails from the Sunni town of Tikrit, north of Baghdad, and has long been a committed member of the secular Ba'thist party, he has commissioned posters of himself riding a white stallion. White is a sign of purity, and the white horse is a familiar image associated with the Imam Husayn, martyred in the fields of Karbala in 680, who became the quintessential Shi'i hero (al-Khalil 1991:11, 14). In Karbala itself, a shrine city of immense spiritual signficance to Shi'a throughout the world, Saddam's giant portrait stands next to the silver door to the tomb of the Imam 'Abbas, and a nearby banner proclaims that "The visitors to the holy shrine in Karbala ask God to preserve Saddam Hussein." The shrine of the Imam Husayn also sports a banner asking visitors to "embrace and thank the President for taking care of the holy shrine" (Cockburn 1992:13).

Other common ways for Muslim political leaders to assert their religious credentials and to affirm their sacred authority is undertaking the *hajj* and the public performance of prayer. With an eye to Indonesia's 1992 legislative elections, President Suharto (b. 1921) made a highly publicized pilgrimage in 1991. Similarly, President Hafiz al-Asad (b. 1920) of Syria, concerned that his 'Alawi background would make him appear heterodox to the country's Sunni majority, prayed in public with King Faysal (ca. 1904–75), the devout king of Saudi Arabia. Both Syrian and other Arab media featured extensive coverage of the event. In 1973, al-Asad also obtained a *fatwa* from the head of the Higher Shi'i Council in Lebanon, the influential Imam Musa al-Sadr, declaring that the 'Alawis constituted a branch of Shi'i Islam (Seale 1990:173).

Like states, religious actors often manipulate symbols to enhance their struggle with governments over who speaks for Islam. One group opposed to the Saudi and other Gulf monarchies, for example, employed a logo on its publications suggesting that it, rather than the House of Sa'ud represents Islam (see fig. 6). The logo features the Ka'ba, the focal point of the pilgrimage in Mecca, from which arises a globe and a rifle in a clenched fist. Underneath is the name of the group, Munazzamat al-Thawra al-Islamiyya fi-l-Jazira al-'Arabiyya (Organization of the Islamic Revolution in the Arabian Peninsula), and above the picture is the Qur'anic phrase referring to the Prophet's injunctions to his followers to proceed against Tabuk: "Go forth lightly and heavily [equipped] and strive with your wealth and persons in the cause of God" (9:41).

In Egypt, many Islamists have attacked the pyramids, Egypt's paramount national symbol, as a celebration of the pre-Islamic "era of ignorance" (*jahiliyya*).[3] They find inspiration for their views in the Qur'an, which memorializes the Pharaoh as "arrogant" (*istakbar*) and "insolent [*junudahu*] in the land beyond reason [*bi-ghayr al-haqq*]" (28:39; see also 22:38; 69:24). Similarly, commenting on the Qur'anic story of Moses' confrontation with Pharaoh, Sayyid Qutb made Pharaonic rule the template for tyranny and implied that a courageous confrontation with tyrants (*tawaghit*)—those who had usurped God's power—was needed today (Qutb 1985:3:1330–31). Some activists go so far as to demand that the pyramids be razed (Walker 1992), seeing them as an offensive representation of a moral order that was destined to perish with the advent of Islamic revelation. For these Muslims, the identity of the state is compromised by the pyramids because the state, in celebrating Egypt's archaeological heritage, appears to support the ideals of the *jahiliyya*. Despite the sensitivities of the activists, the government, intent on promoting the special place of Egypt in the Arab

Fig. 6. Opposition groups appropriate Islamic imagery
and Qur'anic verses to legitimize their causes. Logo
of the Islamic Revolutionary Organization in the
Arabian Peninsula.

and Mediterranean worlds, has deployed Pharaonic and even Greek
images—Nefertiti, the pyramids, a Greek amphitheather—on bank
notes and stamps (Sivan 1990a:1007). It is not surprising, therefore,
that, immediately after Sadat's assassination, the assassin linked the
un-Islamic nature of the modern state with the *jahili* society prior to the
seventh century: "I am Khalid Islambuli; I killed Pharaoh, and I am not
afraid of death" (Kepel 1984:184).

Roy Mottahedeh has written of the outrage Iranians felt at the im-
prisonment by the shah's security apparatus of one young *mullah* (a
junior religious authority) who wore the black turban of the *sayyid*, a
descendant of the Prophet. Upon the *mullah*'s release from detention,
he was warmly greeted by the congregation of his mosque, one of
whom summarized the general and politicized feeling: "It's not right,
a learned sayyed like you in prison." With conscious irony, the *mullah*
replied, "On the contrary, it's my heritage as a sayyed" (Mottahedeh
1985:265).

Symbols may also be manipulated in the contest among various
nonstate Muslim groups. For example, from 1975 to 1990, Lebanon

Fig. 7. The words underneath this AMAL-inspired tree of martyrs, painted on the side of a house on the road to Sur (Tyre), indicate that it is nourished by the blood-soaked "land of the south"—Israeli-occupied south Lebanon.

was locked in a devastating civil war, often thought to have pitted an entrenched Christian elite against a dissatisfied Muslim majority. Yet many divisions existed within the Muslim ranks, as they do within Christian ranks. Among the Shi'a, in particular, a relatively accommodationist group, Afwaj al-Muqawama al-Lubnaniyya (AMAL, the Lebanese Resistance Battalions) and a less compromising movement influenced by Iran, Hizbullah, have been bitter opponents. Both movements manipulate Islamic symbols. As figure 7 shows, the AMAL painting of a tree whose branches indicate the names of "martyrs" to the cause invokes an Islamic symbolism of *shahada* (martyrdom). The logo attached to many Hizbullah publications (fig. 8) depicts the arm of Husayn holding an automatic rifle, a Qur'an, and a globe arising from the Arabic words denoting "party of God." Over this is the Qur'anic verse, "For truly the party of God will be the victors" (58:22), and beneath it, "The Islamic Revolution in Lebanon." The effect of this representation is to suggest the divinely ordained and universal nature of the movement's struggle and to link it with the successes of the Iranian revolution, thus distinguishing it from other groups in Lebanon in order to affirm its superior claim to sacred authority.

Fig. 8. "For truly the Party of God will be the
victors." Hizbullah logo, Lebanon.

Networks of Authority

The preceding discussion makes clear that no one group in Muslim
societies possesses a "monopoly on the management of the sacred"(Kane 1992:9). Kings, presidents, military officers, bureaucrats
(dealing specifically with religious issues and otherwise), 'ulama, Sufi
shaykhs, and nontraditionally educated intellectuals are all competitors
for sacred authority. To complicate matters further, several or all may
exercise authority simultaneously—one individual's sacred authority
is not exclusive of another's. We describe below several themes common to all of them.

First, all Muslim leaders are conditioned by the modern world, and
distinctions between "fundamentalists," "traditionalists," and "modernists" are misleading if they ignore the common ground on which
they all stand. Very real differences in type of education, social posi-

tion, and ideology exist among them, but none has remained unaffected by the normative and technological changes that have swept the world in this century. Chapter 2 demonstrated how the constitution of revolutionary Iran acknowledges the contemporary emphasis on popular sovereignty while reaffirming the traditional, and formerly exclusive, principle of divine sovereignty. From the perspective of analyzing Muslim politics, judgments as to whether the coexistence of these two ideas is contrived or valid are less helpful than noting the tendency to invent and reinvent tradition.

Political change is complex and differs according to political ideas and the need to persuade others to share them and their associated organizational structures. Actors always have available the vision of alternative "imagined" communities. An important component of understanding politics consists of recognizing how these alternative visions alter or replace currently dominant and authoritative ones. The fact that proponents of credos, beliefs, or ideologies may assert that their values and visions are timeless and immemorial should not obscure the fact that they are subject to constant modification and change. Muslims assert their continuity with the past while coming to terms with a modern intellectual terrain.

As Chapter 5 will explain, Muslims use modern technology for their own purposes. That this is so is obvious and would be unexceptional but for the entrenched characterizations of "fundamentalists" as committed to a virtually unchanged Islamic law (Heritage Foundation 1984:4) or intent on creating "priestly theocracies" that would be at once "fanatical" and out of touch (Reagan 1990:409). Similar ideas also prevail among the secular Arab left. Samir Amin, for example, has declared that "rationalism [and] fundamentalism constitute two states of mind irreducible to one another, incapable of integration" (1990:184). In terms of ideas and technology, Muslims are not living in a reconstructed past, nor are they turning the clock back. As Ahmad Moussalli writes, "although [Islamic] fundamentalism appears conservative, it is actually a progressive program" that demonstrates an "understanding of science as well as its impact on the structure of society and its values" (1992:9).

Second, objectified understandings of Islamic beliefs and practices have irrevocably transformed Muslim relations to sacred authority. Of crucial importance in this process has been a "democratization" of the political process of Islam and the development of a standardized language inculcated by mass higher education, the mass media, travel, and labor migration.

Throughout this century, Muslim intellectuals have articulated a powerful indictment of the un-Islamic nature of their societies. This censure is predicated on a belief that existing authorities—political rulers and their allies, the ʿulama—have failed in their guidance of Muslims and that each Muslim has the right to direct access to and interpretation of scripture. To justify this view, writers frequently invoke the Qurʾanic phrase (50:16) that God is closer to man than his jugular vein; priestly intermediaries are not required. ʿAli Shariʿati spoke disparagingly of the idea of an official clergy as "long-bearded demagogues." He said that a clergy should not exist in Islam, and he specifically criticized Iran, where the religious scholar (ʿalim) has a higher status than persons "accomplished" (fazil) in such subjects as the Qurʾan, Islamic history, and the Prophet's biography (sira). In his view, Iran's ʿulama were "second-class scholars" who have erroneously claimed hereditary and "monopolistic" powers (Shariʿati 1979:41,115–16). Habib Boularès, a former Tunisian cabinet minister, distinguishes between "the power of the ʿulama" and the "ʿulama of power." The latter, in his view, inhabit the unprincipled world of compromise and have abdicated their responsibility to speak truth to established authority: "The tragedy of the Muslim world is that this religious hierarchy prefers the flickering light of the candle to the blazing flame of the spirit" (1990:69).

In southwest Nigeria, Muhammad Jumat Imam (1896–1960), proclaimed himself the "Mahdi-Messiah" in December 1941 and proceeded to construct a new movement. It has assumed the style of a Sufi tariqa (religious order), including a shrine for its founder that has become the focal point for regional pilgrimage. Imam nominated himself as the preeminent religious authority, regarding others as lacking a knowledge of English and Arabic, which he possessed. "That such a view met with the support of many is an indication of how both the expansion of Western education and the improvements in Islamic education . . . were altering the traditional criteria for leadership" (Clarke 1988:159). The spread of British colonial education, with its access to employment in the colonial government, had begun to influence profoundly Islamic education by the 1930s. Through the establishment of Islamic educational organizations such as the Ansar ud-Deen (Companions of the Religion) and the Islamic Reformation Society in the 1930s, not only were new educational forms introduced but acquisition of this kind of education also became a standard of authority rivaling seniority and virtuous character (Clarke 1988:159–63).

Third, the combined effect of criticism of the religious status quo and the belief that sacred texts are directly apprehensible has been a potent challenge to exclusivist ideas of authority, resulting in a fragmentation of sacred authority. Like Martin Luther at the Diet of Worms (1521), Muslim writers have "claimed to be attached to the authority of the Word of God alone and . . . in public asserted the relative unimportance of all who claimed to come between God and the believer's conscience" (Lienhard 1989:96). This has led to an opening up of the political process and heightened competition for the mantle of authority.

As with the peasants' revolt (1524–25) in the wake of Luther's dissent, the effect at times has been a rejection of the infidel state and its apparatus. Members of al-Jama'at al-Islamiyya have proclaimed Egypt the land of unbelief, and Shaykh 'Umar 'Abd al-Rahman (b. 1938), has lashed out at 'ulama who appeased the government and allowed such un-Islamic practices as the drinking of alcohol, adultery, and gambling (R. Ahmad 1991:150, 160–74). The 'ulama have been clearly forced on the defensive, declaring publicly that they act only on behalf of "true Islam" (al-Islam al-sahih), seeking to combat the errors of both those who are "ignorant" (jahilin) of Islam and those who reject it altogether (see, for example, al-Ghazali 1989:1). Since Muslims need to create a more Islamic society, they argue, it is "madness" (hamaqa) to fight over furniture before the house has been rebuilt (al-Ghazali 1989:2).

Part of the explanation for this political struggle lies in the process of objectification discussed in Chapter 2 and noted above. Because Muslims around the world possess an intensified awareness of Islamic ideas and practices, they are more assertive in their judgments of what constitutes proper Islamic conduct and who is a true believer. Ironically, from the perspective of governments whose Islamic credentials are often found wanting, the educational system they foster has been pivotal in developing this new consciousness.

The impact of modern mass education is pervasive. Students are taught about the unity of Muslim thought and practice in a set national curriculum that includes Islamic studies as one subject among many. Instead of sitting at the feet of a recognized master of traditional learning, an impersonal relationship between students and teachers, who have become employees of the state, is stressed. Even while teaching that Islam permeates all aspects of life, the formal principles of Islamic doctrine and practice are compartmentalized and made an object of study. The traditionally educated religious authorities sometimes adapt to this form of education, but some resist it.

As an example of how intricate the basis of contemporary Islamic authority has become, the training of one qadi (religious judge) in the Malaysian state of Kedah combined traditional Islamic learning with a modern-style university education. Born into a family of religious scholars, Syeikh Marzuki received six years of primary education at his father's school, and then he attended the Islamic college in Alor Star and a Middle Eastern university. Informally given the title of *shaykh* in recognition of his training in the Middle East, Marzuki joined the religious bureaucracy, the Department of Religious Affairs, and eventually became a district Islamic judge. In short, he derived his authority from competence in both traditional and modern Islamic learning and the formal patronage of the state (Hassan 1993).

The beneficiaries of modern mass education are often less willing to collaborate with the state system that made their education possible in the first place. Many are attracted to Islamist groups such as the Muslim Brotherhood (in Egypt, Jordan, and the Sudan), Tunisia's Hizb al-Nahda (the Renaissance party, formerly the Mouvement de Tendance Islamique (MTI) in Tunisia), FIS in Algeria, ABIM in Malaysia, or the "Muslim Parliament" created in Great Britain in January 1992. These groups are led by "new" intellectuals, who have usually not received a traditional religious education. They include the Nahda's Rashid al-Ghannouchi, a secondary school teacher; FIS's ʿAbbasi Madani (b. 1931), who has a doctorate in education from the University of London; and the Muslim Parliament's Kalim Siddiqui (b. 1931), a former subeditor of *The Guardian* in London.[4] The groups and their leaders have become self-conscious Islamic actors who inevitably compete for authority with other self-proclaimed Islamic actors—especially the ʿ*ulama* and, increasingly, the state.

Sufi groups as well are never apolitical. They challenge the ʿ*ulama*'s exclusive control over religious knowledge and sometimes challenge the state's self-ascribed right to speak for Islam. This constitutes part of the fragmentation of sacred authority in Muslim societies. But, as we indicate throughout this book, dichotomized understandings—in this instance, Sufi *shaykh*s versus ʿ*ulama*—are distorting. It is often the case that eminent members of the ʿ*ulama*, even as they uphold the standards of orthodoxy, participate in Sufi movements. A celebrated example is the Sudanese Mahdi, Muhammad Ahmad. He was not only a religious scholar but also the founder of a religious order in which his descendants have continued to play a major role. Thus "the Mahdi himself was hard to classify in [a] Sufi-ulama dichotomy" (el-Affendi 1992:40).

In some contemporary societies, such as parts of West Africa and Central Asia, Sufi orders have increasingly taken on a pronounced political role. These orders—and opposition to them—contribute to the fragmentation of authority (Abduvakhitov 1993:80–81; Launay 1992:86–88; O'Brien 1988). In the late nineteenth and early twentieth centuries, Sufi orders throughout the Muslim world were seen as potential templates for transregional political action threatening colonial rule. French colonial authorities were concerned that the orders could be used by the Ottomans and rival colonial powers to weaken French rule in the Maghrib and sub-Saharan Africa. In practice, the authority of Sufi religious leaders was less than total, as indicated by the fact that many individuals belonged to more than one order and only a few orders required that their members join no other. As a whole, however, the hierarchies of dominance established by Sufi *tariqa*s formed a pervasive and popularly understood organizational framework in some countries, including Morocco and Afghanistan. In Morocco, for example, the language and organizational structure of the protonationalists of the 1930s was adapted from religious orders (Rezette 1955).

In contemporary West Africa, the role of the Muridiyya in Senegal in organizing economic production and framing political action from the colonial era to the present is well known (O'Brien 1971, 1975). Elsewhere, the influence of Sufi orders is more subtle but no less pervasive. As Launay (1992:179–95) writes, the basic hierarchical structure of orders such as the Qadiriyya, which spread throughout the region from the eighteenth century onward, and the Tijaniyya, which dates from the nineteenth century, requires a formal initiation, implying acceptance of the authority of a *shaykh* (religious teacher and leader) and one's own role as *murid* (pupil). This hierarchical link can be extended to transcend the life of the *shaykh* and to include more disciples than oneself. Although the authority of the *shaykh* lasts, in principle, throughout his lifetime, his knowledge and *baraka* (grace) become institutionalized and thus serve to attract and guide followers long after his death. The success of this institutionalization owes much as well to the funding that the more prestigious Sufi orders often receive from wealthy traders and industrialists, who, like philanthropists elsewhere, acquire social prestige from their charitable donations (see, for example, Tahir 1975:28, 83, 159, 165–71).

The hierarchy inherent in all Sufi orders implies that they have some degree of centralization, although a number of orders—such as Egypt's Muridiyya order—are more centralized than others. It also means that when Sufi orders lend their support to political movements or goals, as they have done on occasion, they can be highly effective (see fig. 9). The multiplicity of movements, however, means that if one order lends its support to a party or group or opposes government policy, rival orders can be manipulated to oppose it. This was clearly the case in the Sudan when President Numayri (b. 1930; r. 1969–85) exploited Khatmiyya suspicions of the Mahdiyya to bolster his rule (Cudsi 1983:52–53).

In Algeria, pilgrimages to saints' shrines and festivals associated with them were banned by the Algerian government from 1962 until 1989. The shrines and the maraboutic cults associated with them were

Fig. 9. Sufi orders in Egypt and elsewhere, long considered apolitical, are increasingly seen as part of a wider political resurgence. Procession of the Rifa'iyya order on the Prophet's birthday, Cairo, 1987.

popularly seen as symbols of refuge from government oppression. In 1989, following widespread antigovernment demonstrations and suggesting an awareness of the potency of symbolic politics, local authorities dropped the ban, in part to counter the popularity of FIS. FIS activists, like the earlier Wahhabi movement in Saudi Arabia, saw the shrines (and their networks of supporters) as potential rivals and destroyed many of them as a way of "purifying" Algeria (Goytisolo 1994). Thus, the competition over sacred authority is not just between religious movements and the state but among Muslim activists as well.

Even where Sufi orders are seen as weak or politically peripheral, as in Burkino Faso and the Ivory Coast, the rivalry among types and styles of authority is politically significant. At the end of World War II, Manding-speaking pilgrims returning from the *hajj* began to preach against local religious traditions. Exposed to reformist thought, they challenged the authority of established scholars and denounced saint worship as well as the tombs of the founders of leading scholarly families. Derided as "Wahhabis" because of their links with Saudi Arabia, they nonetheless acquired a significant following.

French colonial authorities were hostile to the "Wahhabi" movement, especially because the established local religious scholars accepted a distinction between "religion" and "politics" of which they approved and did not challenge French colonial rule. Thus, although the threat to the traditionalist 'ulama was direct, the French interpreted the Wahhabi attack against the local 'ulama and the appeal to Middle Eastern–trained ones instead as an indirect threat to their rule. Some saw a link between the Wahhabis and the Rassemblement Démocratique Africain (RDA, the African Democratic Assembly), the major West African nationalist party. Although most Wahhabis were "sympathizers, if not militants," of the RDA, they distanced themselves from formal support (Launay 1992:86–88). Nevertheless, the organizational structure of the local Wahhabi movement and its ability to claim transregional religious legitimacy was seen as a significant political threat to both the religious and the political establishments.

Whether from the perspective of state or nonstate actors, therefore, belief and practice in the Muslim world are now expressed in public and often in unanticipated forms. Social categories sometimes overlap and common interests may be discerned, but the competition over sacred authority increasingly pits governments, 'ulama, Islamist groups, and Sufi shaykhs against each other.

Fourth, the contenders for Islamic authority have been predominantly male, but women are not entirely excluded. 'Ulama and preachers of sermons (khatibs) are exclusively men in both Sunni and Shi'i traditions, but women in some regions play influential roles in Sufi movements. From the early days of Islam, female mystics, who were ascetic, celibate, and often slaves or former slaves, were prominent. Like Rabi'a al-'Adawiyya (717–80)—"the first true saint of Islam" (Schimmel 1975:42–60; also see L. Ahmed 1992:96–98)—many of these mystics were thought to produce miracles (karamat) and were invested with intercessionary, saintly qualities. As with their male equivalents, many of their tombs became places of pilgrimage. The shrine of Sayyida Nafisa in Cairo is a notable example, but smaller shrines, from which men are often excluded, are found in Anatolia, Iran, North Africa, and South Asia. Mary (Maryam), the mother of Jesus, figures in Sufi poetry as an exemplar of the individual incandescent with divine enlightenment, and her supposed tomb near Selçuk (Ephesus) in Turkey attracts pilgrims (Schimmel 1975:426–35; Elias 1988).

Women mystics have also had defined social roles and contributed to the communal organization of Sufism. In Aleppo, there were seven "convents" (khanaqas or ribats) between 1150 and 1250, at which women congregated to pursue their spiritual mission. Wealthy women, such as Bibi Fatima in the Sind in the early eleventh century or the daughter of the Mughal emperor Aurangzeb in the eighteenth century, became patrons of convents and endowed them with food and money. In Ottoman Turkey, the Bektashiyya order accepted women as equal adepts who joined men at ceremonies and meals.

In the northern Caucasus after the Russian revolution—principally Daghestan and the Chechen Ingush Republic—women's groups arose in affiliation with the Qadiriyya and, to a lesser extent, the Naqshbandiyya.[5] In Central Asia, small offshoots of the Yasawiyya have had women's sections with female spiritual leaders (Benningsen and Wimbush 1985:67–69).

In the case of Africa, "Even though women are refused access to the principal functions or public places of worship, nothing prevents them from having *baraka* [grace], worshipping saints, or becoming agents of a particular *marabout* [person thought to possess *baraka* and able to transmit it]" (Coulon 1988:116). Women often play significant roles in religious education, as in the schools associated with the Niassène Tijaniyya of Senegal, and, at times, in propagating the activities of religious orders. Many become involved in organizing women's groups associated with the *tariqa*s. Moreover, as with the Muridiyya in Senegal, even if women have no formal position in a religious order, their prestige and status are guaranteed by their inheritance, equal to that of their brothers, of their father's *baraka*: "Women not only possess *baraka*, they also consume it; and they perpetuate it" (Coulon 1988:121).

In some cases, women have acquired their own disciples. In Mamluk Egypt, convents had *shaykha*s (female *shaykh*s) who served as prayer leaders, and in Sind in South Asia, women became *faqira*s (Sufi mendicants) and *murshida*s (spiritual guides) (Schimmel 1975:432–33). Moreover, the Qadiriyya in Malawi was established between 1920 and 1930 through the activities of a *shaykha*.

In Senegal, Sokhna Magat Diop, eldest daughter of a Muridiyya leader, succeeded her father and led a branch of the brotherhood for decades. Although she did not officiate at mosques or at marriages, she was regarded as possessing "the normal powers of a *khalifa* [leader of a brotherhood branch]" (Coulon 1988:130). In southwestern Nigeria, the junior wife of the founder of the Mahdiyyat accompanied him as he traveled throughout the region promoting his message, which included the doctrine that—contrary to local practice—women were allowed to attend mosque prayers and were not required to veil. God, he said, had indicated that his wife, Shaykha Mahdi, was to serve as lieutenant and to succeed him. She did so, although not with universal approval (Clarke 1988:158, 164, 171–72). In the western Sudan and West Africa since at least the sixteenth century, women have become religious scholars (*faki*s [*faqih*s]), established their own religious schools (*khalwa*s), and initiated new members into the orders (al-Karsani 1993:137).

As these examples indicate and Chapter 4 will elaborate, women participate, albeit to a limited extent, in the contest over authority. In

Pakistan, for example, Prime Minister Benazir Bhutto (b. 1953) became a major participant in the public debate over what constitutes an Islamic order. Because she opposed a constitutional amendment that would make the Qur'an and the *sunna* the supreme law of the land and criticized the *shariʿa* courts, the Minister of Religious Affairs, Abdus Sattar Niazi, proclaimed her an infidel (*kafir*) and "liable for the death penalty." Bhutto replied that she believed in the Qur'an and the tradition of the Prophet, but "the law of God should not be subordinate to that framed by hand-picked individuals of the shariʿa court" ("Nearer, my God" 1992:38). In this contest over boundaries, a woman politician was transformed into a symbol for those who wished to extend the control of the religious establishment and those who wished to curtail it.

Muslim women have also become "new" intellectuals and activists involved with such groups as the Muslim Sisters in Egypt. Zaynab al-Ghazali (b. 1917) is an influential writer in the tradition of the Muslim Brotherhood, and her writings are avidly followed by both men and women (see, for example, al-Ghazali 1992). When the Brotherhood reorganized in 1959–69, after a period of repression under Nasser, the major leaders of the movement regularly met in al-Ghazali's home (Ayubi 1991:136)—a sign of the enormous respect in which she was held. Maryam Jameelah (b. 1934), an American convert to Islam who has resided for decades in Pakistan, is a prolific author on a wide range of Muslim topics (see, for example, Jameelah 1980, 1982b, 1982c) with a broad international readership.

The Lower House of the Muslim Parliament of Great Britain has 24 women among its 155 members, and of its four deputy speakers, two are women. The parliament was created to deal with such issues as education, job discrimination, the availability of social and medical services, and personal status (Siddiqui 1993; "Eighth Session" 1994)—issues of prime interest to women. One deputy speaker, Adeela Rashid, affirms that the role of women in the parliament will be assertive: "The chauvinism in Islam happened because women were not educated—only men knew the laws. But now we know our rights given to us by Islam and we're not going to be satisified with anything less" (Rabinovitch 1992). Indeed, the other woman deputy speaker, Zainab Ali, suggests that a specifically Muslim path for women is required: "We must not allow British society to influence our Islamic identity. Assimilation is not the right way: the model handed on by Western women is not acceptable to Muslim women" ("Western Women" 1992). It is clear that women are thus able to use Muslim institutions, including the Muslim Women's Institute affiliated with the Muslim Parliament, to advance their own agendas. It is ironic, how-

Fig. 10. Opening of the Muslim Parliament in Great Britain, May 1992. Muslim institutions in Europe and North America often consciously build on existing political traditions in these societies.

ever, to note that, although assimilation appears undesirable, the conscious imitation of British traditions is pronounced—"Parliament" with its speaker, deputy speakers, and committee structure; and the "Women's Institute," a common feature of British life (see fig. 10).

Women also participate in religious authority in less obvious, but no less important, ways. Female teachers are influential in inculcating, and perhaps subtly subverting, Islamic traditions in such women's religious schools and colleges as Maktab-i Zahra in Shiraz, the women's division of al-Azhar university in Cairo, and the women's faculties at Saudi universities.

Women are more likely than men to engage in shrine visits and occasions such as the Turkish *mevlûd*, the celebration of the birth of the Prophet Muhammad. In these activities, they establish "an intimate link" with the Prophet. The effect of this perceived spiritual and emotive intimacy is enhanced solidarity with other women as well as the acquisition of authority—over children, other women, and, to a certain extent, over husbands and other male family members. As Nancy and Richard Tapper (1987:83) explain, until recently, the state in Republican Turkey has constrained men's religious expression by limiting them to enacting "state-established orthodoxy." Women's activities, in contrast, have been relatively unregulated because of their "inferior status vis-à-vis past and present religious establishments." The political consequence is that women acquire sacred authority: Women "preserve a domain of religious enthusiasm, reworking old forms as symbolic vehicles for defining relations between women and men, man and God, the local community and the state" (Tapper and Tapper 1987:83, 86).

The nexus between women and sacred authority is thus firm, even though it has been overshadowed by the preponderance of male authorities. The relationship is also subtle, and considerations of family and kinship are integral—and are likely to become more important—to a conceptualization of Muslim politics that avoids the stereotypical division of "public" and "private" domains.

4

THE "FIRMEST TIE"

AND THE TIES THAT BIND:

THE POLITICS OF

FAMILY AND ETHNICITY

IN NORTHERN NIGERIA, a young Hausa-speaking woman, Ladi Adamu, obtained the most votes in the 1987 local government elections in Kano state (fig. 11). To the obvious discomfort of the political establishment (masculine and older), she became one of the 350 councilors in the state. Only one other councilor was a woman. Many Nigerians were incredulous that Adamu's husband would permit such a departure from a woman's characteristic role and assumed, as Ladi Adamu explained, "that a woman who speaks out must not follow tradition and must be a prostitute." While Adamu insisted that no contradiction existed between her official duties and family obligations, she was conscious of the paradox that her unprecedented conduct created and took care to frame her words and actions in conventional, deferential terms: "My mission is to emancipate women. Men cannot block my path because I follow all the religious injunctions in dress and behavior." She appeared in public only with a headscarf, and her campaign poster showed her in Fulani dress, holding a newborn daughter whose feet were dyed in henna. Explaining that this presentation conveyed that she was "a respectable married woman" (Brooke 1988), Adamu implicitly understood that the manipulation of conventional symbols endows legitimacy, especially in a changing society.

In Nigeria and throughout the Muslim world, periods of rapid economic and political transformation give new meanings to shared social understandings and tradition. Among these understandings, which evolve over time and acquire ideological meanings in the thinking of both Muslims and non-Muslims, are the controversial and emotionally charged issues of family, gender, and ethnicity. The Muslim family and the role of the woman as mother is offered as the ideal of social solidarity in many Islamic self-representations, whereas Western—

Fig. 11. This 1988 photograph of Ladi Adamu, one of the first female local government councillors in northern Nigeria, displays a headscarf, Fulani dress, and her newborn daughter, whose feet are dyed with henna. These elements suggest that her role of politician is compatible with that of a respectable married woman.

and some Muslim—feminist writers view the Muslim family as the embodiment of repression. These symbolic understandings contribute to the negotiation of boundaries in a moral universe, which, as we suggested in Chapter 1, is integral to Muslim politics. For Muslims, the boundaries are drawn between the good family and the corrupted one; for feminists, between the empowered woman and the subjugated one. Little is neutral in these moral debates, and they form part of the complexity of Muslim politics.

At particular issue is the utility of drawing a line between "public" and "private." The former is conventionally thought to be the realm of politics, a realm dominated by formal institutions and men; the latter, the realm of the nonpolitical, is dominated by family and particularist identities in which women have their greatest scope for activity. However, the line between these realms cannot be so clearly drawn, and, as many have suggested, the public-private distinction is a subject of contention (see, for example, Philips 1991:92–119; Nicholson 1992; Rogers 1975).[1]

The relationship among politics, family, and ethnicity, moreover, is not fixed. In the Arab/Persian Gulf, for example, it appears self-evident that family identity determines political power. The Al Saʿud and Al Khalifa control the financial and symbolic resources of Saudi Arabia and Bahrain respectively. But to describe the role of such forces as family and kinship in terms of the "genes of politics" (Bill and Springborg 1990:85–136) is to assume that their influence is unidirectional. Rather than assume that family and kinship determine politics, political power may also construct family, kinship, and ethnicity, as the Bosnian case illustrates. Bosnian Muslimness is largely the result of competing Serbian and Croat nationalisms and such externally defined notions of ethnicity as those offered by the European Union and the Organization of the Islamic Conference.

Our point of departure is the concept of "elementary" identity used by sociologist Émile Durkheim (1858–1917). Avoiding any implication that the term referred to the primitive or primordial, he regarded kinship and religion as the irreducible elements for social organization and the creation of shared categories of thought in less differentiated societies, such as those of the Australian aborigines. In more complex, multireligious and multiethnic societies, educational systems performed this role (Durkheim 1977; Cherkaoui 1976; Bourdieu 1988). While accepting the crucial role that mass education has played in transforming societies throughout the Muslim world, we hold that kinship, family, and ethnicity retain crucial influence in all societies.

Consistent with the discussion of modernization in Chapter 2, therefore, these elements of personal and collective identity—the ties that bind—have not been diminished by processes of social, political, and economic change. Rather, they persist and, in multiple ways, interact with Islam—the "firmest tie" (Qurʾan 2:256; 31:22). Indeed, the Qurʾan offers the view that kinship and Islamic loyalties operate on several levels. Family obligations and loyalty to one's parents and kin are morally sanctioned (e.g., 4:36), yet loyalty to the community of believers—the "brotherhood" (ikhwa)—united in submission to the one God, must take clear precedence (for example, 9:71, 49:10). The story of Abraham's willingness to sacrifice his son Ismaʿil, and of Ismaʿil's willingness to be sacrificed, carries resonance: The father-son relationship, while undeniably strong, was subordinated to God's wishes. In the end, a merciful God "ransomed him" (fadaynahu) and the family was spiritually transformed (37:99–111).

The Politics of Family

The Family as Microcosm of the Moral Order

Societies worldwide invest the family with sacred significance and base other interpersonal relationships, including community and political obligations, on its model. The family is a primary unit for ritual observance as well as an influential site of religious and secular education and the transmission of religious and worldly knowledge from one generation to the next (Hardacre 1993:129–40). It serves as a locus for developing notions of trust, authority, and responsibility. In short, the family—and its primary expression in domestic space, the household—is frequently taken as a microcosm of the desired moral order: "When husband and wife take up to live together as a family, they in fact lay the foundation of culture and civilization" (al-Mawdudi 1982:84). The competition and struggle over the meaning and centrality of the family thus inevitably loom large in what we call Muslim politics.

The 1979 Iranian constitution makes the political role of the family explicit in Principle 10, which states that the family is "the fundamental unit of the Islamic society" (Iran 1980:190). In many societies, phrases such as "father of the nation" or "elder brother" indicate how the metaphor of family pervades political life and is used to legitimize individual political leaders and by extension the political institutions with which they are identified (Schatzberg 1988:71–73). In his message celebrating the 1993 peace agreement, Yasser Arafat called on his "family and beloved people," his "brothers and sisters," to show unity in supporting the accord (BBC SWB ME/1798 MED/7, September 20, 1993). King Hussein of Jordan is one of many leaders who refers to himself and is often referred to as the father of his national "family" (al-Dustur editorial, in FBIS-NES-93–217, November 12, 1993, p. 48). President Suharto of Indonesia is often referred to as Papa Bangsa ("father of the people"). Likewise, the basic unit of many Islamist groups is the "family" (usra), and the leaders monitor their members until convinced they are fully committed to the movement (Drayf 1992:238).

The idea of the family is so central that only with difficulty do societies alter its conventional images and public forms. What James Scott (1992) calls the "public transcript" of the family role of women, and women as mothers—the stereotypes of what families are supposed to stand for—is often regarded as "ground zero" for society. Pressures to change the official and often legally endorsed view of families and family roles are often regarded with great suspicion. This is in part, as we have noted, because the family provides a powerful idiom for expressing core national and religious values (see, for example, Doumato 1992).

Until at least the nineteenth century in the West, the family was a common economic enterprise, and marriage in the Middle Ages was contracted not between principals but between households. The major family concerns were with survival and the transmission of property rights, not with nurture or shared sentiment (Bourdieu 1976). Since the late nineteenth century, however, a shift of major proportions has occurred in various parts of the world, including the Muslim world, to viewing the family—in particular the nuclear, middle-class family—as providing a safe haven from the harsh world. The family provides a domestic space in which emotion can be expressed, and support—between siblings, genders, and generations—can be taken for granted (Schneider and Smith 1973). Some writers have gone so far as to suggest that the nuclear family was particularly suitable to the needs of an industrial society (Parsons and Bales 1955), although others, including Elizabeth Bott ([1955] 1971), who studied working-class districts in London in the 1950s, discovered that over a century of industrialization and the dislocations of World War II left complex networks of extended families intact.

The defenders of traditional values often feel threatened, even shocked, by public acknowledgment of the ways in which social practice deviates from their ideal of the family. As a result, in the United States and Europe, many conservatives advocate a return to "basic values." This is an explicit component of the Conservative platform in Britain. Conservatives thus place the family at the center of a political ideology that is intended to justify their own claim to power. In Muslim societies, as in Western ones, it is difficult to talk about changes in family values because the "family" means many things and has different political connotations.

The Political Meanings of Family

The implicit contrast between the politics of "traditional" societies, presumably dominated by family concerns, and the politics of the "developed" world is particularly distorting. Such a contrast ignores or understates the influence exerted by extended families in "modern" societies. Prominent examples include the Kennedys and Roosevelts in American politics, *nomenklatura* families in the former Soviet Union and its successor states, and the Churchills and Macmillans in Britain. Some scholars suggest that in the case of the Muslim world, the importance that family networks play is conditioned by the nature of the political system and the extent of the governmental sector's intrusion into the economy and society (see, for example, R. Springborg 1982:243–44; Denoeux 1993:17–18). Yet, in the sense that family members in Western as well as Muslim societies follow one another in the civil service, politics, or the military, the assumption that families play a important role uniquely in Muslim societies is undermined.

As in all societies, ideas of kinship and family are not fixed but are modified in response to different situations. They are understood in the context of complementary, locally held notions of patronage, neighborliness, friendship, and ties of work and school (see Eickelman 1989a:151–78). It is only to be expected, therefore, that no one idea of family and kinship describes Muslim societies from the southern Philippines to Tajikistan, Pakistan to Morocco, Germany to Canada. The "Muslim family" is an abstract category, which, like the subject of women and Islam, "has for a long time been dominated by ahistorical accounts of the main tenets of Muslim religion and their implications" (Kandiyoti 1991:1).

In light of variations throughout the Muslim world, it is clear that the family does not possess uniform political significance. "The centrality of the family in Islam" is often assumed (see, for example, Esposito 1982:x). Indeed, Muslims—like Christians, Jews, Hindus, and Buddhists, among others—routinely affirm the great value they attach to family. Yet the *political* roles of the family depend on such other factors as gender, ethnicity, economics, and nationalism.

Family and kinship relations play salient political roles, but these relations are not unique to Muslim societies. Family leaders, government elites, and religious officials may promote marriages between members of different families as a means of enhancing or defending their political and social status, of gaining property and other wealth, or of extending business contacts and networks. Family networks facilitate survival where "society is fluid and political institutions unstable." In Latin America, for example, the family network of elites "was not some relic of Iberian traditions; it was a protection racket. Without a firm institutional fabric, individual members were exposed and individual enterprise was hazardous" (Carr 1985:515). The same can be said for nonelite families.

While the ability to manipulate marriages for political ends may be limited by other factors such as race and descent, such alliances often affect the social, economic, and political status quo to such an extent that they become matters of state concern. In Saudi Arabia, the foundation of the state and much of its continuing legitimacy rests on a calculated marital alliance between the Al Sa'ud, local *amir*s (princes), and what is now called the Al Shaykh—the descendants of the eighteenth-century Islamic reformer Muhammad ibn ʿAbd al-Wahhab. In Morocco, marriages between families of senior military officers and leading merchant families are so sensitive that officers are expected to seek approval from the palace. In revolutionary Libya, the "people's committees," which in principle govern the country, are overlaid on a complex web of tribal alliances and intermarriage, so that national leaders operate through governmental cadres, tribes, and extended families, a combination of "meritocracy and gerontocracy" (Davis 1987:71–72). Most cadres try to sustain ties with friends in Tripoli so they can bypass or counterbalance, when necessary, the formal governmental apparatus, and marriage is a key means of securing such ties.

In Syria, ʿulama families have intermarried in the recent past with urban trader and artisan families, and their surnames—such as al-ʿAttar ("perfumist") and al-Tunji ("goldsmith")—often reflect these unions (Batatu 1982:15). In Iran, families of the higher religious officials, the "sources of imitation" (marajiʿ-i taqlid), have intermarried. Ayatullah Muhammad Husayn Burujirdi (d. 1961), for instance, was able to find five prior marajiʿ in his family genealogy, and the Shirazis, a prominent religious family, have had influential religious leaders in various branches of their extended family. In the period immediately prior to the Islamic revolution, all seven "sources of imitation" shared common family connections. Several of these key religious families have also intermarried with the political and economic elites, including bazaris, the military, and professionals (Fischer 1980:88–97). The effect of this interweaving of family networks is to solidify and extend political influence.

Marriages become "a means by which political and economic conflict and competition in the wider society are negotiated and managed" (N. Tapper 1991:xv, 91–93). A Moroccan example suggests how these strategies change over time. In the early 1940s, a young religious scholar from a Berber-speaking town, the deputy to his elder brother, who served as Islamic court judge (qadi) for the region, married the daughter of the region's French-appointed native chief (qaʾid). This was a marriage which attenuated tension between the chief, appointed from outside the region, and the judge's family, influential in local politics. The marriages of both brothers forged alliances among provincial notables.

After Morocco's independence in 1956, the older brother was appointed to the first Constitutional Council and in 1963 became a member of the first parliament. His younger brother was appointed qadi in a provincial center elsewhere in Morocco. In the 1960s—we emphasize the dates because familial strategies change over time—his oldest daughter married a schoolteacher from the same town, who eventually became a senior Ministry of Education official. His eldest son also married into a local family. Both these marriages solidified the judge's standing in the town to which he was appointed.

In contrast, the marriages and alliances of the judge's younger children, which took place in the 1970s and 1980s, reflected postindependence Morocco's changed economic and political circumstances. A son who completed secondary school in the early 1970s (when few Moroccans went to university) secured a post in Casablanca through family connections in the provincial town where he grew up; he met his wife at his workplace, not through family ties. He later became a key administrator in a leading Casablanca holding company. A third son was selected for schooling with Morocco's crown prince; he now holds a position of considerable responsibility in an important ministry in Rabat and serves in the prince's inner circle of advisors. A fourth son, a secondary schoolteacher, lives in the same provincial town as the father (who retired from his judgeship in the early 1970s) and is active in local politics. In an earlier generation, each of these marriages would have had a calculated strategic significance. These more recent marriages show greater flexibility but indicate a range of connections that further collective family interests in both governmental and private, regional and national, spheres of influence.

Although this Moroccan example is modest and unspectacular, a similar pattern prevails in Iraq, where key positions in the regime and control of major sectors of the economy are linked to intermarriages with Saddam Hussein and ties formed in his village of origin, al-Tikrit. So sensitive has the public acknowledgment of these ties become that the Iraqi government has banned the use of names (such as al-Tikriti) which identify villages of origin. In Syria as well, the ʿAlawis, the sect to which President Hafiz al-Asad belongs, wield influence disproportionate to their demographic strength. Although conflict and tensions have occurred among the Tikritis in Iraq and the ʿAlawis in Syria and remain a source of instability, family and ethnic networks are intertwined with formal structures of power and patronage in both Baʿthist regimes.

Similarly, in Malaysia, family relationships and marriage alliances have pronounced political implications. This is as true of Malay business elites as it is of local and national political elites. Family relationships create a moral system whereby responsibility for one's close kin is both automatic and expected: "Consanguinity as defined by Malay tradition and Islam creates broad social ties within which people should observe basic moral tenets" (Idris 1991:13). At the level of national politics during the premiership of Tun Abdul Razak (1922–76), a core group within the cabinet consisted of individuals of "high status parentage" from two families from the states of Pahang and Johore (Idris 1991:28). The Minister of Culture, Youth, and Sports was married to the Prime Minister's sister, while the Prime Minister was married to a daughter of the fomer president of the Senate. His other daughter was married to the Minister of Education. These marriages not only created family alliances but also helped to facilitate interstate connections within the Malaysian federation. In addition, the Deputy Prime Minister and the Minister of Education were also related by marriage: The sister of the Minister of Education was married to an army general whose sister was in turn married to the Deputy Prime Minister. Malay observers did not find it surprising, therefore, that this particular general was promoted over his colleagues (Idris 1991:26).

The instrumental significance that may be ascribed to the family in Muslim politics reveals only part of the story, however. Families constitute ideological clusters that carry meanings and values ascribed to them by both family members and those external to the family. The rationale of the Saudi regime is that the Sa'ud family, as custodian of the holy places of Mecca and Medina, must constitute an exemplary Muslim family, standing at the apex of aggregations of families that collectively comprise Saudi society. It is precisely because of this royal self-representation that critics of the regime often focus their attempts to delegitimize it on alleged improprieties in the family life of the House of Sa'ud, such as corruption and illicit sexual activities (see, for example, 'Abduh 1990:31–36; also Jadhakhan 1992:esp. 24–38).

Parallel to a pattern seen in Western societies, the family has become the ground on which ideological battles are waged. Questions frequently heard in the religious and political discourse of Western societies include: Do the conditions of modern economic life and social mobility require adjustments in the ideal of the nuclear household in which mothers raise children while fathers earn the family income? What are proper gender relations within the household, and who does the housework and raises the children? How can poor and dysfunctional families cope, and what are the implications for society of increasing numbers of illegitimate children? Is society undermined by the recognition of homosexual rights? In the face of significant economic and social challenges, must the family unit be reaffirmed as the repository of morality in a world that has become increasingly morally diffuse and relative?

Islamists have responded to such questions much like Christian, Jewish, or other "fundamentalists" have done: Social changes that weaken "family values" are deplored and resisted. The social reality, however, is not as clear as these Islamists present. On the one hand, there has been a shift among elites and the emerging middle class from households composed of extended families—that is, more than one conjugal family and more than one generation of married couples—to separate households for each married couple or polygamous marriage. This trend has been documented for Istanbul since the late nineteenth century (Duben and Behar 1991), for Morocco since the late 1930s (Eickelman 1989a), and for the Arabian peninsula since the 1970s (al-Thakeb 1985; Eickelman 1991).

On the other hand, whatever patterns of formal authority households present to the outside world, household decisions emerge through internal negotiation, disagreement, conflict, and bargaining. Decisions to marry, to build a house or establish a separate household, to take in a relative, to hire a servant, or to move are seldom made by a single individual within a household. Not all household members have an equal voice, but it would be rare for a single family member to be responsible for a decision, even if the public "face" of a household might impute absolute authority to its male head (Laslett 1984:368–74). Indeed, studies of the Arab Gulf suggest that women seek out their mothers for information and advice, and a significant number of brothers and sisters rely on one another in addition to their fathers (Dhaher 1981:28–29). Moreover, the trend toward nuclear households is partially mitigated by the simultaneous tendency for extended families to live in the same neighborhood (Eickelman 1989a:154–70) and to rely on each other for business contacts and various kinds of financial and social support.[2]

Women in the Muslim Political Imagination

If the family is inherently politicized, it follows that the status of women and questions of gender are also politically contentious. Islamist representations of Western and Westernized women are often unflattering, suggesting that woman's emancipation "is actually a disguised form of exploitation of her body, deprivation of her honour, and degradation of her soul" (Doi 1989:10).[3] Yet, although Islamic discussions of cultural authenticity often present the West as the morally inferior "Other," such discussions mask the real target of moral censure—local elites and their Westernized practices or ethnically distinct groups and their "deviant" conduct. Islamist discourses on women that uphold the authenticity of tradition thus seek to draw boundaries not only between the Muslim and non-Muslim community but also between the "true" guardians of community and the "internal Other" (Kandiyoti 1991:7–8).

Veiling

As we indicated at the outset, perhaps no issue so inflames discussions of gender relations in Islam as that of the veil (*hijab*) and veiling (*ihtijab*). From Malaysia to Morocco, the choice of dress for Muslim women, both married and unmarried, is a complex political statement (see Hoffman-Ladd 1987; Taarji 1991). In some societies it is a matter of personal choice; in others it is virtually prescribed by government, social convention, or peer pressure. In Sufi orders such as the Bektashiyya in the Balkans, it has been customary for women attending meetings with men not to veil (Norris 1993:95), but even in supposedly secular societies such as Turkey, some women wear a headscarf while attending religious ceremonies and Islamist women regularly wear the veil. As we indicated in Chapter 1, Muslim girls in both France and Egypt—although the proportion in the respective cases varies markedly—have turned to wearing the headscarf in the classroom. In cases where veiling is prescribed socially or officially, the decision to do so or not involves status. Veiling is also politically ambiguous, involving competition, not simply among groups and institutions within the state but also among international human rights organizations, minority rights groups, and nongovernmental funding agencies. For example, the social agendas, whether implicit or explicit, of a Western developmental agency and a Gulf *da'wa* organization would not necessarily be the same.

Arlene MacLeod writes of working women in Cairo, whom she describes as "lower middle class." By veiling, she means the adoption of the headscarf and "modest," ankle-length dresses, not the complete covering of the face (although some women do so even in Cairo). She argues that women's presence in the workforce and in public places in Egypt is not new in itself. Most lower middle-class working women in Cairo have rural origins, and in rural areas, up to two-thirds of a woman's time is spent in agricultural labor outside the house (1991:50). In Cairo and its suburbs, women, benefiting from the public-sector employment opportunities created in the Nasser era, engage in low-paying, routine clerical work. Many of them say they would quit their jobs if they could, but they need the income to support their families.

In the late 1970s, the adoption of "Islamic" dress was confined to Islamist students on university campuses. By the 1980s, however, a significant number of lower middle-class women had also adopted Islamic garb (MacLeod 1991:113). This had little to do with re-Islamization—their faith remained strong and unquestioned—but Islamic dress conveyed the social message that a woman could hold a job in the government bureaucracy or in a bank without abandoning her roles of wife and mother. Wearing *hijab* showed respect for the boundaries of a well-ordered, moral society without inhibiting social change. Veiling is thus a means for women to assert some control over the ambiguous moral situation created by new economic and social pressures (MacLeod 1991:139–41; Hijab 1988:53–55). Moreover, by blurring distinctions between lower middle-class dress and the expensive and unaffordable "Western" clothes of wealthier Egyptians, "Islamic" dress—often subsidized by Islamic groups—becomes a means of asserting respectability in difficult economic circumstances (MacLeod 1991:98–113, 133). Because of its affordability, Islamic dress empowers lower middle-class women and thus enhances their claims to status in society.

In the Muslim politics of Algeria as well, the veil has been transformed into a symbol of contention. As in Egypt, women in popular urban quarters have increasingly adopted Islamic dress, although in Algeria more than in Egypt, Islamists frequently back verbal persuasion with threats of violence. A number of secular modernists attack this trend by asserting that Islamists wish to subjugate women and remove legal rights accorded them in recent decades (Boudjedra 1992:74–87). Muslim activists (including veiled women), on the other hand, argue that only through the full implementation of Islamic norms and precepts will women be fully liberated (Aniba 1991:257; Lemu 1978:30). This debate has come to the fore with the political ascendancy of FIS and other Islamist groups.

Contesting Gender Boundaries

Women are thus central to the larger political and moral imaginaton, essential to the upholding of civic order and virtue. For Islamists, a woman's role as mother—producing, nurturing, and educating children—is crucial. In response to a government request in July 1985, Kuwait's Committee for Qur'anic Interpretations and Legislation recommended against allowing women voting rights, saying that "the nature of election processes befits men, who are endowed with ability and expertise. It is not permissible that women recommend or nominate other women or men" for public posts, such as membership in Parliament. The decree contended that women could exercise indirect influence within their families on their husbands and male relatives. The decree concluded that "Islam does not permit women to forfeit their basic commitments" of bearing and rearing children (Associated

Press 1985). Women do, however, vote in Kuwait's neighborhood co-operative societies (jama'at ta'awuniyya) without, apparently, forfeiting their "basic commitments."

In Bangladesh, despite entrenched notions of female segregation (parda [purdah]), the number of women who head households and work outside the home, particularly in rural areas, is growing. Figures are difficult to obtain, but one indication of the increasing trend is that in 1982 women headed 16.5 percent of rural and 6.9 percent of urban households. There seems little doubt that this pattern has continued (Islam 1991:1), and because of increasing poverty and tension between the landed and landless, extended families have been less able to support these women. The formation of women's cooperatives, which provide loans and training in jute craftwork, has encouraged the mobility of the poorest women, while in the past it has also tended to reinforce the class and gender domination of well-off men (Rosario 1992:106–19). But agencies such as the Bangladesh Rural Advancement Committee (BRAC), the Grameen Bank, and international nongovernmental organizations have assisted more women from diverse backgrounds to become self-reliant. By upsetting traditional economic relations and in sending their children to BRAC-run schools, they have thus directly challenged the power of village leaders, including the 'ulama, who have had defined influence in educational matters. One consequence of this crossing of conventional boundaries has been a proliferation of fatwas against women who have been denounced as "impure" ("A Religious Backlash" 1994). At stake is the integrity of the traditional moral and political economy: "Bengali notions of honour, shame and purity are important not only to maintain a sexual hierarchy but to maintain group boundaries, status structures, distribution of power—the overall structure of domination" (Rosario 1992:179).

Women Islamist intellectuals and activists often contribute to the defense of traditional female roles. Maryam Jameelah, who has been closely associated with the Jama'at-i Islami in Pakistan, wrote: "Although I believe that every woman should be educated [to] the fullest sense of her intellectual capacities, I certainly question the advantages of taking women out of the home (particularly those with young children) to compete in business offices and factories with men and substituting nurseries and kindergartens for a home upbringing" (Jameelah [1969] 1982a:17). Zaynab al-Ghazali, a leader of the Egyptian Muslim Sisters, an organization closely allied with the Muslim Brotherhood, argues that women may be educated, but their primary duties are as wife and mother. She also argues that society is harmed if mothers do not remain at home until their children mature (Hoffman 1985).

It is precisely because women are placed at the center of civic order that the contest over family legislation has so often become a matter of high politics.[4] In Pakistan, for example, the controversy over Islamization has focused on such matters as women's rights in divorce, inheritance, and legal testimony, and sections of the conservative religious establishment have been pitted against the Women's Action Forum and women's professional associations in attempting to reform *shari'a*-based family law. One political organization of *'ulama*, Jamiyat Ulama-i Pakistan (Society of Pakistani 'Ulama), has made family law issues central to its program. In the early 1980s, the government of Zia ul-Haq (r. 1977–88) proposed several reforms that were opposed by educated professional women as restrictive and un-Islamic. One key reform was the *qanun-i shahadat*, the law of evidence, which would have equated the testimony of two female witnesses to that of one male. Women were also to be excluded from cases involving the *hudud* (Qur'anically prescribed punishments) (Weiss 1986). Moreover, fierce debate has ensued over whether the Muslim Family Laws Ordinance of 1961 should be repealed. It has irritated many Islamists because of its relatively liberal provisions on women's rights in marriage and divorce (Patel 1986:91).

Muhammad Reza Shah Pahlevi, influenced by his sister, Princess Ashraf, promulgated Iran's Family Protection Act of 1967, which strengthened women's rights, especially those involving marriage. This act was technically repealed and recast in even more liberal terms in 1975, yet by then it had become a focal point of opposition. Ayatullah Khomeini targeted it as symptomatic of the regime's decadence, and soon after he came to power it was suspended (Keddie 1981:179–80, 240, 266). Ironically, some of the reforms first proposed by the shah have been reintroduced by the Islamic Republic since 1991—a reinvigorated family planning program, state-sponsored prenuptial contracts that give women the right to initiate divorce proceedings, and greater opportunities in the workplace and in higher education.

In the period from 1915 to 1916, the Sudan became the first country after Ottoman Turkey to allow women to institute judicial proceedings for divorce. After Sudanese independence in 1956, *shari'a* and civil court judges were at first exclusively male, but in 1970 a woman, Najwa Kamal Farid, was appointed to the *shari'a* court, followed by three others in 1973 and 1974, with more women in the civil courts.[5] Despite the amalgamation of the civil and *shari'a* courts in 1980, coups, and Islamization programs, women remain in the Sudanese judiciary, principally hearing cases in the appeals courts. In part due to pressures from the Sudanese women's movement, liberalizing reforms were introduced in the 1960s and 1970s allowing women the right to contract for themselves in marriage (1960), increasing maintenance (*nafaqa*) payments, and liberalizing the law regarding divorce because of cruelty (Fluehr-Lobban 1987:50, 100–102, 138, 278). Sudan's first Permanent Constitution, adopted in 1973, also granted equal protection to men and women, as well as equal protection for adherents of Christianity and other "heavenly" religions (Fluehr-Lobban 1990:618). Although the Permanent Constitution has never been formally rescinded, Sudan's radical Islamization beginning in 1983 rendered many of its provisions moot.[6] Nonetheless, in January 1990, six months after an Islamist military government seized power in the midst of civil war, it convened a Conference on the Role of Women in National Salvation. This conference resulted in a 1991 code of personal status that, although only minimally innovative, reaffirmed women's increased authority in marriage and other improvements of women's status (Fluehr-Lobban 1994:133–35).

In Morocco, women work in both the state and the nonstate sector and are strongly represented in higher education. In an August 1992 speech, King Hassan, after encouraging women to participate in the municipal and parliamentary elections, said: "I have understood and listened to your complaints concerning the *Mudawwana*" (the 1958 *shari*ʿ*a*-based legal code that is the basis for Moroccan laws regarding marriage, family, and inheritance). It was within his powers, he said, to change this code, and he invited women to write to him and to a judicial committee entrusted with revising it. In spite of the promises of change contained in the king's speech and the fact that a process of wider consultation was set into motion, the alterations appeared to some Moroccan legal specialists as insignificant ("Recevant" 1993; Mayer 1993:93–105).

Perhaps because family law is one of the most conservative of all institutional spheres, the changes that have occurred in it have met with more resistance than major transformations in other spheres of activity that affect women throughout the Muslim world. Education is a pertinent example. To be sure, the gap between men's and women's education has grown in some places, such as among Afghans after the Communist coup in 1978 and the Soviet invasion in 1979. Reacting to the needs of the resistance as well as the government's mandatory literacy campaign for both men and women, which appeared to many an unwarranted intrusion into private lives, the number of schools, and specifically the number of female students, declined significantly. Moreover, among the 2.8 million Afghan refugees in Pakistan, of whom 75 percent were women and children, girls constituted only about 7 percent of the total student population in primary and about 3 percent in secondary schools (Majrooh 1989:89–92). Although there continues to be a gap between women's and men's access to higher education in virtually all Muslim societies, this gap is closing in wealthier countries, and in others it has narrowed dramatically in recent years (Eickelman 1989a:198–200).[7]

In Iran as of 1994, 30 percent of government employees were women, and 40 percent of university students were women, up from 12 percent in 1978 (Ghazi 1994). In the past few decades, women have thus made significant, but uneven, strides in access to education and health care, and to participation in the labor force. Women also increasingly participate in formal and informal *political* processes, whether these involve organizing community relations with the occupying forces during the Iraqi invasion of Kuwait, transforming the rural economy in Bangladesh, campaigning for elections in Turkey, or demonstrating against the ban on women driving in Saudi Arabia. In Iran, Faezah Hashemi, the eldest daughter of President Rafsanjani, acted as a spokesperson for Iran's women's movement during Women's Week in 1994 (Ghazi 1994).

Hasan al-Turabi claims that women in the Sudan "have played a more important role in the [National Islamic Front] than men recently" in all aspects of the party, in Parliament, and as ministers and judges. "Segregation of women is definitely not a part of Islam" (al-Turabi 1992:58). Observers may dispute his depiction of the improved situation of women in the Sudan, but it is clear that women elsewhere in the Muslim world—Morocco, Jordan, Egypt, Malaysia, Turkey, Bangladesh, and Pakistan—do hold political office. In the case of Pakistan, Turkey, and Bangladesh, they have served as prime ministers.

The emergence of Muslim women into positions of formal political responsibility is occurring in spite of one interpretation of Muslim tradition that argues that women cannot lead an Islamic state. Abu-l A'la al-Mawdudi of Pakistan (1903–79) insisted that the head of an Islamic state must be male. He invoked a *hadith* that he rendered as a "nation would not prosper which hands over the reins of its government to a woman" (al-Mawdudi 1983:60). This *hadith*, found in al-Bukhari's collection (n.d.:228), refers to the ascension of Khosrow's daughter to the Persian throne in the pre-Islamic era. It is more accurately translated as "A people who entrust their affairs to a woman will not prosper." Al-Mawdudi's translation, supporting his conclusion that only male rulers are legitimate in an Islamic state, thus conveys a particular ideological construction.

Because of views such as al-Mawdudi's, even women who are successful in acquiring formal political roles are careful to portray themselves in ways that suggest they are not radically challenging traditional gender roles. Benazir Bhutto, a member of one of Pakistan's leading political families and at times its prime minister, has avoided photographs that depict her shaking the hands of men in public, and for some time she has preferred to appear in photographs which emphasize her roles as daughter and mother, notwithstanding the bitter political struggle that erupted into a violent clash between her supporters and those of her mother in early 1994 (Kamm 1994).[8] In Jordan's 1993 parliamentary elections, Toujan Faysal became the first elected woman in the lower house, while two women were appointed to the senate. Faysal, a former television journalist, was defeated in the parliamentary elections of 1989, when the Islamists vociferously opposed her and accused her of apostasy. After her 1993 victory, Faysal said, "The Islamists fear me because I can fight them from the inside. I know the Qur'an as well as they do." Yet in public and in photographs, as was seen in the example of Ladi Adamu in Nigeria, Faysal takes care to emphasize her role as mother (Ramadan 1993).

Women's "Place" and Public Life

A key dimension of Muslim politics is the contest over the meanings attached to "women" as a symbol. The underlying belief, common to all ideological formations, is that women must remain "in their place" for political and social harmony to prevail. Unlike social conservatives, liberals and feminists, however, believe that women can remain "in their place" and still have roles equal to men in all spheres of activity. Throughout Islamic history, they point out, women have exercised considerable political influence, sometimes as rulers (Mernissi 1990; Peirce 1993). Analyses that assume that women have simply played subordinate roles thus need to be challenged. Indeed, some Muslims have argued that "no hope is possible for Muslim societies without the positive participation of women, whose full rights have been assured by religion" (Elmandjra 1992:172–73). Others argue that the Qur'an "illustrates explicitly the correlation between the female and bearing children," but it does not describe the "psychological and cultural perceptions of 'mothering'" as "essential created characteristics of the female" (Wadud-Muhsin 1992:22). Wadud-Muhsin argues that the liberation of women began with the Prophet's message in seventh-century Arabia and did not end at his death, and that God spoke equally to men and women. "If a woman was not a judge (*qadiya*) during the Prophet's lifetime or did not attain a political position, this does not mean that she was forbidden from doing so for all time" (Shahrur 1992:593, 596). Such arguments jettison the centuries of legal interpretation developed by male Islamic scholars and suggest that Qur'anic texts must be interpreted in each generation (Wadud-Muhsin 1992:12; Shahrur 1992:44).

Notwithstanding the support that these reformist interpretations have acquired, a more prevalent view, echoed throughout the centuries of Islamic history, argues that the just Islamic society exists in a delicate balance (*mizan*) or complementarity of genders. "Nature has made men and women different, adapted to different natural functions, and capable of different duties in life. . . . Thus cooking, laundering, shopping, washing-up are the responsibility of one person" (Tabandeh 1970:40–41). As the wife of Iranian President Rafsanjani, Effat Marashi, said of her domestic relationship: "The entire responsibility of the children and house rests upon my shoulders," leaving her husband free to fight "for the cause of Allah" ("Tales of Love" 1993).

If women do not adhere to this moral order, society runs the risk of degenerating into *fitna*, a term which means temptation or, more importantly, rebellion, social dissension, or disorder. A saying of the Prophet, which appears to have been codified between the late eighth and the early ninth century, holds that there is "no *fitna* more harmful to men than women" (cited in Spellberg 1991: 51). Women are so potentially powerful that they are required to submit to their husbands,[9] segregate themselves from men to whom they are not immediately related, and restrain themselves, lest the pattern of gender relations, which is at the core of a properly ordered society, be overturned. One Sufi order in Turkey, the Aczmendis, decrees that women cannot be present at a dervish lodge because "it is forbidden for women to be in a place where men are present" (Yilmaz 1994). In Nigeria, Ibraheem Sulaiman, a "new" Muslim intellectual, writes of the role of women in the Sokoto caliphate, which prevailed in West Africa from 1817 to 1837 and represents for him the ideal Islamic state: "In so far as women are seen by most men as symbolizing the ultimate in joy and comfort, women could play a key role in stemming the tide of social decay, or accelerating it. In fact, society as a whole is, in the ultimate sense, saved by the self-restraint and moral discipline which women display" (Sulaiman 1987:130).

The view that women's assertiveness may be tantamount to *fitna* is consistent with the elaboration of a public-private dichotomy in which the role of women is restricted to the private, nonpolitical realm. However, the public-private dichotomy is misleading for several reasons (compare Philips 1991:119). First, women may play strong, even central, roles in modern society provided that they work through men. Even in Saudi Arabia, women operate in finance, banking, and transnational charitable organizations, often facilitated by their male relatives, and can teach and practice medicine. Consistent with his view that Islam is inherently political, Ayatullah Khomeini commemorated the role of women in the Iranian revolution, while reaffirming traditional male-female relationships: "They confronted a despot with a clenched fist while holding their child in their other arm, thus ensuring the success of our revolution" (Khomeini 1988:6). In Indonesia, the Lembaga Konsultasi & Bantuan Hukum Untuk Wanita & Keluarga (LKBHUWK, the Institute for Consultation and Legal Aid for Women and Families) in Jakarta is committed to stimulating "the legal awareness [of women] of [their] social rights and duties" and to obtaining for them "equal opportunities in the areas of education and employment." Although Muslim "women have the equal status and position as men, both spiritually, intellectually, socially, as well as morally," they are not to "forget their predestinational status as wom[e]n"(Yamin 1984:7–11; compare LKBHUWK n.d.). The Institute of course is careful to seek the approval of the ʿulama—its sponsors include the Majelis Ulama Indonesia (the Assembly of Indonesian ʿUlama), and its office is located in a mosque.

Second, through complex social networks of their own, women may entertain friends and kin and thereby cement social ties and serve as channels of information and communication. In times of social tension, these channels of communication may help to resolve disputes. In the Iranian village of Aliabad in 1978–79, for example, women acted to defuse a difficult situation: "Because women could be seen as somewhat removed from a conflict and because they had lower status, they were used as messengers or intermediaries in delicate sociopolitical negotiations" (Hegland 1991:222). The consequence of women acting in such roles is that the political goals of the father or husband may be advanced.

In addition, women's contribution to achieving the goals of the extended family is salient. In the case of Oman, women and men jointly further the aspirations of their family clusters (*hayyan*) in maintaining and extending claims to status, property, and education (C. Eickelman 1984:80–111). Extended families thus provide women with access to authority, and, in this regard, family/nonfamily distinctions are more useful than private/public ones.

Finally, some social institutions erode distinctions between the private and public. The *diwaniyya* in the Arab Gulf, a regular, informal gathering of relatives, professionals, members of the same religious group, workmates, or those sharing political goals, is not limited to extended families. A wide range of topics is usually discussed, such as sports, literature, and cars, and political discourse certainly does not dominate. But because they constitute the arena for nonstate activity and discussion, interlocking networks of *diwaniyya*s form the backbone of civil society. Male and female *diwaniyya*s have existed side by side (although male ones have predominated in the past), but with women increasingly educated (and to higher levels) and their greater partici-pation in roles outside the household, women's *diwaniyya*s have be-come more common. A few *diwaniyya*s now include both men and women. In the parliamentary elections of 1992, the Kuwait Democratic Forum, which advocated greater rights for women, helped to break down gender divisions by inviting two women to speak in a predomi-nantly male *diwaniyya* setting.

Although the barriers between men and women in a society such as that of Kuwait remain formidable, "the diwaniyya is the means by which the public space enters the home" (Tétreault 1993: 280), and it thus qualifies the idea of a public-private dichotomization correspond-ing to male-female relations. Neither public nor private can adequately describe its complex functions. The term *diwaniyya* is limited to the northern Gulf states, but such social and discussion circles are also common elsewhere, including in Iran, where they are simply called "circles" (*dawra*s).

The social picture, as we can see, is far from settled. Precisely be-cause of this uncertainty, the family, and the role of women in it, is invested with diverse ideological meanings. The regime, established religious authorities, and counterregime Islamists all claim to be the defender of family integrity and of the roles and rights of women in an Islamic society. In so doing, each makes the ideas of family and women pivotal to contemporary Muslim politics.

Ethnicity

Similar to the ways in which family and women have become subject to explicit ideological contention, ethnicity, another "elementary" identity, is controversial and carries various political meanings. The controversy is sometimes compounded by an explicit linkage between gender and ethnicity. In a village in Selangor in Malaysia, a young reli-gious student who had studied at al-Azhar in Cairo delivered a ser-mon in 1979 that drew a connection between the defense of women's traditional domestic and family roles and the promotion of Malay eth-nicity. He said that the problems affecting Malays, such as drug use and the intrusions of television, had at their root new social roles that took women outside their traditional duties. Wage labor was particu-larly objectionable because it exploited women and encouraged baser instincts. "This call for strengthening of the Malay race required women to adhere to a stricter, Islamic version of male authority and of women's roles as mothers and wives" (Ong 1990:268).

As with family and gender, however, ethnicity influences political events, but ethnic relations are themselves shaped by political and other considerations. Here, too, the relationship between Muslim politics and "the ties that bind" is reciprocal. Many Muslims argue that the ties of Islamic community created through common submission to God supersede those of ethnicity and kinship. As the Qur'an says, God distinguishes believers only by their piety: "The most honored among you is the most pious (atqakum)" (49:13). The idea that Islam and ethnicity are antithetical and antagonistic also appears in the thinking of Islamists such as Egypt's Sayyid Qutb, who consigns ethnicity, tribalism, and nationalism to the category of the *jahiliyya*. In using this term, which originally referred to the pre-Islamic "age of ignorance," he powerfully criticizes the validity of particularist ties (Qutb 1981:159).

Western social scientists have also politicized ethnicity, by which most mean "the way individuals and groups characterize themselves on the basis of their language, race, place of origin, shared culture, values, and history" (Banuazizi and Weiner 1986:2–3). Ethnicity is often thought to be a matter of birth because of the notion of shared descent. The "liberal expectancy" was that ideas of the territorial state and nationalism would displace ties of kinship and ethnicity as the sources of political community. Marxists assumed that "proletarian internationalism" would displace ethnicity and that class would determine identity (Moynihan 1993:27–28). Common to all views is the transformation of ethnicity into an ideology.

Ethnicity is an enduring social and political force, constructed and reconstructed as circumstances and contexts change. Yet, ironically, the post-Soviet world order has given rise to virulent ethnonationalisms that remind us that political boundaries are not fixed. Rather than simply determining the nature of political organization, as "tribe" was thought to determine politics in some societies, ethnicity is formulated in relation to diverse political and social forces. "External" opposition—the opposition of one social group to others—is paramount among them. To take a familiar non-Muslim example, African "tribes" were created in the context of colonial rule. One scholar went so far as to say, "The Luyia people came into existence between approximately 1935 and 1945. . . . It was clearly due to the reaction of younger and more educated men to the exigencies of the colonial situation" (Southall 1970:34). This objectification of the tribe—in which both colonial authorities and politically active Luyia colluded—has its parallel in the objectification of ethnicities in Muslim societies. The formation of identity is sometimes inadvertent, however. Elsewhere in Africa, for example, Sufi religious orders—formally intended to advance universal Islamic identities—have at times promoted the rise of ethnic consciousness. This has been the case with the Muridiyya and the rise of Wolof ethnicity in Senegal (Launay 1992:237).

In Saudi Arabia, Oman, Yemen, the Gulf states, and Jordan's East Bank, notions of ethnicity and tribalism are virtually indistinguishable. They are usually framed in terms of genealogy, although claims of tribal descent are better thought of as invented traditions (discussed in Chapter 2), rather than as historically verifiable accounts. Indeed, the fact that peoples and groups can change tribal and ethnic affiliations under certain conditions indicates the flexibility of these supposedly fixed identities. The Kwatzba, for example, left their original tribal grouping to join the Rwala, located in Jordan, Saudi Arabia, and Syria. Although this move did not fit into the existing Rwala genealogy, tribal history has been reformulated to include them as part of the larger tribal confederation (Lancaster 1981:24–25). In another example, the Al Sa'ud, a house (*bayt*) of the Masalikh subdivision of the Awlad 'Ali tribe of the 'Anayza confederation, have at times been invested with a political and national role. As the Al Murra in the Empty Quarter said at the time of King Faysal (d. 1975): *Al Murra Al Faysal*, "Murra people [are] Faysal people." They distinguished between the *dawla* (state), by which they meant the bureaucracy, and the *hukuma* (government), by which they meant the Al Sa'ud, whom they regarded as the "rightful leaders of the Islamic nation" (Cole 1975:109).[10]

In a similar manner, groups such as the Sindhi- (and Arabic-) speaking Shi'i Liwatiyya of coastal Oman have also claimed Arab descent, explaining their "temporary" loss of Arabic (and tribal identity) by centuries of residence on the Indian subcontinent. With India's independence in 1947, the Liwatiyya in Oman were given the choice of becoming Indians or Omanis. Most chose Omani nationality, recognizing the precariousness of their position if they chose Indian nationality but resided outside of India. Once this choice was made, Liwati intellectuals began to "discover" Arab antecedents and one produced a manuscript purporting to document these Arab origins. In addition to the Liwatiyya, ex-slaves (Arabic, *khuddam*) attached to tribes and ruling families throughout the Arabian peninsula and other groups lacking tribal descent have traditionally had an inferior social status, as shown by occupation and the lack of intermarriage with other groups, but modern economic conditions are rapidly eroding these distinctions. To some Arabs in the peninsula, visible African features may imply descent from slaves, but it may also indicate descent from earlier ruling families that possessed slave concubines.

As with the Liwatiyya example, contemporary Arab identity suggests that ethnic claims need to be placed in historical context. Many Arabs assert that they are a "race," although for centuries populations have mixed and intermarried throughout the Arab world. Despite the claims that first appeared in the nineteenth century that the Arabs constituted a nation, although divided politically, Arabs still maintain that they are unified in language and culture. Many regional dialects of Arabic, however, are mutually unintelligible. Arabs from Saudi Arabia and the Gulf states understand colloquial Moroccan Arabic only with difficulty, and vice versa. The spread of mass higher education throughout the region since midcentury has facilitated communication among Arabs from different regions through "modern standard" Arabic, which is modeled on classroom and the broadcast media. Still, major differences of dialect and situational identity remain. One is not just Muslim in the Middle East, but also Arab, Berber, Nubian, Circassian, or Kurd.

The ways in which Muslim identities are shaped and reshaped are strikingly illustrated in the case of Bosnia. Throughout the Balkans, Sufi orders like the Bektashiyya, the Khalwatiyya, the Naqshbandiyya, and the Qadiriyya provided significant frameworks for religious identity from the sixteenth through the early twentieth centuries (Norris 1993:82–137; compare Popovic 1986). In the period of the Titoist Yugolsav state (ca. 1945–91), religious identity and nationality were legally separate, although in practice, Catholic Bosnians were officially Croatians and Orthodox Bosnians were Serbs. Until 1961, individuals could register only as Serbian, Croatian, or undeclared. With the 1961 census, however, Muslims were allowed to register as Muslims for the first time. In the Bosnian constitution of 1963, they were accorded the status of an ethnic "nationality" (nacija), and in 1964 the Communist party in Bosnia "declared explicitly that Muslims had the right of self-determination" (Lockwood 1975:27). State and party action helped to formalize Muslim identity as an ethnic one. Later events sharpened the Bosnian dimension of this ethnicity. By the mid-1980s, two contradictory trends had emerged. One was a renewed emphasis on common Muslim practices—distinctive dress for women, more public celebration of religious festivals such as Ramadan, participation in the pilgrimage, and election of the first non-Bosnian religious leader for all Yugoslavia (ra'is al-ʿulama). The other trend, following the rise of anti-Albanian sentiment, was the incipient distinction between Bosnian and non-Bosnian Muslims (Sorabji 1988, 1993).

The collapse of the Yugoslav state and the advent of civil war in 1992 added a further defining dimension. Partly as a result of ethnic designations formulated by the European community and partly as the result of support from Muslims elsewhere in the world, the identification "Bosnian Muslim" was solidified. The transformation of a Muslim identity in Bosnia into a Bosnian Muslim ethnicity was thus in large measure due to an "architecture" of external groups and pressures (Berman and Lonsdale 1992:330–32).

The phrase "Muslim ethnicity" may appear to conflate two separable kinds of identity, yet our use of the term is deliberate. The Malaysian constitution (Article 160:2), for instance, specifies that Malays are Muslims (see Mutalib 1990:2, 9, 31). In other cases in which the constitutional order is not so clearly prescriptive or has not yet been defined— as in Bosnia and, as we shall argue, in Pakistan—identities and self-designations have been transformed as circumstances have changed, sometimes dramatically. Anti-Muslim sentiment may heighten a sense of Muslim identity, but this at first may not be synonymous with an ethnic identity. Yet, as events unfold, religious and ethnic attachments may begin to converge. A Muslim ethnicity may emerge.

The transformations of identity that occurred among Pakistani Muslims suggest that a divergence of religious and ethnic ties may also occur. In prepartition India, Muslim intellectuals such as Muhammad ʿAli Jinnah (1876–1948) accented an Islamic identity to distinguish themselves from the Hindu majority. Pakistan, a romanticized "land of the pure," would demarcate the boundaries of an Islamic realm juxtaposed to secular India. After partition in 1947, however, "Muslim ethnicity . . . outlived its original purpose" (Alavi 1986:43), with Jinnah, now the father of the nation (Quaid-i-Azam, "the Great Leader"), openly articulating his secularist suspicions of an Islamic state or particularist identities. Punjabis became the dominant ethnicity in Pakistan, while Sindhis, Baluchis, Pathans, and Bengalis pressed their claims as well. In the particular case of Bengali Muslim society, "the weaknesses of a[n elitist] religious identity which provided at best an unsatisfactory basis for an incomplete cohesion in society" led to the creation in 1971 of Bangladesh as a "nation state on the basis of a separate linguistic-cultural identity" (R. Ahmed [1981] 1988:xi–xii).

Although Pakistan's official ideology encourages the preeminence of Islamic identity, ethnic and tribal identities continue to be a major force in national politics. In November 1991, a friend of Benazir Bhutto was raped by a gang that, the victim said, was sent by the son-in-law of the president. Bhutto claimed that the motivation for the rape was political intimidation directed at her, and she and various women's groups demanded that Islamic justice be applied. State institutions proved irresolute in dealing with what quickly became a major public scandal, however. Although families usually conceal the "shame" of rape, in this case the victim's father and her supporters turned to a convocation of the family's tribal leaders (*jirga*) to elicit support in pressing her case to the authorities (Pitchford 1991; Rashid 1991a; Hussain 1992).

Ethnicities are thus also constructed in part by an "internal architecture" of rivalries within collectivities (Berman and Lonsdale 1992: 346–50), but it would be a mistake to draw too sharp a distinction between "internal" and "external" factors. In the case of the Kurds in northern Iraq, clan divisions organized around traditional leaders (*aghas*) such as Mustafa al-Barazani (1903–79) provided one framework for loyalties and alliances. Another was provided by younger, urban professional leaders such as Jalal Talabani. These social cleavages crystallized into political parties, but the ostensible ideological differences between the parties—called at various times the Kurdish Democratic party (KDP) and the Patriotic Union of Kurdistan (PUK)—were more apparent than real. Often internal Kurdish rivalries eclipsed Kurdish opposition to the Ba'thist (and therefore Arab nationalist) government in Baghdad. In addition to the internal social rivalries, external sponsors such as Iran, Syria, the United States, Israel, and the Iraqi government exploited the differences among Kurdish factions and helped to create rival senses of Kurdish nationalism. The picture is further complicated by many Kurds, especially migrants and the educated, who identify themselves as Arabs (or, in the cases of Kurds in neighboring Turkey and Iran, as Turks or Persians). Others stress their identity as Muslims, as opposed to secular Kurdish nationalists (Van Bruinessen 1992a:54).

This process by which a Muslim ethnicity is affected by internal rivalries is clear in the case of the southern Philippines, where Moro nationalism has been in an uneasy alliance with Islamic identity. Muslim Moros constitute 4 to 7 percent of the population of the Philippines, but they are divided into three major and ten minor ethnolinguistic groups. Of the twenty-two provinces of the southern Philippines, where most Muslims live, they constitute a majority in only five. Although some Muslim notables argue that the Muslims of the Philippines have worked toward autonomy since the Spanish colonial era, most historians note that rivalries among the various traditional Muslim rulers largely coincided with a peaceful coexistence with the Spanish. During the period of U.S. colonial rule (1898–1946), however, common schooling for the sons of Muslim notables (*datus*), which paradoxically introduced notions of Islamic tradition and history, fostered an early sense of self-awareness as Muslims (McKenna 1993). This identity became intensified in the early 1950s, when notables assumed control of American war-damage payments. These elites, promoting their own authority, channeled much of the money into mosque construction, which encouraged a heightened religious identity but not an overtly politicized one.

Moro nationalism, based on a common Muslim identity, began to emerge out of the several local, ethnolinguistic identities in the region. This "Moro-ness"was given concrete expression with the imposition of martial law in September 1972, partly in response to a separatist rebellion in the south. Strengthened Muslim identity occurred as an indirect result of transnational Muslim connections, which provided Filipino Muslims with work opportunities in the Middle East, where they acquired some knowledge of Arabic, formal training in Islamic studies, and financial assistance. From 1955 through 1970, the government of Egypt provided more than two hundred scholarships for Moros, many from *datu* families, to study the religious sciences. These students began to return to the southern Philippines in the 1960s. Gradually, they acquired wider political and religious roles, and by the 1980s they had become firmly linked to the separatist movement (McKenna 1993). Many members of the Moro National Liberation Front (MNLF) central committee "were recruited from among Moro students who were studying in various Arab universities at the time" (Che Man 1990:128). The consolidation of the separatist movement also coincided with material support from the Libyan government.

Members of the traditional elite, disadvantaged as a result of the central government's land reform and modernization program and partly educated in the Middle East, stressed the idea that Moros were fighting for the cause of Islam. Thus a Moro-Muslim identity was promoted, and the major groups used Islamic symbolism to recruit and mobilize followers. The MNLF emphasized the obligation to participate in both the Islamic *jihad* and *bangsa* (identifying with one's ancestors). The Moro Islamic Liberation Front (MILF), for its part, declared that "the ideology of the MILF is *La illaha illa Allah Muhammad rasul Allah* ('There is no God but Allah and Muhammad is the messenger of Allah')" (Che Man 1990:88). This language indicates the importance of symbolic notions such as *jihad* and the *shahada* (the declaration of faith) to Muslim politics. Here, Islamist groups, rather than the state or religious authorities, constitute the institutions that control symbolic production and its articulation.

Despite the accent on a Muslim-Moro identity in the Philippines, significant family differences account for the formation of separate nationalist groups. The MNLF (formed in 1969) represented more secular and nontraditional tendencies, although it also contained elements of the traditional religious leadership and aristocracy. Many of its leading cadres received military training in Malaysia. In contrast, the leadership of the MILF (formed in March 1984) was dominated by the religiously educated, many of whom had become increasingly discontented with what they regarded as the leftist agenda of the MNLF.

The general population has remained divided by class, subgroup, language, and territory, such as the divisions between the Tausug and Sama in one area of the south. These divisions and rivalries complicate the search for an all-encompassing Moro-Muslim ethnicity (McKenna 1993; Horvatich 1993:35). All subscribe to the idea that Islam constitutes a vital component of their identity, and followers are aware of being "discriminated against as Muslims" (Che Man 1990: 89). There is, however, substantial disagreement over the degree of Islamization of the nationalist movement, the desirability of autonomy within the Filipino state or independence from it, and the extent of reliance on external patrons.

As the politicization of Islamic identity in the Philippines suggests, the instrumental importance of Muslim ethnicities may increase in situations where Muslims constitute a minority. Governments, for example, may use ethnicity to advance foreign policy goals. In China, the government allows Muslims to participate in the pilgrimage to Mecca as a way of currying favor with Muslim states such as Saudi Arabia and of securing construction and military contracts. The government also seeks to present a favorable image of its treatment of Chinese Muslims by refurbishing Muslim shrines, mosques, and religious buildings and by encouraging the visits of foreign Muslim delegations to such institutions as the China Islamic Association in Beijing (Piscatori 1987).

Ethnic groups within a society may also use ethnicity in their competition for status and entitlements. The population of the Hui and nine other officially recognized Muslim groups increased by an average of 30 to 40 percent between 1982 and 1990, as opposed to a mere 10 percent increase for the dominant Han population (Gladney 1994c:186). These officially recognized minority groups have used their Muslim "nationality" (*minzu*) to press their claims for greater recognition of Muslim rites and legal practices from the Communist government in Beijing. For example, Muslims are permitted to marry at age eighteen, whereas the age for Han Chinese women is twenty-five and for men, twenty-eight. Muslims are also exempt from government pressure to cremate the dead. In addition, they receive time off from work for religious festivals, and some workplaces provide separate eating facilities (Dreyer 1982–1983:52–53).

In 1989, the publication of a book that discussed the sexual customs of Muslims inflamed Muslim sensibilities. Predominantly Hui Muslim students, joined by representatives of other Chinese Muslim nationalities, staged protests in Beijing and elsewhere. On May 12, some three thousand protesters marched in the capital, and significantly larger demonstrations occurred in the provinces. Unlike the student pro-democracy movement that was to culminate in the Tiananmen Square protests a month later, the government on June 4 provided the protesters with transportation, banned the offending book, and publicly burned copies of it. The official media stressed that the Muslims' protests were legitimate because they were conducted by legally recognized representatives of a world religion (Gladney 1991:1–7).

There have been more violent Muslim protests in China when the government was less accommodating. In 1975, toward the end of the Cultural Revolution (1966–76), when mosques were closed and religious activities proscribed, villagers in Shadian, in southern Yunnan, reopened their mosque and resumed congregational (Friday) prayers. Branding this as "counterrevolutionary," the government dispatched troops. Many casualties resulted, and eleven Muslim villages in the area were destroyed (Wang 1992:371). In April 1990, Chinese television reported that a separatist group in Xinjiang province declared a *jihad* against the government and hoped to establish an independent "Islamic Republic of East Turkestan." The government purged the fourteen rebel villages and issued a new set of regulations that required *imams*, along with other religious leaders, to support socialism and the People's Republic before they could be examined on religious matters and licensed (Mirsky 1990). In June 1993, a group demanding an independent East Turkestan claimed responsibility for exploding two bombs in Kashgar, southern Xinjiang (Gladney 1994c:183).

The process of constructing ethnicities suggests that they are formed by the wider political processes and are inseparable from them; ethnic identities are not simply the creators of the political process. The ethnicities so developed serve as agents of Muslim politics, however. Ethnicity can empower peoples, widening the horizons of individuals as participants in a larger enterprise and providing them with a sense of a distinct political boundary between themselves and others. These boundaries may overlap, but not necessarily, with those of "Islam." Ethnicity can also be used against peoples, setting them apart and disenfranchising them, and it can be used to support or delegitimize states. The reason why ethnicity can serve as an instrument of politics is that it may be seen as the "natural" source of political and social cohesion, thereby "deepening" the language and imagination of politics (Berman and Lonsdale 1992:317, 347).

5

PROTEST AND BARGAINING

IN MUSLIM POLITICS

M USLIM POLITICS has attracted immense, and largely unfavorable, attention. Interest—one might even say obsessive interest—has focused on such undeniably significant events as Shiʿi unrest in countries of the Arab/Persian Gulf in the early 1980s, the assassination of Egyptian state functionaries throughout the 1980s and early 1990s, Shiʿi suicide bombings in southern Lebanon since 1982, the bombing of the World Trade Center in New York in February 1993, and the murder of journalists, intellectuals, and foreign tourists in Egypt and Algeria in the early 1990s. These acts, carried out in the name of Islam, earned Muslims a reputation for violence and radicalism, but the relationships between Muslim groups and governments are more varied and less coordinated than such an unnuanced negative image implies. Because actors always have available the vision of alternate "imagined" communities, an important component of understanding politics consists of recognizing how these alternative, oppositional, and purportedly peripheral visions revise or replace currently dominant and authoritative ones.

If one were to look at the Muslim world in the 1950s, the politically active element of the population was more limited, despite the emergence in some countries such as Egypt and Iraq of student and trade union groups. One observer of Iran has commented that the 1953 coup d'état, facilitated by American and British intelligence, was only possible because no more than 10 percent of Iran's population was politically active. Most Iranians "entertained little thought of challenging the traditional elite structure" (Cottam 1993:21–22). Since then, major economic and social changes have widened the political base and provided new challenges to traditional elites.

Among those who are politically engaged today, a range of activities exists. Some Muslims may become protesters but only in the sense that they engage in the "politics of silence" or in everyday forms of resistance (Scott 1985). That is, their actions—such as resort to alternative banking associations (Singerman 1994) and reliance on Islamic private voluntary organizations (Sullivan 1994:57–98)—suggest dissatisfaction with state-defined policies and institutions, although they do not necessarily imply direct confrontation with the regime.

Accommodation and opposition are often juxtaposed, but these terms mask more finely calibrated positions. Since Sadat's coming to power in 1970, the Ikhwan al-Muslimun (Muslim Brotherhood) in Egypt—as opposed to "neo-Ikhwanist" groups—may have largely accommodated itself to the the political status quo. It has participated, for instance, in various elections, including parliamentary ones, under the banner of legally recognized political parties such as the Hizb al-Wafd al-Jadid (the New Wafd party) in 1984 and the Hizb al-ʿAmal (the Labor party) in 1987. Yet it has also urged major changes in policies affecting social matters such as family legislation and in foreign policy concerns such as the peace treaty with Israel and Egyptian participation in the Gulf war of 1990–91. By the same token, opposition covers a range of activities—from working within the system to change it, as we have just mentioned, to rejection of the status quo as un-Islamic and violent confrontation with the existing political establishment. Therefore, the distinction between accommodation and opposition, as with other issues we have questioned in this book, cannot be sharply drawn and must be put into the perspective of local and shifting contexts.

Protest is a useful, if more general, term to refer to the spectrum of activities of Muslims, especially the politically active Muslims we refer to as Islamists. By definition, Islamist groups are involved in protest. They have resolved that the wrongs of society must be righted, but the corrective means are not restricted to one kind of activity. Protest may be "accommodative" (MacLeod 1991) in the sense of a desire to assert moral distance from and to criticize aspects of a political and social system whose foundations are basically accepted. This approach is not inconsistent with a process of bargaining between Islamist movements and the government or groups they criticize. Protest may also be "non-accommodative" in the sense of either an unwillingness to abide by the rules of the game, or a desire to change the rules—although, as we shall see, even these approaches involve tacit bargaining.

Membership and Organization

All contemporary Muslim protest movements share certain elements. One is that they appeal to the same categories of persons who sense a gap between the status quo and their aspirations. They need not be materially deprived to feel discontent, but the perception of deprivation—relative to other groups in the society or to the globalized economy—is what matters. In fact, evidence suggests that those attracted to Islamist projects are often, but certainly not always, in what might be called the "lumpen middle classes"—the lower to mid–middle classes (Ibrahim 1980:438–39; see also, Goldberg 1992:211–13)—that include petit bourgeois traders and artisans (see Birtek and Toprak 1993:199) but also professionals who feel that their upward mobility has been thwarted by economic and political policies and conditions. In this broad socioeconomic grouping, many, if not most, see in their Islamist activity the chance for a better life. With specific reference to the Muslim Brotherhood, a "surprisingly consistent pattern that persists over almost a fifty year period is that radical groups appeal to, and recruit members from, the urban professional middle class, especially, in more recent times, engineers" (Davis 1984:141, also 142–43). A further indication of the attraction that Islamic ideologies exercise for professionals is the January-February 1990 elections in Gaza, in which Islamist candidates won five of the nine seats in the Engineers' Association; they likewise obtained 43 percent of the votes of the West Bank Engineers' Association in August 1992 (Jubran and Drake 1993:13; Milton-Edwards 1991a:260).

In the case of Shi'i adepts of the Hizb al-Da'wa al-Islamiyya (Islamic Call party) in Iraq, one study indicates that the majority have come from the urban lower middle classes, and include university students, soldiers, and small businessmen (Baram 1994:536). In Pakistan as well, members of the Jama'at-i Tulaba (Students' Association), the student wing of the Jama'at-i Islami (Islamic League), come from small towns and rural areas, but are primarily from the urban lower middle classes (Nasr 1992:72–73). Although the Jama'at-i Islami itself has expanded its base, particularly since the 1970s, into rural areas, its core constituency is still from the lower middle classes in towns and cities (Nasr 1994:81–100). In Uzbekistan's Ferghana Valley, the growth in Islamic activism that has occurred since 1989 has been fueled by "social and economic problems, especially in the cities, where the lower and middle classes are concentrated" (Abduvakhitov 1993:89).

This is not to suggest that the poor, especially the urban poor, are entirely excluded from Islamist groups. Indeed, young people in the towns of the Ferghana Valley, fearful of the future and without certain job prospects, have been attracted to the idea of Islam as the solution to their problems. In northern Nigeria as well, the millenarian movements of the 1980s attracted marginalized "lumpen" laborers, such as seasonal workers and street peddlers, many of whom were impoverished migrants from other parts of the country and neighboring countries who had been attracted by Nigeria's oil economy (Lubeck 1987; Nigeria 1981:79).

Islamist groups may also appeal to the rural peasantry. One group in upper Egypt, broadly inspired by the teachings of Shaykh ʿUmar ʿAbd al-Rahman in the early 1990s, were led by individuals from wealthy families but attracted a large following of the poor—"a mix of peasants, seasonal workers, fishermen, drivers, and people in rural, petty service delivery" (Auda 1994a:402; see also Buccianti and Claude 1992:1, 3). Similarly, a revolt broke out in the Delta region of lower Egypt in August 1992 in which most participants appeared to be drawn from largely illiterate artisans, day laborers, sharecroppers, and the unemployed (Auda 1994b). In Turkey, the Refah Partisi (Welfare party, RP) drew particular, though not exclusive, support from a squatter-house district in Ankara, where it won the majority of seats in the munipical council elections of March 1994. In seven prior elections, the RP and its predecessor, Millî Salâmet Partisi (National Salvation party, received most of their support in the least developed provinces, particularly in eastern Turkey, of those in which they were successful (Akinci 1994). The discontents that followed economic restructuring and massive urbanization doubtless played a large part in their success.

One general explanantion for this socioeconomic and class diversity among activists is the process of objectification that we have discussed. Mass education opens the way to "democratized" access to sacred texts and overcomes restrictions as to who is "authorized" to interpret them. As a consequence, the monopolistic control by elites—whether attained in fact or merely aspired to—is countered by the greater number of would-be interpreters from diverse backgrounds yet commonly possessing modern-style education.

To this class dimension, youth and education must be added. Muslim activists are overwhelmingly young, often, though not always, following leaders in their forties or younger. They are usually educated as well, often to tertiary level. In some parts of the Ferghana Valley, Islamist groups dominated by young people have taken over responsibility for public order from the central government. The leader of one Islamic militia told Abduvakhitov (1993:89) that he had "8,000 young believers organized into patrol groups." In Pakistan, the Youth Force of one Wahhabi-style political organization, Jamiyat Ulama-i Ahl-i Hadith (Society of ʿUlama of the People of the Hadith), was active in expressing opposition to Saddam Hussein during the Gulf crisis of 1990–91. Mobilizing Pakistani as well as Saudi and Kuwaiti students, the Youth Force declared its willingness to defend the Holy Places threatened by Saddam's aggression (M. Ahmad 1991:164–65).

The youthfulness of participants in Islamist movements is not surprising when the demographic trends of Muslim nations—those forty states with a Muslim-majority population or with significant Muslim minorities (25 to 49 percent)—are considered.[1] Over 43 percent of the population of these countries was under fifteen years of age (Weeks 1988:13), with over 50 percent in Gaza and the West Bank, 44 percent in Algeria, 40 percent in Morocco, 39 percent in Egypt, and 37 percent in Indonesia (Omran and Roudi 1993:15; Population Reference Bureau 1993). In one town in India's western Rajastan in 1991, 45.72 percent of the Muslim population was fifteen years old or less. If the population nineteen and below is considered, the figure rises to almost 56 percent. These figures are comparable to other parts of India (Ahmad 1994:121; see also Ahmad 1993:99–103). The youthful profile of many Muslim communities does not directly translate into support for Islamist movements, but can contribute to it when, for example, state policies or political rivalries eliminate a more experienced, older leadership through violence or exile. For example, some observers speculate that the December 1992 deportation of 418 Hamas and Islamic Jihad leaders from the West Bank and Gaza opened the way "for a younger, less experienced breed of leaders . . . prone to internal divisions and splits" and more liable than older ones to be "trapped in an untimely showdown with the Israeli [and now Palestinian] authorities" (Abu-Amr 1994:129).

These young Islamists are often well-educated. In the case of the Daʿwa movement in Iraq, 61 percent of one list of martyrs (*shuhada*) to the cause in the early 1980s—victims of Saddam Hussein's repression—were university educated (Baram 1994:536). Student elections, sometimes even at the secondary school level, are also a barometer of Islamist support, particularly in areas where other means of electoral expression are restricted or absent. In the West Bank, for example, Islamist groups won approximately 40 percent of the student vote between 1978 and 1987, and in the Gaza Strip, 65 to 75 percent (Legrain 1990; Abu-Amr 1994:19–21). Between 1992 and 1994, Hamas and Islamic Jihad participated in student elections at various universities throughout the West Bank and Gaza. Their success varied, depending in large part on community reactions to the stages of the peace process and to electoral alliances that student activists forged on each campus. It is clear that Islamists have a distinct constituency on university campuses, but the size of the constituency and the strength of Islamist appeals vary.[2]

In Egypt, a 1988 survey of students at the Cairo University by Samia Mustafa al-Khashab demonstrates the disenchantment that university youth feel toward the official religious establishment and implies a substantial degree of attraction to Islamist groups. Seventy-five percent of the students surveyed regarded al-Azhar as "either partially or wholly ineffective" in responding to the needs of young people, while 70 percent wanted it to become more directly concerned with social problems. Nearly 75 percent of the students felt that Sufi orders made little contribution toward resolving social difficulties, and 68 percent believed that the orders were unnecessary. Concurrently, almost 75 percent of the students believed that the Islamist groups were responsive to the views and needs of Egyptian youth. Eighty-two percent believed that such groups should not be proscribed because they contributed to the improvement of social conditions and the "Islamic awakening" (cited in Starrett 1991:325–26). Such statistics, however, only partially capture the underlying tensions that accompany rising Islamic activism among the educated young. Patrick Gaffney's narrative of mounting campus tensions at Egypt's Minya University in 1978–79 suggests that Islamic activism in provincial universities possessed a more intense strength than was indicated in official and media reports. The role of Islamist sermons and religious "lessons" in spreading alternative and highly popular interpretations of current events was particularly underemphasized (Gaffney 1994:94–112).

Unsurprisingly, the Islamist movements that have become prominent in the 1970s and 1980s often have leaders who are relatively young, in their thirties and forties. The reason for this is not a supposed political tension between generations, and it is due to more than the changing demographic profile of the Muslim world. The reason lies in part in the higher educational level among the young, often enhanced by formative years overseas—stimulating negative as well as positive impressions—and in the fact that a good number of the older political activists already occupy important positions within existing parties or institutions. It is possible that individual members of this generation may break with the establishment for a number of reasons. Yet, younger people who have not been politically co-opted clearly do not need to be careerist in their politics, and can therefore afford to give voice to protest. Given demographic growth, it is this generation that is finding it hard to be assimilated into governmental and private sectors, and the grounds for their protest are considerable.

'Abbasi Madani, one of the Western-educated leaders of FIS in Algeria, was a member of the revolutionary-era Front de Liberation Nationale (FLN, National Liberation Front) but came to believe that it needed to be reformed in Islamic directions. Until his arrest in mid-1991, he showed a willingness to cooperate with the regime and to participate in multiparty elections as well as to endorse democratic ideas. Yet ʿAli Belhadj (ʿAli bin al-Hajj) (b. 1956), another major FIS leader and *imam* of the al-Sunna mosque in the Bab al-Oued district of Algiers, articulates the disenchantment of his generation with the failures of the socialist and secular revolution. He has thus been harsher than Madani in criticizing the FLN and has been more openly skeptical of the idea that the Islamic state must be democratic (Belhadj 1991:87–94).

The youthfulness of Islamist leadership has also been apparent in Central Asia. One of the first Islamist leaders in Uzbekistan, referred to in conventional Uzbek usage by his personal name only, Rakhmatullah (1950–81), came to prominence in his late twenties. In 1979, he publicly denounced his own religious teacher for having sold out to the Communist regime. Rakhmatullah, a mechanic by trade, and another young leader, Abduwali, argued that young Muslims should be thoroughly conversant in Marxist and Leninist doctrines in order to understand the politics of the state, but that students should also have direct access to printed literature on Islam. Muslim missionaries traveled to towns and villages throughout Central Asia and gradually won concessions from the Communist-era government. Although the movement slowed after Rakhmatullah's death in 1981, officially attributed to an automobile accident, what began as an apolitical Islamic "educational" movement in the late 1970s (see fig. 12) gradually became transformed into a political movement, known in Russian as the Islamskaia Partiia Vozrozhdeniia (Islamic Renaissance party), recognized by some but not all of the Central Asian republics.

We recognize, of course, that leadership, like the movements themselves, crosses generational lines. Rashid al-Ghannouchi, the leader of Tunisia's Renaissance party, became politically active in his thirties and continues to exercise influence in his fifties. Other leaders, however, acquired political prominence only later in life, as the obvious case of Ayatullah Khomeini indicates. Another example is Ahmad Yasin (b. 1937), a religious scholar and Islamic leader in Gaza who is associated with the Muslim Brotherhood and now Hamas. In the early 1980s, when Yasin was in his mid-forties, the al-Mujtamaʿ al-Islami (Islamic Assembly) which he founded became a vehicle for Islamization, and in the mid-1980s he incurred the wrath of the Israelis (Yusif ca. 1989; Abu-Amr 1994:64–69). Shaykh Abubakar Gumi (1922–92), chief *qadi* of Kaduna in Nigeria, had long preached against the deviations of the Sufi brotherhoods, but he became politically prominent from the early 1970s, when he was in his early fifties. His political activity intensified from the late 1970s when the Izala reform movement (Jamaʿat al-Izalat al-Bidʿa wa-Iqamat al-Sunna [Society for the Removal of Heresy and Reinstatement of Tradition]) was founded.

Fig. 12. In Central Asia, the apolitical Islamic educational movements begun in the 1970s gradually acquired political overtones. Religious class at a new mosque, Karshinskaia oblast, Uzbekistan, 1992.

The rise of the Izala is explained in part by another feature of the modern Islamist experience—urbanization. The traditional Nigerian economy had been dominated by agriculture, contributing 65.9 percent to the gross national product in 1958–59, but by 1980 agriculture's share had dropped to 18 percent. Droughts in the 1970s took their toll, but the impact of oil was more pronounced. Particularly under the first military regime (1966–79), revenues were disproportionately applied to urban projects, resulting in a substantial exodus from the

:. The consequence of such rapid economic dislocation was
\mong the new urban residents whose aspirations for a
erous and secure life were largely disappointed (Kane
).

rapid urbanization also contributed to the rise of religious activism
in Algeria. FIS appeals to the large number of individuals in the cities
and their shantytown (*bidonville*) peripheries—which some observers
call the *non-villes* (non-towns) (Labat 1994:55–56). Although the Algerian state and the FLN controlled the countryside, the shift in state
investments away from agriculture toward heavy industry in the 1960s
and 1970s contributed to massive emigration from the countryside to
the shantytowns that grew up around Algiers, Constantine, and major
urban centers. By 1988, the result was that 44 percent of Algeria's population was living in cities, with most of the new immigrants living in
inadequate housing. Many people were further impoverished as a result of the economic liberalization implemented beginning in 1988 by
the regime of Chadli Benjedid (b. 1929; r. 1979–92). A 1991 survey of
Algiers indicates the extent of the economic and social crisis. Three-
fourths of the youth aged sixteen to twenty-nine were seeking work,
and each year the educational system produced 270,000 additional unemployed diploma holders. Some 80 percent of the youth of this age
group continued to live with their families, often eight persons to a
room (Daoud 1991).

Islamists in Algeria have found sympathetic audiences in these
bleak milieus. In the early 1970s, the state liberalized the laws that reg-
ulated voluntary associations and authorized the construction of
mosques. In other cases, authorities turned a blind eye to converted
garages and other buildings serving as mosques. In the shantytowns,
poorly supplied with any form of government services, most of these
activities were carried out by Islamists, and thus their activities were
not limited to mosques (fig. 13). As the quality of government schools
deteriorated, Islamists provided schooling through mosques, sports
facilities, and health services. In the earthquake that struck the Algiers
area on October 29, 1989, FIS gained wide attention for the effective
relief operation that it mounted. The net result was that Islamic groups
took over many local functions the state was unable or unwilling to
provide (Rouadjia 1990:34, 59, 77, 111). Between unemployed educated
youth and members of an older generation who saw their agricultural
lands confiscated under a 1971 agrarian reform law, there was no
dearth of candidates for leadership.

The overall profile of other countries in which Islamist movements
have taken hold since the 1970s is remarkably similar to those of Nigeria and Algeria. In Egypt, there has been a rapid urban growth in Cairo

Fig. 13. Prior to 1992, the offices of the religious parties in Algeria, which were accessible to citizens and followers, had already begun to offer services that the government was unable to provide. Storefront headquarters of the Islamic Society Movement (Hamas), Oran.

and in provincial centers such as Assiut that has not been matched by the economic opportunities or hope for advancement available to earlier generations. Large areas of greater Cairo are deprived of effective governmental services, and in many poor areas Islamist groups offer basic medical and social services the government cannot provide. As in Algiers, these groups provided important, and publicly recognized, emergency assistance after the October 1992 earthquake in Cairo. Although education was once seen as a means of personal and social advancement and educational opportunities grew significantly in Egypt from midcentury onward, educational quality has declined and diplomas are no longer a guarantee of employment. In the decade of the 1970s alone, the number of students in Egypt doubled (Sivan 1985:51). These "declassed, proletarianized students" form what Roy (1992:70, 73) has called a "lumpen-intelligentsia" for whom Islamist organizations and doctrines have much the same appeal as did Communism to western Europeans in the 1930s.

The situation is much the same in large cities elsewhere. Between 1976 and 1986 alone, Tehran's population doubled from four to eight million inhabitants. The greatest rate of increase was from refugees and poor rural immigrants flowing into the slums of south Tehran

Fig. 14. Women in Istanbul campaigning for the Welfare party, which was
victorious in the 1994 municipal elections in Istanbul and elsewhere.

(Hourcade 1987:68). As bleak as the living quarters of recent immigrants may appear, cities and towns offer considerable material and
educational advantages over their villages of origin as well as the
promise of a better future. In Turkey, Pakistan, Tunisia, and elsewhere,
Islamist strength is centered in the larger cities and towns (fig. 14). Islamic activism knows no geographical limits, but it often finds considerable support among recent urban immigrants and the lower middle
classes who find their economic and social status increasingly threatened. Islamism offers an educated, unemployed younger population
the hope of a way out of their difficulties and a reassuring sense of
their own place in society.

Although the urban dimension is clearly important, the significance
of rural areas should not be overlooked. Recent urban immigrants remain deeply influenced by their rural origins and maintain their links
with the countryside through family and economic connections (Nasr
1992:73; Early 1992:49; Khuri 1975:184–86). In the specific case of secondary schoolteachers who join Islamist groups, a large number move
from rural areas to provincial towns (see Mardin 1983:154) or the
metropole—or indeed both, in a two-step process of internal migration. Although they may change jobs once in the urban environment,
the traditional religious education to which schoolteachers are ex-

posed in the rural areas continues largely to shape their worldview (Davis 1984:141).

Protest groups organized in the name of Islam possess broad appeal and attract large numbers of followers and sympathizers. It is impossible to specify membership figures with any precision, however, and many claims, either of the government or the groups themselves, must be treated cautiously. The Muslim Brotherhood in Egypt, founded in 1928, appears to have been a broad-based movement, expanding from four branches in 1929 to around 2,000 branches and between 300,000 and 600,000 "active members," with possibly another half million sympathizers in the movement's peak years between 1946 and 1948 (Mitchell 1969:328). Whether this figure is accurate or not, the Free Officers who planned the 1952 Egyptian revolution were acutely aware of the Brotherhood's strength and made a tactical alliance with it (el-Sadat 1957:79–81).

Although Islamist movements pursue a power-seeking strategy that includes building a popular base in society, their membership is usually not mass-based, thereby providing another reason why it is difficult to do more than estimate their strength. Although they claim to speak for the Muslim community (umma) as whole, they depend on a cadre of committed activists supported by outer circles of supporters and sympathizers. Groups may distinguish between grades of membership, generally differentiating between the core of activists and others supportive of the goals of the movement. For instance, the Egyptian Muslim Brotherhood in the period of its founder, Hasan al-Banna (1906–49) distinguished among active, assistant, affiliated, and combatant Brothers. In the Daʿwa party of Iraq, social and professional associations of Shiʿi sympathizers are called "the companions" (al-ansar)—the term used to refer to the Prophet's first supporters in Madina; they act "as a protective shield around the hard-core cadre" (Baram 1991:32).

Lebanon's Shaykh Fadlallah and other religious leaders are disingenuous when they speak of Hizbullah "in the broad Qurʾanic sense" of the totality of Muslims and deny that it is "an organized party" (hizb tanzimi), for it is clear that an institutional structure exists with gradations of membership (Fadlallah 1985; al-Shiraʿ [1984] n.d.:147). Regular membership (al-intizam) is not open to large numbers of individuals—it involves special training and socialization, particularly for militiamen—but there are constellations of adherents or fellow travelers around this core ("Hizbullah" 1986). In essence, while the movement may attract popular support, depending on circumstances and issues, its membership may be seen to constitute concentric circles of sympathizers around a relatively small, though effective, group of committed adherents.

The Bangladesh Islami Chatri Sangshtha (Bangladesh Islamic Organization of Female Students), a women's Islamic movement, parallels the male-only Muslim student movement, the Islami Chatra Shibir, and is active on university campuses and among the educated. Islami Chatri Sangshtha has six levels of membership, and progress through these is determined by a combination of mastery of a "syllabus" (consisting of reading, memorizing, and explaining the Qur'an; learning *hadith*; reading a specified set of Islamic books; and inviting others to join the movement), advancement of the movement's goals, and obedience to the organization. Teaching sessions stress that "obedience to the *Amir* or head of the organization . . . implies obedience to the Prophet Muhammad which in turn indicates obedience to God himself." Discussion of politics is introduced in the upper levels of the movement, and advanced members recognize that the movement raises women's political and religious consciousness and prepares them to take active political and social roles (Huq 1994).

In seeking a direct political role in society, some groups follow the model of organized political parties that seek to attract formally enrolled members and present a public platform of goals and policies. Such is the case with the Jamaʿat-i Islami parties in Pakistan, Bangladesh, and India, which have fielded candidates in elections and participated in government. In Lebanon as well, AMAL has organized along political party lines that are familiar to Lebanon where multiparty elections have occurred since the founding of the republic. AMAL's charter (*mithaq*) identifies itself with the Harakat al-Mahrumin (Movement of the Dispossessed)—begun in 1974 by the Shiʿi religious leader Musa al-Sadr—and maintains that it is "a movement of all the people" and, as such, a national, Lebanese, organization (cited in Norton 1987:166). Yet AMAL simultaneously sees itself as a movement committed to improving the particular circumstances of the Shiʿa. To this end, it holds regular party conferences, produces policy statements, and issues membership cards. In Turkey, the Rafah Partisi evolved, according to Soncer Ayata, from a loosely-knit "confederation of Sufi groups" into an organized, professional party apparatus with a strong leadership and committed grass-roots support. This structure has helped them to get out the vote as, for example, in the March and July 1994 municipal elections, when they secured notable victories in Ankara, Istanbul, and elsewhere (cited in Akinci 1994).

Because of their claims to broad representation, however, Islamist groups such as Hizbullah assert that they are not like parties and do not depend on formal organization (*tanzim*). Yet, in practice, the movements are divided into public and secret organizations and are hierarchical and cellular, with rank determined by level of commitment. In some cases, as in the Iraqi Daʿwa and in Afghanistan's Jamaʿat-i Islami, led by Gulbeddin Hikmatiyar (b. 1947?), the cell (*khalwa*) organization is inspired by the secular Baʿthist or Marxist-Leninist structures in which some Islamists formerly participated. The Daʿwa is divided into two "wings" (*janahs*), one military, the other, political. The military wing has supervised the training of members in Iran, Lebanon, and Syria. Among other activities, the political wing has engaged in a vigorous publication program (ʿAbd al-Hadi 1983:19).

In other cases, the model for inspiration and legitimation is the cell-like structure of Sufi orders, which have layers of initiation and commitment, some of which are concealed from external view. The Muslim Brotherhood, for example, was based on cell-like organization, and its leader was referred to as *murshid* (guide), a term used of Sufi *shaykhs*. As with the Iraqi Daʿwa organization, the secret wing of these Islamist groups is sometimes called the combatant (*jihadi*) wing, which may employ violence that would be deniable by the group's public, or "civilian" (*madani*) wing (Drayf 1992:237–41). The Muslim Brotherhood developed a "special organization" (*al-tanzim al-khass*), which was responsible for such acts as the assassination of Prime Minister Nuqrashi Pasha in December 1948 and other similar acts of violence.

The Technologies and Culture of Protest

In 1994, the film *al-Irhabi* (The Terrorist) created fierce controversy in Egypt and elsewhere in the Arab world. Starring ʿAdil Imam, one of Egypt's most popular actors, it cast Muslim activists in a violent light and portrayed them as simpleminded and boorish, with their leaders manipulative and authoritarian. Bourgeois life, by way of contrast, was depicted as cosmopolitan and tolerant. Liberal media professionals, unhappy with the Islamist project in Egypt, did not require instruction in the socializing or propaganda potential of mass communications—particularly in the video version of the film which could be viewed in the privacy of the home. Moreover, while the Mubarak government may not have produced the film, it could not have been unhappy with its message.

Muslim critics of the status quo also make use of the technological instruments of the modern mass culture. Television, radios, cassettes, videos, personal computers, photocopiers, facsimile machines, and electronic mail are frequently, if not routinely, found in the homes and offices of Muslim activists, *ulama*, and Sufi *shaykhs* as well as those of government officials. The use that Ayatullah Khomeini and his supporters made of the direct-dial telephone and cassettes to incite revolutionary sentiment in Iran is well known, and was prefigured in the utility that Jamal al-Din al-Afghani (1838/39–1897) saw in secretly printing and distributing leaflets to agitate against the Qajar ruler, Nasir al-Din Shah (r. 1848–96). Moreover, opposition to the tobacco concession, which al-Afghani and others among the *ulama*, merchants, and townspeople expressed in 1890–91, was encouraged by resort to the telegraph. This new device allowed opponents to maintain contact with each other and Shi'i religious figures in Iraq, and to coordinate their activities (Keddie 1981:65–67).

Such ready usage of available technologies is not, however, unique to Iran. Indeed, Islamic groups from Southeast Asia to Europe publicize and propagate their message in sophisticated ways that seem unremarkable. Groups responsible for the kidnapping of Western hostages in Lebanon were referred to as "telephone" organizations, and the Egyptian magazine *al-Musawwar* reported that a raid on a software import firm disclosed the structure of the clandestine wing of the Muslim Brotherhood ("Structure, Aims of Muslim Brotherhood Detailed" 1992:5). The organization used sophisticated coded computer records to track members who had infiltrated the police, judiciary, press, medical, and other professions.

Dar al-Arqam (House of Arqam), a Malaysian millenarian group that was outlawed and its leader arrested in October 1994, was adept at creating a financial empire in several countries. It ran bakeries and bookshops among its diversified activities in Malaysia and elsewhere in Southeast Asia, but it also operated technology service and desktop-publishing businesses. It paid for its members to acquire technical as well as other training overseas, and one of its posters proclaimed: "With advanced technologies, Muslims can manage the world according to Allah's law" (Karp 1994).

Technology is of course neutral, but its use subtly alters the disseminated message. Print and other technologies create new forms of community and have transformed authority and social boundaries, defeating conventional assumptions of a "great divide" separating "tribal" and urban, nonliterate and literate. The collected essays in *Literacy in Traditional Societies*, edited by Jack Goody (1968; see also, Goody 1977, 1986) made a significant step toward recognizing the religious and political implications of the written and printed word, and Benedict Anderson's *Imagined Communities* (1983) subsequently noted the transformative value of writing and printing and demonstrated their contribution to the formation of national and religious identities.

A succession of new media technologies has profoundly contributed to Islamic political movements in Afghanistan, beginning with "print Islam" (Eickelman 1989b:17) in the course of this century. As David Edwards explains, the development of print communication in Europe over five hundred years appears leisurely in contrast to Afghanistan, where its development is compressed into little more than a century. Print and telegraph communications transformed the ways in which people were governed, thought about one another, and conceived of their religious identity (Edwards 1995; also see Edwards 1993).

The first Afghan newspapers of the late nineteenth century had a limited circulation, although, as in Central Asia at about the same time (Khalid 1992:116), they reached a small literate elite that had an influence far beyond its numbers. Newspapers provided a focus for the development of political ideas that were at least partially independent of the previously influential circles of court, tribe, and mosque (Edwards 1995:171–73). Indeed, by the late 1920s and 1930s, newspapers had become a major vehicle for advancing political causes. For example, a weekly four-page newsletter, *Irshad-unNiswan* (Guidance for Women), appeared in 1921 (Majrooh 1989:94). Such publications gave prestige to the government internationally and offered employment to graduates of Afghanistan's secondary schools and *madrasas* (religious schools). Through the judicious use of subsidies, newspapers restrained potential dissidents by keeping them on the government payroll.

By the late 1940s, secular modernists had begun to speak out against the traditional religious establishment. Religious leaders were initially on the defensive, as they were unskilled in dealing with the ways in which secularists disseminated their ideas. Although by the 1960s leftist newspapers flourished, only one major independent religious newspaper, *Gahiz*, had emerged by 1968. Leftist newspapers and pamphlets, supplemented by Soviet radio propaganda in Afghan languages, provided arguments for secularists to use against Islam. In turn, *Gahiz* and religious tracts in Afghanistan, as with publications elsewhere in the Muslim world in the 1960s and 1970s, provided crucial texts and arguments for Muslim intellectuals to use against those whom they regarded as antagonistic or less committed. In Kabul University and elsewhere, religiously minded students formed study groups in which many of these publications were discussed, their goal being educational rather than explicitly political.

Whatever the major differences between secular leftists and religious modernists in the 1960s, both had parallel experiences. They had both been educated in government schools and constituted the first generation to acquire literacy. Political radicals encouraged confrontation and polarization in Afghanistan through both their organizations and their newspapers and pamphlets. These publications emphasized loyalty to the authority of the *organization*, not to the authority of the state or traditional elites. Muslim groups, notably the Muslim Youth Organization at Kabul University, followed the lead of the leftist groups and the Muslim Brotherhood, which Afghan students in Cairo had observed firsthand in the 1950s. These Muslim groups thus used their publications to affirm not only the validity of Islamic solutions but also the necessity of allegiance to the Islamic organizations themselves. The larger Islamic mission became dependent on prior obedience to the movement, and the routinized expression and promotion of this linkage became essential for success. This process helps to explain how Muslim groups, initially organized for the purpose of education or spiritual improvement, became transformed into more formal political organizations such as the Hizb-i Islami Afghanistan (the Afghanistan Islamic party), dedicated to overthrowing the post-1978 Marxist government.

Although the various resistance groups, including Jamaᶜat-i Islami, two rival Hizb-i Islami groups, and Shiᶜi organizations, all opposed the Soviet invasion and the Marxist government, and notwithstanding appeals to Muslim solidarity, their common goal did not lead to close integration. Most Afghans saw the Marxist takeover in April 1978 as having little to do with ideology, but as a triumph of the Ghilzai Pashtu, to whom many of the coup leaders belonged, over the Durrani Pashtu. In simple terms, it was read as the victory of one traditional *qawm*, or ethnic group, over another. By 1980, the Marxists had dropped most of their ideological propaganda, sought to persuade Afghans that they were not against Islam, and tried to play on traditional tribal rivalries. This was in contrast to earlier efforts at land reform and other initiatives that ignored traditional tribal and religious structures (Korgun 1993:106). The Islamic resistance groups failed to unite, even when urged to do so by their foreign supporters—including Saudi Arabia, other Gulf states, Pakistan, and the United States; rather, each group relied on a particular set of tribal and ethnic ties. These divisions became more pronounced after the Soviet withdrawal in 1989 as each group now saw the opportunity to seize power at the expense of its traditional rivals (Roy [1985] 1990:215–21; Canfield 1989).

As we described in Chapter 4, tribal, ethnic, linguistic, and kin divisions persist, despite Islamist aspirations. In some respects, resistance to Marxist rule and the Soviet invasion of Afghanistan provided one of the most clear-cut opportunities for *jihad* against a clearly defined "infidel," yet this did not result in higher unity in the name of Islam. The "routinization" of Islamic ideas through print and pamphlets and through higher educational levels helped institutionalize ideas of shared Islamic identity, but it did not in itself suffice to transform an oppositional movement into one capable of exercising state authority.

In Afghanistan and elsewhere, audiocassettes, easy to smuggle and readily duplicated, have begun to replace, or at least supplement, pamphlets as a form of religious debate. The pamphlet has the advantage of greater anonymity for the author, but the cassette has other advantages. Cassettes are inexpensively and easily reproduced, and they may be played virtually anywhere—in the home, automobile, mosque, or other meeting places. Perhaps the greatest advantage of cassettes is that they provide access to currents of Islamist protest outside of one's own society. The sermons of Lebanon's Shaykh Fadlallah, Egypt's Shaykh ʿAbd al-Hamid Kishk, and Malaysia's Haj Hadi Awang are widely available beyond their country of origin and are often found in Europe and America where Muslim students are located. "Voiced Islam" (al-Islam al-sawti) has thus become a formidable force rivaling "print Islam."

In earlier generations, the exposure of students to Islamic ideas would have been through the Qurʾan and religious treatises. Increasingly, however, it is the pamphlet, the popular sermon (khutba), the cassette, the telephone, and the electronic mail news service (J. Anderson 1994) that distribute information and ideas to all parts of the Muslim world. The National Research and Fatwa Center in Ann Arbor, Michigan, has set up a toll-free telephone line so that individuals may seek direct advice and fatawa on issues of concern from "knowledgeable Sheikhs and Students of knowledge." One can telephone, fax, post, or electronically mail questions, and answers are given in English or Arabic (IANA 1995). One result of such use of modern technologies is a new awareness of larger trends in the Islamic world, which, as we will discuss in the following chapter, involves the creation of a Muslim transnationalism. Another consequence of the use of modern technology is a kind of empowerment of protest groups within each society. Conscious now that Islamic groups elsewhere bear similarities to their own situations, and influenced by transformations in the Islamic political vocabulary that others may have crystallized, protest movements may find a bolder voice and be encouraged to more decisive activity in pursuit of their goals.

In the cassettes that record the sermons of Shaykh ʿUmar ʿAbd al-Rahman, who has been influential in the Islamic Associations (al-Jamaʿat al-Islamiyya) in Egypt and who was charged with complicity in the bombing of the World Trade Center in New York, one hears that sovereignty belongs to God alone (al-hakimiyya li-llah). In a commentary on Surat al-Kahf (18: "The Cave") of the Qurʾan, for instance, he does not directly name his target, the Egyptian government. Yet, he makes an unambiguous political point when he argues that no congress or party has the right to make laws. The audience hears, "Anyone who makes such laws are not believers" ('Isa 1992), and would understand that governments that infringe on God's sovereignty are illegitimate and undeserving of allegiance.

Cassettes that transmit sermons vary considerably in content, but most are similar in form and often echo the authority of the mosque.[3] The preacher (khatib)—and mosque preachers are exclusively male—chooses as his text Qur'anic verses that are to be explicated. Moral instruction is the primary purpose, and often most of the sermon deals with standards of ethical conduct or matters of ritual practice and dress. Yet, as the above example illustrates, political matters are not absent, although the preacher rarely deals directly with such questions. Rather, the argument proceeds by indirection. For example, an approving reference to the probity of the "rightly guided" caliphs of early Islamic history would not be lost on the audience as a veiled attack on the injustice and immorality of present-day leaders.

Sermons also invoke a range of authorities that may be surprising. Invocations of the Qur'an and hadith are unexceptional, and references to classical Muslim thinkers such as Ibn Taymiyya (d. 1328) and al-Ghazali would be common as well. Yet preachers frequently resort to citations of both contemporary Muslim intellectuals such as Sayyid Qutb, al-Mawdudi, Kishk, and Shaykh 'Abd al-'Aziz ibn Baz of Saudi Arabia, but also Western writers and publications.[4] For example, in Saudi sermons distributed via cassettes during the 1990–91 Gulf crisis, preachers explicitly invoked such sources as the memoirs of Richard Nixon, the Voice of America, the *Financial Times*, the Cable News Network (CNN), and the writings of George Bush, in addition to such contemporary Arab periodicals as *al-Hayat* and *al-Watan al-'Arabi*. These references were invoked to support the case that the United States harbored nefarious intentions in the region. This has notably been true of Shaykh Safar al-Hawali, whose pronouncements during the crisis have been compiled as *Kashf al-ghumma 'an 'ulama al-umma* (The unveiling of distress about the *'ulama*) (al-Hawali 1991: for example, 16, 69, 71, 75–79, 83, 101, 131).

The consequence of this rhetorical style is the emergence—objectification, in our terminology—of an Islam that is manifestly political and ostensibly modern at the same time. Without directly advocating sedition, therefore, the preacher is able to deliver a political lesson that appears at once traditional and, because of the reference to both modern Muslim and Western intellectual trends and writings, "rational." Although denouncing the West and Western values, many preachers thus implicitly employ Western arguments to convince their audiences of their own modern and contemporary focus.

The security implications of the dissemination of religious cassettes—and videos—are obvious, and government efforts to staunch their flow across borders are ineffective. Up to 1992, the Arab Postal Union banned the sending and receiving of audio- and videocassettes. Although by 1993 this formal restriction had been lifted (for example, Royal Mail International 1993:236, 390, 480), cassettes sent through the post are still subject to inspection and delay and often fail to reach their destination, and customs inspectors routinely seize such materials until they can be reviewed by censors. In one Gulf country in 1988, the head censor himself was implicated in smuggling radical Shi'i videocassettes. In Egypt, proscribed material has not necessarily been smuggled from outside sources. Sections of larger towns and cities have become difficult to control, to the degree that the Egyptian press reports a clandestine arms industry, which, although it has crossborder links with Libya and the Sudan, appears mainly home-grown (Subhi 1993). If arms can be clandestinely produced and distributed, how much easier it is to circulate cassettes and pamphlets. The effect may be significant: If cassettes are passed hand to hand, this may increase the solidarity of oppositional groups.

Although some of the videos and cassettes explicity advocate violence against the state, the vast majority, as we have said, stop short of this. Cassettes are used, for example, to transmit *nashids* (anthems), which are widely circulated and often reflect national or regional styles. *Nashids* build on such musical traditions as the *quwwali* from South Asia and rhythmic chanting from the Middle East, especially as practiced in Sufi traditions (see Waugh 1989). They typically have a martial air and involve male choruses that repeat, often to drum beats, variations on standard Islamic phrases such as *Ya Allah Allah, Allahu akhbar* (O God, God, God is most great) ("Nasyid Iran" n.d.) or the *shahada*, the profession of faith in the one God and His Prophet. Lyrics attesting to the greatness of Islam and the special mission to purify it are added (as in the *nashids* of the Muslim Brothers, for example, "Nasyid Ikhwanul Muslimin" n.d.), but at times explicitly political themes also emerge. Yusuf Islam, a British Muslim convert and a former popular singer, recorded a *nashid* in support of the *jihad* in Afghanistan:

> O victory is coming
> and history will tell
> 'cause the disbelieving army
> is heading for hell.

And paradise belongs
to the pious and firm,
to God we belong
and to Him we return.
Afghanistan and Islam,
Afghanistan and Islam,
Ya Muslimun, ya Muslimun

(Islam n.d.)

In the United States and western Europe, rap music has become tantamount to the *nashid*. Rap and hip-hop groups in Europe articulate a sense of disquiet with their societies and use their songs to highlight and implicitly protest against the racial and social discrmination that Muslims often feel. In the process, they attract audiences among both Muslims and non-Muslim youth, the latter primarily from racial or ethnic minorities. The group Cash Crew projects a particularly resonant message of protest in "Thatcherite," Conservative-led Britain:

I ask you a question
Who is your master?
Islam says it's time to wake up
In this place called England . . .
The sun will rise in the West
And will bring them to one God,
Allah the Magnificent
Who has no partners
The truly Beneficent. . .
Englishman is funny . . .
Worshipping the money . . .
In this system you can't be happy,
But this is all you know
Since you come out of your nappy

(Cash Crew 1994)

In the United States, Public Enemy is more outspoken in its denunciation of white-dominated society and has allied itself with the Nation of Islam faction led by Louis Farrakhan, who has often been accused of intolerance toward whites and Jews. The acknowledgments on its recordings contain the invocation, "All praise is due to Allah," and the *shahada*, the profession of faith, is evoked in the following lines:

Listen Christian, Muslim, Jew
Here's a little something that I thought you knew
There's only one God and God is one

(cited in Wells 1990:43)

In its song, "Don't Believe the Hype," Public Enemy equates the initially skeptical reaction to Elijah Muhammad (1897–1975), the founder of the Nation of Islam, and Malcolm X (1925–65) to the hostility that greets Farrakhan in both the African-American community and the wider American society. In performance, the group appears with a bodyguard reminiscent of the Fruit of Islam, the security force of the early Nation of Islam and of Farrakhan's faction today. Members of Public Enemy at times also display the star and the crescent. They urge followers to listen to their message directly:

> The follower of Farrakhan
> Don't tell me that you understand
> Until you hear the man
>
> (Public Enemy 1988)

As the former "Minister of Information" of the group, Professor Griff, said: "If you say that black people have been robbed of their name, their language, God, culture and religion and stripped of their very being—can you say that we are ourselves?" Farrakhan's Nation of Islam is attempting to rectify the situation in part through its "Do for Self" program: "We don't steal, We don't step on the poor. Black Americans have got to stop begging white Americans" (Wells 1990:43).

The importance of the *nashid*s and rap music is that they represent the ways in which popular cultural forms can be mobilized to foster claims and counterclaims in Muslim politics. The insistent rhythms, assertive refrains, and often mocking tones are especially effective in articulating protest. Hannah Arendt reminds us: "To remain in authority requires respect for the person or the office. The greatest enemy of authority, therefore, is contempt" ([1969] 1986:65). Like humor, music can be subversive. It is a popular representation of Muslim symbolic politics, but, as we would expect, it may also be ambiguous in its political message. Even the intemperate language of Public Enemy leaves one uncertain as to whether the group possesses an exact political program. The ambiguity of these recorded messages makes it all the more difficult for governments to prohibit them.

Governments also worry about the use of such technologies as the fax and electronic mail. One group in Algeria, the "Fax Group," has been charged with antistate activity (for example, BBC SWB, ME/1688, A/10, May 14, 1993). Often using the United States as a base, electronic mail networks also disseminate information and points of view across the world and are particularly used by university students at both the undergraduate and the postgraduate level. They relay news stories collected from various media—for example, on the status of Muslims in Bosnia, FIS in Algeria, and Kurds in Turkey—and comments on these stories. Many of these networks are specific to countries, including Israel, Palestine, Turkey, Egypt, Saudi Arabia, and Algeria. In some cases, officially disseminated news bulletins, such as those offered by the Algerian embassy in Washington, are immediately countered by opposition groups. In other cases, electronic networks aim for a broader audience by referring to themselves as "Islamic." One example is the Islamic Information and News Network, a subsidiary of the Pakistan News Service, which has regularly reproduced sermons and speeches of Hamas leaders, among others.

The self-representation of these networks expressly devoted to Islamic issues is unambiguous. *Islamic World Journal*, produced by the International Muslim Students Union (based in Seattle, Washington), says that it is "committed to raise awareness and enhance the unity of Muslim communities while providing an inside view of the Global Islamic Movement." To this end, it provides extended commentary on such contemporary issues of Muslim concern as the Kashmir conflict ("Censoring the History" 1994). These networks also often call for action in support of "moral," though not necessarily Islamic, causes. For instance, one electronic news service reported that Williamson County commissioners in Texas refused to give Apple Computer a tax abatement because Apple had granted health benefits to the partners of homosexual employees. The service called upon Muslims to write to the county commissioners to support them in their stand against "shrinking morality and [the] rampant indecency of sexual promiscuity" ("Williamson County" 1993).

The globalization of information is an inescapable part of the modern world, and, as elsewhere, in the Muslim world it may enhance the abilities of protest groups while increasing the vulnerability of governments (Sreberny-Mohammadi and Mohammadi 1994:28–31; Scholte 1993:47–49). In Saudi Arabia, for example, the government has recognized the potentially negative effects of satellite communications systems. Pressured by the ʿ*ulama*, it has banned the use of satellite dishes, which had become popular during the Gulf war in order to receive CNN broadcasts. The dishes continued to grow in popularity, and the regime feared that Saudis would be able to obtain morally and politically harmful material that avoided state censorship ("Saudi Arabia Bans All Satellite Dishes" 1994; "Antennes paraboliques" 1994). Although the Ministry of Interior, responding to opposition from the middle classes, has quietly let the ban go unenforced, the Saudis are spending a substantial amount of money to develop a cable system which would compete with other cable systems—Arab and Western—and which would be easier to censor (Khalaf 1994). The Iranian Majlis also ratified a ban on satellite dishes in December 1994. In another indication of the importance of symbolic politics, some Iranians, angry about the domination of American cultural programming, compared satellite dishes to the American flag ("Iran Prohibits Satellite Dishes" 1994). Although the Constitutional Council soon declared the Majlis bill impermissible on narrow constitutional grounds ("L'Interdiction des antennes paraboliques" 1995), the fear that outside transmissions may undermine the cultural and political order remains apparent.

The Fragmentation of Authority

As we argued in Chapter 3, common to contemporary Muslim politics is a marked fragmentation of authority. The *'ulama* no longer have, if they ever did, a monopoly on sacred authority. Rather, Sufi *shaykhs*, engineers, professors of education, medical doctors, army and militia leaders, and others compete to speak for Islam. In the process, the playing field has become more level, but also more dangerous.

Two conceivable outcomes of this fragmentation are possible. One is the intensification of dispute and contest; in the metaphor of the market, the "price" of Islamism may be pushed upward by a number of keen, and uncooperative, bidders. This is the scenario that many, if not most, Western observers—and a good number of Muslim commentators—believe is likely. The political forecast for Egypt, Algeria, Saudi Arabia, the Sudan, and sometimes Indonesia, among other countries, is often unfavorable because it is assumed that they will succumb to the centripetal tendencies of conflict within Muslim societies.

Evidence can certainly be marshalled to support this line of argument. *Takfir*, the proclaiming of a fellow believer as an infidel, and the transformations in the concept of *jihad* so as to accord primacy to the enemy *within* the Islamic state or *umma* are ideological currents of marked potency in the current age. Moreover, the use of violence to support these currents is an undeniable fact of life. Ministers of Awqaf, presidents, *amirs*, and *'ulama* have all been targeted for attack, but so, too, have Muslim "liberal" critics such as Faraj Fuda, the Egyptian writer who was murdered in June 1992 for his supposedly anti-Islamic views, and Taslima Nasreen, the Bangladeshi woman writer who is accused of suggesting in print that parts of the Qur'an need to be revised (Philip 1993; Brown 1994). In Algeria and elsewhere, Islamists have targeted intellectuals, journalists, novelists, teachers, and others identified with the propagation of values contrary to their own. In Egypt, a parliamentary deputy attacked the government for promoting anti-Islamic values and "immorality," citing as evidence the publication six months earlier of a photograph of a nude by the

Austrian painter, Gustav Klimt (1826–1918), in a cultural monthly. Following this attack, several Egyptian intellectuals, including the Nobel Laureate Naguib Mahfuz, spoke out against "intellectual terrorism in the name of Islam" ("Le Terrorisme intellectuel au nom de l'Islam" 1994:1).

Such activities have polarized Muslim societies, with authoritarian governments ironically assuming the mantle of liberalism against Islamism. The ʿulama may simply be instruments of the regime in this process, but very often they agonize over both the degree of what they regard as the radicalization of Islam and the extent of the government's heavy-handed response. In Egypt, for example, Shaykh Muhammad al-Ghazali has spoken of his worry about Islamist groups at the same time as he has been anxious about the regime's response. Curiously, for a member of the official religious establishment, he has also appealed for equal time in the media:

> There are those who hate all Islamic trends, whether moderate or extremist. They are waging wars against Islam, both secretly and openly. They make derisory pronouncements (al-taʿalim bi-l-ghamaz) about it. All we want is that the callers to Islam (duʿat al-Islam) be accorded the [same] opportunity [to air their views] that their rivals (khusum) have. (al-Ghazali 1989:1)

Such descriptions come close to suggesting that civil war looms on the Muslim horizon.

But this is only one way of looking at the situation. A second, alternative, view is that the multiple centers of power and contenders for authority come to various accommodations; in the market metaphor, the price is negotiated to the relative satisfaction of all. If we take just the Islamist groups as our example, it is apparent that they must interact with four sets of actors: the government, external patrons such as Saudi Arabia or Iran, other Islamist groups, and the masses or the target audiences from which they wish to attract sympathizers. The Muslim Brotherhood in Egypt, for example, has at times vigorously, even violently, opposed the government, but over time it has adjusted its strategy to the prevailing political winds. It has had to take into account both the suppression and the enticements of the government; the relatively conservative concerns of financial backers such as the Saudi monarchy; the pressure from other, more demanding Islamic groups that may regard it as having sold out to the establishment; and the amorphous, often illiterate masses whose religious and political formation they hope to control. An intricate politics of compromise and give-and-take may thus result and be as likely as civil war.

In several Muslim societies, Islamist groups—when indeed they are allowed to do so—have even routinely participated in electoral politics. In Egypt, the Muslim Brotherhood, not officially recognized as a political party, participated in electoral alliances in the parliamentary elections of 1984 and 1987, winning 12 and 32 seats respectively. Along with other groups, it refused to participate in the elections of December 1990. In Tunisia, Islamist candidates won 14.5 percent of the national vote in April 1989 and up to 30 percent in major cities. Partly as a result of this strong showing, the government has refused to legalize the main Islamist movement, Hizb al-Nahda. In Jordan, where King Hussein initiated a process of political reform in November 1989, Islamic candidates scored an unanticipated victory in the first parliamentary election in twenty-two years. Islamists took 34 out of the 80 seats, with the Muslim Brotherhood securing 22 of these seats and other Islamists winning 12 more. In the November 1993 parliamentary elections, following the adoption of a one-person, one-vote system, the number of Islamists elected declined to 16. Yemen's first elections occurred in April 1993, and al-Tajammuʿ al-Yamani li-l-Islah (the Yemeni Gathering for Reform), while failing to win a single seat in the south (formerly the People's Democratic Republic of Yemen), won 62 seats in the north. It came second to the 121 seats of the General Popular Congress, the president's party that governed the north prior to Yemeni unification in 1990 (Dresch and Heikal 1994).

In the August-October 1992 parliamentary elections in Lebanon, Muslim groups such as Hizbullah and AMAL fared relatively well. Boycotted by a number of groups, especially Maronite ones, and tarnished by allegations of voting irregularities, the elections were nonetheless an indicator of Islamist strength in the southern Jabal ʿAmil and eastern Biqaʿ Valley areas. Out of a total of 128 seats in the Majlis al-Nawab (Deputies' Assembly), Hizbullah took 8 seats out of the 27 Shiʿi deputies elected. Four other non-Shiʿi deputies—two Christian and two Sunni—appeared on Hizbullah's lists and vote with it in parliament. Hizbullah has specifically used its parliamentary platform to oppose any Lebanese-Israeli peace treaty. AMAL, which has been more willing to accommodate itself to the Lebanese state, took four seats in the elections. Its leader Nabih Birri became speaker of the assembly, after the long-serving Shiʿi speaker, Husayn al-Husayni, resigned his post in protest at what he saw as Hizbullah vote rigging in the Biqaʿ. In addition to Hizbullah and AMAL members, three deputies were elected from two Sunni Islamist groups (el-Khazen and Salem 1993:48, 419–33, plates 12 and 13).

In Indonesia, the Partai Persatuan Pembangunan (PPP; United Development party), was founded in 1973 as a government-approved coalition of Muslim parties. In the 1977 elections to the House of Representatives, PPP won 99 out the 360 seats, and 94 in the 1982 elections. In 1984, however, Nahdatul Ulama, the most important component of the coalition, withrew from the coalition and PPP's share of the vote declined accordingly. In the 1987 elections, it took only 61 of the 400 parliamentary seats, and in 1992, 62. Malaysia has a well-established parliamentary tradition, and Parti Islam Se-Malaysia (PAS; Pan-Malaysian Islamic party) has participated in national and state elections, with mixed success. Although it had cooperated with the ruling party between 1973 and 1977, it became a sharp critic of official policies. On the national level, PAS won five parliamentary seats out of 154 in 1982; one out of 177 in 1986; and seven out of 180 in 1990 when several other smaller Islamically oriented parties participated. In the October 1990 elections, the ruling Barisan Nasional (National Front) coalition lost all 39 state assembly seats and 13 parliamentary seats in Kelantan to PAS and its ally, Semangat '46 ("Spirit of '46"). PAS has since cautiously promoted an Islamic social agenda there.

Rather than assuming that protest politics inevitably ends in confrontation, therefore, it is useful to recognize that the dynamics of interaction among the various political actors who are seeking power and influence generates de facto rules of the game. These rules need not overlap with constitutional, formalized precepts, but they suggest that competitors, including the government, engage in bargaining. Governments prefer to obscure the fact they are dealing with Islamist groups in this way, but there is no denying that they do so. It would be exceptional if they did not. The implication is that this tacit bargaining, the working out of implicit rules for a modus vivendi, creates a form of short-term stability—even though this may not be desirable ultimately. Indeed, each protagonist hopes that in the long run such de facto interaction will induce favorable changes in the conduct of competitors (Mitchell 1981:123–25, 197; also Auda 1994a:374–75).

Tacit bargaining is a more common occurrence than is normally acknowledged. The fact the British government and the Irish Republican Army are unalterably opposed and advocate very different resolutions of the Irish problem has not prevented their quietly talking to each other and devising procedures for limiting the effect of violence. Likewise, French authorities, who have steadfastly claimed in public that they would not meet with representatives of FIS, labeling them as "terrorists"—and who tried to persuade the Americans to break off "dialogue" with FIS in mid-1994—were somewhat embarrassed by press revelations that Charles Pasqua, the Minister of the Interior, had met secretly in Germany with FIS leader Rabah Kébir and that the government maintained other contacts with FIS representatives (Cuau 1994; Lesieur 1994).

It would be foolhardy to predict the result of the protest politics of Muslims. Neither alternative that we have outlined is inevitable. Without question, politics is localized and subject to particular and changing circumstances. But, given the broadly held assumption that Muslim politics is inherently revolutionary, it is important to note that there is nothing preordained or permanent about its radicalization. Indeed, some observers believe that the radicals' "moment" may have come and gone (Roy 1992). Whether that is the case or not, politics in the Islamic world belongs alongside other political orders: Protest and bargaining constitute its two, intimately interconnected, sides.

6

MUSLIM POLITICS:

A CHANGING POLITICAL GEOGRAPHY

A

S INDIVIDUALS AND SOCIETIES struggle to make sense of the global processes of rapid social, economic, political, and technological change, standard conceptual maps of the social and political world become obsolete and the necessity for new guideposts obvious. Geopolitics—the "art and science of understanding and predicting spatial aspects of the shifts in political power among groups, particularly states" (Demko and Wood 1994:3)—once primarily focused on physical frontiers and the control of territories. Now it increasingly involves a politicized geography of groups and movements with competing claims and counterclaims. For nearly three decades, geographers have used terms such as "spatial awareness" (Wheatley 1976) to invoke the multiple levels of perceptions involved in understanding loyalties, opportunities, and affinities among persons and groups. Yet in recent years, a Brooklyn rabbi, Menachem Mendel Schneerson (1902–94), who never set foot in Israel, became a major voice in Israeli politics (Friedman 1994:328–30, 351–53; compare Kepel 1994a:140–90). Likewise, Morocco is only one of many states to recognize the continuum with its emigrant community. State authorities seek to promote a sense of "home" by encouraging emigrants to vote in national elections and by showing solicitude for their interests while living abroad.

Location and space have undergone such transformations that it is possible to argue that "primordia . . . have become globalized." Where once territory was the root of one's identity, ethnicity and religious activism have become "deterritorialized" (Appadurai 1990:11, 15) to the point where adherents, such as Sikh or Muslim activists, identify with each other as much as, if not more, than they do with the fellow citizens of their national homeland. Migration in search of work or political freedom, socialization through the defining literature and practices of a new movement, and immersion in the global culture contribute to this reorientation and reorganization of religious identifications—and, by extension, of Muslim politics.

The political geography of Muslims operates at multiple levels. At the micropolitical level, it involves the ways in which households, families, neighborhoods, small communities, and sects weigh opportunities and chart courses of action that affect their well being. Even at this level, "locality" may refer to persons physically removed: Somalis in Cardiff or Turin may be consulted regularly on decisions affecting their families or households in Mogadishu. Other levels involve the calculations of regional and national elites, and the "market" forces of politics and economics as groups formulate their interests and plan their future on the basis of incomplete and shifting information. In the past, these various layers of political and moral awareness could be envisaged as separable spheres of activity, but the advent of mass education and mass communications has facilitated their intercalation.

In African-American Muslim households, for example, domestic space may serve as a way simultaneously to distance a Muslim family from its non-Muslim milieu and to breach the distance between the American Muslim and larger Muslim contexts. Curtains tend to be drawn, and the decorating of front doors with Arabic calligraphy signifies that in such houses "the hostile environment of racism, discrimination, and religious intolerance [is] locked out." Internal decoration, particularly in middle-class homes, is a mélange of Middle Eastern, African, Asian, and Western styles: "African American Muslims have thus taken small portions of various Muslim cultures and woven an interesting tapestry that transcends (without denying) both their American nationality and their ethnicity" (McCloud 1995:106, 110).

Geography is clearly not merely a physical construct; spatial relations may preeminently be a state of mind. Connections and disconnections, distance and proximity are notional, and perhaps all the more significant for that. Through television, images of political and religious authority as well as community are daily projected into domestic space (Ossman 1994); as we discussed in Chapter 5, other cultural technologies are also crucial to the dissemination of ideas and information. If, through these means, Muslims in Moroland in the southern Philippines and in Nigeria, as well as different Muslim groups within each society, acquire a sense of linkage between and among them, the implications are potentially immense.

First, the "decentering" of Islam away from a preoccupation with the Arabian peninsula allows an awareness of the myriad forms of relations—economic, cultural, political, social—that have developed among Muslims worldwide and that have little to do with their position relative to the supposed center (see, for example, von der Mehden 1993). One does not need to subscribe to the view that a "global ecumene" has emerged to recognize that at times "the peripheries talk back" (Hannerz 1989:70). Westerners flock to Indian mystics, dance to reggae music, and read the magical realist novels of Latin American authors. In the Muslim world, Arab states formulate questions of moral censorship on the basis of novels written by Salman Rushdie in Britain and Taslima Nasreen in Bangladesh. The long-term impact of the permeability of borders is not certain, but there is no doubt that Muslims are reshaping their identities and political agendas while becoming increasingly mindful of the manifold economic, communications, and social links among them.

Second, the "reduction" of distance may encourage those who hold minority views—as radicals, moderates, or conservatives—to join forces with like-minded persons elsewhere to accomplish common goals. The new political geography, blurring conventional social distinctions, empowering new groups, and challenging governments, may in the long run facilitate the emergence of pluralism, even as some forces in society vigorously resist it. In the sense that symbolic and political connections across national and other political boundaries may be encouraged, conventional understandings of "external" and "internal" appear doubtful.

Transnational Linkages

The ability of Muslims and Muslim states to adapt to changing circumstances is not in question, as we have indicated from the outset of this book; the compatibility of Islam and nationalism is beyond doubt. The appeal to Muslim unity—a doctrinal byproduct of *tawhid*, or the oneness of God—has masked accommodations in practice and ideas to the overwhelming reality of political decentralization and variety. Over the centuries, Muslims have been able to adjust to the superior power of the infidels, and hence to a territorially demarcated international system; moreover, they have adjusted to the existence of multiple centers of power, including multiple caliphs, within the broad *umma*. The result has been an elite—and perhaps popular—willingness to come to terms with the nationalist sentiments that have emerged since the nineteenth century and, increasingly in the mid– to late twentieth century, to deploy Islamic themes to buttress nationalist discourse (Piscatori 1986).

This de facto pluralism explains why pan-Islamic political integration has been minimal, despite the longstanding aspirations of Muslims such as Muhammad Iqbal who longed for Muslims "in their totality . . . [to] range themselves under the Caliph" (Iqbal, cited in Esposito 1983:183). Indeed, the prospects for pan-Islamic integration were limited by several factors. Although the term was a European contrivance in the 1880s and was coined partially in conscious imitation of pan-

Hellenism, pan-Slavism, or pan-Germanism, it was promoted by Sultan Abdulhamid II (1876–1909) and supported by Ottoman propaganda and the proliferation of newspapers throughout the Muslim world. Yet the movement was thus identified with the weakening sultanate in Istanbul. When the Young Turks seized power in 1908, they accordingly deemphasized pan-Islam, although the theme was revived during World War I for tactical reasons. Moreover, colonial officials feared, and manipulated, pan-Islamic movements (for example, Landau 1990:54–64, 95–96, 103–29), and Muslim political elites, ruling at first in an informal alliance with the imperialists, solidified their power by promoting and articulating particular identities such as Egyptian, Iraqi, Nigerian, and Indonesian nationalisms. As a consequence, by the time the Turkish Grand National Assembly abolished the caliphate in March 1924, forceful divisions among Muslim political entities had already emerged. As the century has unfolded, they have become formidable features of Muslim political life.

So entrenched have these divisions become that, for the most part, Islamist groups have not called for the restoration of the caliphate. Rather, they seek to establish an Islamic state or Islamic order within their own national societies. A major exception to this pattern, however, has been Hizb al-Tahrir al-Islami (the Islamic Liberation party), which emerged out of the Muslim Brotherhood movement in Jerusalem in 1952. Its leader, Taqi al-Din al-Nabahani (1905–78), believed that only with the recreation of one Islamic state would the Muslim way of life be able to free itself of the corrupting influence of Western political and cultural imperialism, and only with the restitution of the caliphate would the Islamic state be able to maintain itself against the divisive forces of imperialism, nationalism, and secularism (al-Nabahani 1953a and 1953b; "Supplement" 1994). Because the restoration of the caliphate is an "obligation upon all Muslims in the world," it is an urgent matter for political agitation, and Hizb al-Tahrir becomes the vanguard party that will advance the caliphal revolution (Hizb ut-Tahrir n.d.:1).[1] This notion of a "vanguard" party appears as the basis of the declaration of Algeria's Groupe Islamique Armée (GIA), which announced that it had reestablished caliphate rule in August 1994 ("Le GIA annonce" 1994).

Regardless of the status of the GIA's claim to caliphal rule, pan-Islam may be thought to be advanced by the Organization of the Islamic Conference (OIC), the interstate organization of the Muslim world which was founded in response to an arsonist's attack on the al-Aqsa mosque in Jerusalem in 1969 and, in a larger way, to the alignments of Arab and Muslim politics following the disastrous Arab defeat in the 1967 war with Israel. Consisting of fifty-two members, including several of the Central Asian republics and Palestine, it is committed to the advancement of solidarity among its members (the first objective indicated in Article 2 of the OIC charter). However, union of the Muslim members has not been specifically endorsed, and it has in fact been undermined. Indonesia and Nigeria have been anxious not to appear too closely identified with the organization for fear that it would brand them as "Islamic states" and thus imperil their fragile domestic legitimacy.[2] In addition, the charter is transparent on the need to defend the individual sovereignties of its members. Article 2 affirms the principles of respect for "non-interference in the domestic affairs of Member States" and "the sovereignty, independence, and territorial integrity of each Member State" (cited in al-Ahsan 1988:128–29; Moinuddin 1987:84–100).

The short history of the OIC, moreover, reveals significant fissures: ideological differences between such pro-Western regimes as those in Tunisia, post-1973 Egypt, and Malaysia and relatively pro-Soviet regimes such as those in Syria or Libya; political differences among the monarchies, republics, and military juntas; and economic differences between the oil-rich and the poor, particularly in Africa. The OIC was unable to resolve the Iran-Iraq war (1980–88) or defuse Iraqi-Kuwaiti tension that led to the second Gulf crisis (1990–91). Furthermore, its counsels have been bypassed in the Palestinian-Israeli peace process, and, despite the offer of its Secretary-General to mediate in the dispute, it did little to settle the related difficulties of civil war and mass famine in Somalia. In the case of Bosnia, over which Muslims have been agitated, the OIC in December 1992 gave the United Nations (UN) Security Council a deadline of January 15, 1993, to provide effective support for the Muslims. If the UN failed to respond, it said, unspecified collective measures would be forthcoming from the Muslim world. In the event, no action materialized either in January or in the May 1993 meeting of Muslim foreign ministers at Karachi.

The activities of the OIC need, however, to be put into perspective. As clear as its inability to resolve intra-Islamic disputes or to protect Muslim peoples has been, such purported "failures" are the norm of international organization; no other international agency, with the possible exception of the comprehensive UN system, has distinguished itself in regional conflict resolution. In addition, the OIC can count effective contributions in a number of areas: It helped to galvanize the international consensus against the 1979 Soviet invasion of Afghanistan and support for the Afghan *mujahidin*; its Al-Quds Committee (created in 1975 under the chairmanship of Morocco's King Hassan), concerned with working for the liberation of Jerusalem, has focused attention on Israeli policies in the city and generally the Occupied Territories; the Islamic Solidarity Fund (established in 1974 and based in Jidda) has channelled funds to relief and charitable causes; and the Statistical, Economic, and Social Research and Training Center (created in 1978 with headquarters in Ankara) compiles data on economic interactions, including trade patterns and commercial ventures, of the Muslim states.[3] The most important component of the extensive OIC network is the Islamic Development Bank, which was established in Jidda in 1974. It has proven adept at targeting development projects to finance and it has become one of the most active aid agencies in the developing world (Meenai 1990; Wilson 1995).

While the picture is thus mixed, it is clear that the OIC has not advanced, and in fact does not intend to promote, tight political integration of the Muslim states. An interstate organization like others, it is the creation of its sovereign members and survives as long as it fulfills their interests. In this regard, it has been a success. Pakistan has found in it a convenient foil to India's manipulation of the Non-Aligned Movement, and Malaysia has used it as a way to enhance its voice in world and regional counsels, particularly as neighboring Indonesia evinces a certain wariness toward the OIC. Turkey has never deviated from its commitment to the Western security alliance and is sometimes uncomfortable with OIC resolutions. Yet, after the widespread condemnation of Turkey's invasion of Cyprus in 1974 and the worsening of the general economic situation from the late 1970s, the Turkish regime—particularly during military rule (1980–83)—appreciated the need to turn to the Muslim world for support of its foreign policy and for greater trade. Although at the Casablanca summit of December 1994 the OIC did not recognize the "Turkish Republic of Northern Cyprus" as a Muslim state or accept it as a full member, Turkey has largely been successful in promoting itself as the bridge between the North Atlantic Treaty Organization, to which it belongs, and the OIC. It thereby increases its international prestige while remaining unenthusiastic about more cohesive forms of political integration (Aykan 1994:73–196).

Raising Umma-Consciousness

Just as the emergence of a universal Islamic state is not on the horizon, neither are forms of pan-Islamic activity missing from the political geography of Muslims. As one scholar notes of Catholicism, the development of religious orders such as the Jesuits, Dominicans, and Franciscans constituted a kind of "horizontal" transnationalism, not to mention pentacostalism, that clashed with the "veritcal" transnationalism of the Roman church (Della Cava 1991, 1993). In the case of Islam, vertical transnationalism is lacking, but there are three ways in which a horizontal transnationalism may be said to have political significance.

First, a range of non-state actors has emerged to promote da'wa, the "call" to Islam. Each may have its own particular version of da'wa and Islam in mind, but in common they bind together networks of individuals and groups self-consciously committed to an Islamic community that is at once translocal and transclass.

As the creation and expansion of Sufi networks show, the general process of creating transnational Islamic networks is not new. Sufi brotherhoods have long formed transregional networks. Some, such as the Bektashiyya, founded in the thirteenth century, had a privileged role throughout the diverse lands of the Ottoman Empire. The order was closely identified with the Janissaries, the professional military body that played an important role in maintaining the Empire until Sultan Mahmud II (1785–1839) crushed them after an attempted rebellion in 1826. At the same time, he outlawed the Bektashiyya order, destroying its lodges, publicly executing three of its leaders, and exiling the rest (Lewis 1961:77–78). By the 1880s the Bektashiyya, like other orders, had again become politically influential and remained so through the early years of the independent Turkish republic (Lewis 1961:398–406). An estimated 10 to 20 percent of Turkey's adult male population belonged to it just prior to 1925, when religious brotherhoods were outlawed in Turkey (Birge 1937).

As previously indicated, other orders, including the Tijaniyya and Qadiriyya (Abun-Nasr 1965; Brenner 1988), had extensive links throughout North and sub-Saharan Africa and often wielded significant political influence. Colonial intelligence officers, such as Octave Depont and Xavier Coppolani (1897) in Algeria, may have overestimated the organization of these orders as monolithic "pan-Islamic" conspiracies—their elaborate, multicolored end map showing crisscrossing lines of influence linking brotherhoods across national and colonial frontiers throughout the Muslim world. Nonetheless, these transnational linkages formed important channels for communication. Moreover, the hierarchies of dominance between Sufi masters (Arabic, shaykh; Persian, pir) and their disciples (murids in both languages) formed a pervasive and popularly understood framework of influence and authority. Often new political communities resulted. For example, by crossing existing ethnic and social boundaries of identity, the Khatmiyya in the Sudan "paved the way for the first Sudanese quasi-national movement, the Mahdiyya" (Karrar 1992:170).

Sufi networks may not always be highly integrated. In the Kurdish areas of Iran, Turkey, and Iraq, the Naqshbandiyya maintain a vague sense of loyalty to the supreme mufti in Syria as the order's head, but some Naqshbandi connections are loose at best while others are tighter owing to marital and family ties (van Bruinessen 1992: 226–27). Sufi movements may have stronger links in many regions of sub-Saharan Africa, especially West Africa, and their connections are far from negligible in Turkey and Central Asia. In the Sudan, for instance, the Niassiyya, a branch of the Tijaniyya order, has gained in popularity at the expense of the older orders, especially among West African immigrants. Spiritually centered on Kaolack, Senegal, this hierarchical movement has facilitated linkages of various kinds—social, economic, and political—among its adepts in both the Sudan and the region. One observer estimates that their transnational connections have been so important that "in the 1986 elections [in the Sudan], all members of the Niassiyya were directed by Kaolack to support the candidates of the National Islamic Front" (al-Karsani 1993:141–42).

Contemporary nonstate actors include the Rabitat al-ʿAlam al-Islami (the Muslim World League) and the Jamiʿyyat al-Daʿwa al-Islamiyya (Islamic Call Society), among others (Schulze 1990). The former is especially active in dispensing Qurʾans and other religious material throughout the world,[4] sponsoring religious educational programs, and providing religious scholarships for students to study in Saudi or other Muslim world universities. In but one religious school in Kelantan in northeastern Malaysia in 1989, for example, the Rabita paid for ten student scholarships (out of ninety-four students), with one advanced student going to Umm al-Qura University in Saudi Arabia for more specialized training. Publications bearing the Rabita's imprint were readily apparent in the school's library. The Call Society engages in similar activities, although its work often transmits the particular, and idiosyncratic, thoughts of Colonel al-Qadhdhafi.

A notable feature of these *daʿwa* groups is their vigorous publication activities. The Rabita, for example, publishes a widely distributed monthly periodical in several languages, *Majallat al-Rabita* (League Journal; English title, *The Muslim World League Journal*). A typical issue contains educational and didactic pieces on various aspects of Muslim history and ritual, such as the *hajj*, but it also includes articles on issues of immediate relevance such as the Bosnian crisis and, at times, a review of contemporary intellectual debates in the West such as that inspired by Samuel Huntington's *Foreign Affairs* article on "The Clash of Civilizations" (*Muslim World League Journal* 1994). The Rabita's Southeast Asian affiliate, the Regional Islamic Dakwah Council of Southeast Asia and the Pacific, publishes a regular periodical, *al-Nahdah* (The Renaissance) in thirteen regional languages, including English. The Libyan Call Society has published the periodical *Risalat al-Jihad* (Message of the Struggle), which in characteristically unrestrained language has criticized Muslim and non-Muslim regimes, as well as movements such as the Muslim Brotherhood, for errant behavior (for example, "al-Wihdat" 1984). The Mu'tamar al-ʿAlam al-Islami (Muslim World Congress), based in Karachi, publishes a weekly newsletter, *The Muslim World*, which reports on events throughout the world and urges on readers an appropriate Muslim conduct. For example, in 1994, readers were encouraged to protest against the supposed plans of the Austrian government to award the European Literature Prize to Salman Rushdie's novel, *The Satanic Verses* ("Secretary-General's Letter" 1994:1).

These nonstate organizations, particularly through their formal presentations of Islamic issues and standardization of language and approach, help to create incipient ideological communities that do not overlap neatly with those of state frontiers. The process of objectification is unfolding in the transnational arena as well as within national and local contexts.

A second and related way in which transnational Islam may be said to have political significance is in the increasing concern over the plight of Muslim minorities. In 1936, a new English-language journal, *Genuine Islam*, appeared in Singapore, which transmitted the Sufi ideas favored by its patrons but also regularly reported on Muslim concerns in Germany and elsewhere in the West as well as in Egypt, Palestine, and other largely Muslim societies (Weyland 1990:230–31). Today virtually every Muslim journal—such as *Majallat al-Rabita*, *al-Nahdah*, and others like the London-based *Ahl al-Bayt* (People of the [Prophet's] House), the Arabic and English language periodical of the Shiʿi Rabitat Ahl al-Bayt al-Islamiyya al-ʿAlamiyya (World Ahl al-Bayt Islamic League)—has a section devoted to the problems and prospects of Muslim minority communities throughout the world. In the case of *Ahl al-Bayt*, "minority" often refers to Shiʿi communities within predominantly Sunni societies, as well as Muslim communities within non-Muslim societies. The *Journal [of the] Institute of Muslim Minority Affairs* has been especially effective in providing informed analyses of the diverse Muslim minorities of Asia, Europe, America, Africa, and even Latin America.

The dilemmas of Muslim minorities in the West are of special concern. A standard interpretation of Islamic traditions holds that Muslims must leave (*hijra*) or confront (*jihad*) un-Islamic society (*dar al-harb* [land of war] or *dar al-kufr* [land of unbelief]), and reside in *dar al-Islam*. Yet, because of economic or political deprivations or the desire to obtain education or reunite with family, Muslims have moved to Europe, the United States, and Australia in large numbers and now reside there permanently. This unexpected state of affairs has incited lively debate among Muslim intellectuals, with some arguing that *hijra* is permissible only as a strategy of *da'wa*—a way to propagate Islam— and others suggesting that this kind of migration is not only permissible but obligatory as a way for the *umma* to acquire the technical skills to progress (Masud 1990:42–43). Although a broad consensus appears to have emerged that the Muslim presence in Western societies is an irreversible fact of life, this state of affairs is not often viewed as satisfactory.

The debates within the minority communities themselves over the boundaries of accommodation to and protest against their home societies—the very stuff of their Muslim politics—have thus captured the attention of Muslim majority communities. Iranian publications, for example, follow these debates and speculate on the implications for their own understandings of Islam. Some are outrightly condemnatory, echoing the refrain commonly heard in the Muslim world that Muslim minorities, especially youth, are prey to the immoral and corrupting blandishments of Western materialism and popular culture (for example, "WABIL Warns Muslim Immigrants" 1994). At the conclusion of a conference in London in January 1995 on relations between the Muslim and Western worlds, the intimate connection between the two "realms" of Islam—majority and minority Islam—was foremost in the minds of participants. They praised Saudi Arabia for its ostensible plans to launch a new Islamic satellite network to combat Westen media distortions of Islam. Satellite programming would penetrate Western societies and, by directly providing unbiased information on the Qur'an and *hadith*, link minority to majority. The Saudi Minister of Awqaf, Da'wa, and Guidance, 'Abdallah ibn 'Abd al-Hasan al-Turki, said that it was imperative to find ways to rectify the image of Islam among Muslim minorities so as to help them avoid "the dissolution (*tadhwib*) of Muslim society in the minority country (*bilad al-aqalliyat*) in which they live ("Nadwat al-Islam fi wasa'il al-i'lam al-gharbi" 1995).

In explicitly acknowledging the permeability of frontiers—especially, as we have noted, in this age of globalized communication— Muslim leaders are subverting one of the presumed dichotomies of international relations: internal/external. On one level, it is conceded that *dar al-kufr*—or an intermediate, neutral realm, *dar al-sulh* (realm of truce) to which Western societies are often assigned—is an "external" domain in which Muslims routinely live. Yet, on another level, the defense and guidance of these very same Muslims are regarded as an "internal" Muslim prerogative. In such ways are the transnational dimensions of modern Islam transforming the Muslim political landscape.

A third reason why the transnational *umma* may be said to have acquired some substance is that Muslims are concerned with a number of "Muslim" issues. We do not mean to imply that these issues are Muslim in the sense that everyone understands them in a uniform or doctrinally defined way. Rather, they are Muslim in the sense that they take on symbolic currency and often play a part in Muslim politics. Examples of such issues include Afghanistan, Palestine, the Rushdie affair, and Bosnia. In each, transnational concern is aroused because of the shared perception that Muslims and Islam are under attack and require defense.

Since at least the General Muslim Congress of December 1931, convened after the Wailing Wall riots of 1929 in order to promote protection of Muslim holy places, and more particularly the 1936–39 Palestinian Arab revolt against British rule, the issue of Palestine has exercised Muslim sentiment. The Congress, inspired by the *mufti* of Jerusalem, Hajj Amin al-Husayni (1897–1974), was intent on raising Muslim—and not simply Arab—consciousness about the growing Zionist movement and, of course, on soldifying his own ambitions to lead the Palestinian national movement (Kramer 1986:123–27). Since then and for reasons we outlined in Chapter 1, Muslims from around the world have identified themselves with the aspirations of the Palestinian people, and at times—such as in Egypt in the 1930s (see A. Cohen 1982:140–41)—manipulated the symbolic significance of the issue to validate their own claims to authority in the competition with rivals. "Palestine" has thus become a major element in the symbolic politics of Islam.

In Dhaka, Bangladesh, the Islamic Research Centre produced a characteristic book entitled *The Palestine Issue and the Muslim World*, which was "aimed at providing . . . readers with an idea that it is the matter of faith in Islam and not adherence to the modern concept of Arab Nationalism that will ultimately decide the question of Palestine, nay, the conflict between Islam and the evil forces of Nimrod opposing it" (Jalil 1981:*iv*). The apocalyptic language highlights the depth of concern over the issue that has been felt in Bangladesh, and simultaneously undermines received notions that only the Arabs have an entitlement to the moral high ground in the defense of Palestine.

In South Africa, Muslims have been agitated over the Palestine question from at least 1948, and, in Durban for instance, a Palestine Islamic Solidarity Committee was established. Car stickers proclaiming support for the Palestinians have also become popular. *The Muslim News*, a leading newspaper in the Muslim community from 1960 to 1968, was a vocal critic of Zionism, even incurring an official ban on particular issues because of its inflammatory rhetoric. As sincere as Muslim sentiment doubtless was, another level of interaction was present. Identification with the Palestinians was at once an affirmation of Muslim "kinship" and a demand for justice for Muslims at home:

> The Muslims throughout the world, be they in China or Palestine, see themselves as a single unit, linked by a dynamic that does not allow themselves to remain silent when people, especially those of the same faith, have their human rights trampled upon. . . . We, as Muslims, identify with the oppressed Palestinians because we experience oppression ourselves under unjust rulers in this country. If we are being accused, as Muslims, of importing the problems of the Middle East into this country we don't deny the fact because the laws of South Africa force us to identify more closely with the oppressed people of Palestine. We are Muslims first and last, therefore, whatever happens to our brethren in the Middle East is of dire importance to us. In the same way that their problems are ours, our problems here in South Africa are theirs (cited in Haron 1993:224).

The Bosnian issue has also become a matter of general concern and has rapidly acquired prominence in the symbolic politics of Muslims. To give one example of grass-roots activity, Islamic Relief, the Central Women's Association, and other Muslim organizations throughout Britain have organized fund-raising dinners and drives to assist the Bosnians, and many community leaders have called upon the OIC to send troops to the front ("Focus on Bosnia" 1994). In July 1993, six Muslim nations—Iran, Turkey, Malaysia, Bangladesh, Pakistan, and Tunisia—as well as the Palestine Liberation Organization offered to send up to eighteen thousand troops to support the Muslims (Curtius 1993), and at least Iran and Saudi Arabia seem to have provided covert assistance in the form of weapons, ammunition, and armored combat vehicles (Tabatabai 1993). To mixed effect, Muslim "volunteers" also went to Bosnia, as they had as *mujahidin* to Afghanistan. But Bosnia was not Afghanistan, and many of the volunteers "found the Muslims of Bosnia a peculiar lot, secularists through and through, children of Europe lightly touched by the faith" (Ajami 1994:35). Yet, in a sense, this realization was less important than the general outrage at what has been viewed as a genocidal attack on Islam.

While many Muslims have thus denounced both the parsimony and hesitations of Muslim governments, they have also sharply attacked the West for its reversals of policy and failure to punish the "aggressive" Serbs. Some have even seen in the Western handling of the crisis a profoundly negative commentary on Western values. The Turkish president, for example, accused the West of a double standard in which the obvious aggressor was not punished because of engrained fears of a Muslim state in the midst of Europe (Pope 1993).

As with the Palestinian issue, the transformation of Bosnia into a Muslim issue has not lacked local effects. Turkish outspokenness has helped to enhance Turkey's influence in the Balkan region and, perhaps more importantly, to signal to Central Asian Muslims that it can be counted on as a committed friend. The Malaysian government was the first member state of the United Nations to break diplomatic relations with Serbia, and it has opened refugee camps for Bosnians and channeled humanitarian aid to them ("Malaysia's Stand on the Bosnian Issue" 1992). While thus advancing Malaysia's international standing, Prime Minister Mahathir (b. 1925; r. 1981–) has been able at the same time to solidify his own standing at home, particularly in light of the concern expressed on the issue by such important Muslim groups as ABIM. One indicator of his relative success is the favorable comment his lead has drawn from erstwhile critics of his regime. Chandra Muzaffar, a Muslim intellectual and founder of the reformist, citizens' rights group ALIRAN (Persatuan Aliran Kesedaran Negara, Society for National Consciousness), has in the past been placed under detention, but on this issue he has applauded the prime minister's forthright condemnation of Western equivocation (Khan and Abdullah 1993).

The Significance of Muslim Transnationalism:
Tablighi Jama`at

The nature of Muslim transnationalism may be elucidated by an examination of one transnational movement.[5] Tablighi Jama`at is a movement that began in India in the late 1920s and is devoted to the propagation (*tabligh*) of Islam. It is principally directed toward fellow Muslims whose faith seems to have been corrupted or lapsed. Appealing originally to illiterate or semiliterate peasants but gradually attracting followers in the professions and among the well-educated, Tablighi Jama`at expanded, at first, from the region of Mewat to most of the Indian subcontinent, and, then, from South Asia to the Arab world, Africa, Southeast Asia, Europe, and North America. One study indicates that the growth rate of the movement in Pakistan is higher than that of the *hajj* (Qurashi 1989).

Its rapid expansion may be explained by patterns of migration from the Indian subcontinent and by reliance on nearly worldwide networks of Indian merchants; the doctrinal simplicity and transsectarianism of its ideology; and the tolerance of local governments in response to the movement's avowed apoliticism. Tablighi Jama°at would thus seem to radiate outward from an originating center and to contribute toward the concretization of a religious and social identity not based on the political culture of the nation-state.

As with the earlier examples discussed, however, the transnationalism of Tablighi Jama°at poses certain challenges to conventional assumptions:

CENTER-PERIPHERY RELATIONS

One could possibly argue that a hegemonic center exploits a weak periphery in transnational orders (for example, Baran 1957; Amin 1990). Yet, as we have suggested, the notion of a uniform central focus in Islam appears to be questionable (also see Eickelman and Piscatori 1990:12–14)—as perhaps one could even say of the Catholic church. The "ultramontism" of the papacy in the nineteenth century may in fact have entailed its subordination to French and Italian episcopates. The paramount position of Mecca in Islam is challenged by such other centers as Karbala and Qum (for the Shi°a), Cairo (for the Sunnis), Touba in Senegal (for Mourid Sufis), and, not least, London and Paris (for the large number of European Muslims and Muslim visitors). Moreover, to assume that the center supersedes authentic local traditions may be tantamount to applying stereotyped standards of authenticity and cultural purity; these standards may constitute a caricature of Muslim societies that are constantly changing and, in several though differing ways, interconnected.

The Tablighis seem alternately to accord primacy to the Nizamuddin mosque and educational complex in India, the Arabia of the holy cities, and Dewsbury in Britain where large numbers of Tablighis annually congregate. It may have been the case in many countries that Tablighis hailed from South Asia, and it may be true that delegations routinely go there for inspiration and to participate in the regular international convocation (*ijtima°*). Yet there is no evidence that local branches are either chiefly funded by or directed from an outside center, and, as testified by the examples of Morocco, France, and Belgium where Arab and European missionaries predominate, Indian Tablighis have not always been the direct agents of transmission.[6]

In fact, the Tablighi Jama°at becomes localized over time, much as the Muslim Brotherhood has become "Jordanian" or "Syrian" despite its origins in Egypt, or, in the Catholic world, as churches have increasingly taken on national identities. As Immanuel Wallerstein says, universalist and particularist forces "are not opposites but a symbiotic pair" (1991:167). However present the sense of participating in a great enterprise or of belonging to the worldwide community of believers, Tablighis are so dependent on local—national, provincial, city, and village—resources that they are almost inevitably transformed by the "periphery." In Belgium, the Jamaʿat "remains faithful to the objectives and the missionary principles established by the founder [Mawlana Muhammad Ilyas Kandhalawi (1885–1944)], and it makes use of human resources provided by the secular society which also constitute the human material considered by the founder as targets for Tablighi action" (Dassetto 1988:163).

In contrast to what has often been expected of transnational interactions, local experiences, in time, may thus produce an impact on the wider movement. In Catholicism, Pope John Paul II remains critical of liberation theology in Latin America and elsewhere, but he cannot escape subtle shifts in his social thought as a result of his connections with worldwide Catholic networks. This dialectical relationship between "center" and "periphery" is also present in the Tablighi case. The experience of life in such industrial democracies as France or Canada, for example, may have inspired the general sense that women should be full participants of the movement and the specific provision for day-care centers. The Moroccan Jamaʿat now provides creches for its members, and there is a woman's branch of the Tablighis in Aligarh.

The pattern of localization may also be applicable to exponents of missionary work (daʿis) who begin to identify with those they intend to convert. Although Tablighis from several countries may descend on Muslim communities in Malaysia or Nigeria with the intention of disturbing, and rooting out, supposedly locally inspired mispractices, they have often come to appreciate the force of such specific circumstances as multiculturalism, sectarianism, or an official ethos of secularism that the local inhabitants face.

INSTRUMENTALITY AND COMPETITION OF TRANSNATIONAL FORCES

This localization of a transnational movement suggests that Muslim transnationalism does not simply undercut existing state structures and lead to "denationalization" as might have been assumed from a reading of at least part of the transnational literature (see, for example, Sakamoto 1975:198–99). To the contrary, a dual effect exists. On the one hand, the ideological appeal of nationalism and, to some extent, the autonomy of state policies are diminished by the enhancement of both the sense and the institutions of greater community. The Tablighis, in terms of rhetoric and cosmopolitan membership, direct followers toward the pan-Islamic *umma*.

On the other hand, national regimes attempt to use transnational linkages to solidify or advance their own influence, and the *da'wa* groups mentioned above often project the ideological agenda of their primary state sponsors. The Libyans use the Islamic Call Society to advance their influence, especially in Africa. Although the Muslim World Congress is less identified with the Pakistani government, its positions and those of the Zia ul-Haq regime were complementary.

Saudi Arabia utilizes the Muslim World League and such related organizations as al-Majlis al-'Alami li-l-Masajid (the World Council of Mosques) and al-Nadwa al-'Alamiyya li-l-Shibab al-Islami (the World Assembly of Muslim Youth) to advance its relatively conservative brand of Islam, particularly to counter Iranian-inspired movements and ideas. Recognizing the importance of global communications, moreover, Saudi businessmen, connected to ruling circles though not simply controlled by them, have become major media players in the Arabic-speaking world. In addition to Saudi government plans for an Islamic satellite network, the Middle East Broadcast Centre (MBC) based in London, which broadcasts in Europe and the Middle East and, since September 1993, the United States (via ANA, the Arab Network of America), is tantamount to a Saudi version of Cable Network News. Arab Radio and Television (ART) broadcasts via Cairo and Rome. Like the other Saudi-sponsored cable services, its intent to counter alien cultural influences is clear. In the words of one of ART's managers, "We will do anything we can do to protect our Arab children from the coming invasion from western countries" (Khalaf 1994). Saudi influence over the press is similarly strong. MBC owns the United Press International (UPI) wire service, and the Saudi Research and Marketing Company based in London owns at least ten newspapers and periodicals with an international distribution, including *al-Hayat*, *al-Sharq al-Awsat*, and *al-Majalla* (Khalaf 1994; Marlowe 1992).

The Saudis also less publicly support a variety of groups throughout the Muslim world. It is impossible to track the extent of these financial subventions and to whom they are directed, and the degree of Saudi involvement is almost certainly overstated. Yet there is no doubt that the Saudis have, at various times, provided assistance to groups such as Ikhwan al-Muslimun in Egypt and Jordan, Jama'at-i Islami in South Asia and Britain, Hizb-i Islami in Afghanistan, Hamas in the Palestinian territories, factions of the Front Islamique du Salut in Algeria, Jama'at Nasr al-Islam (Society for the Victory of Islam) in Nigeria, and the Warith ad-Din–led Nation of Islam in the United States (see Black, Pugh et al. 1992; Backmann 1990; Rubin 1995:182–83, 197–98; Legrain 1991:75–79; Kane 1994:495).

The much-vaunted export of the Iranian revolution is another example of how *da'wa* activities may convey the political imprint of their state sponsors. Ayatullah Khomeini left no doubt that the logic of the Islamic revolution required a transcending of Iranian frontiers:

> The Iranian Revolution is not exclusively that of Iran, because Islam does not belong to any particular people. . . . We will export our Revolution throughout the world because it is an Islamic revolution. The struggle will continue until the calls "there is no god but God" and "Muhammad is the messanger of God" are echoed all over the world. (cited in Rajaee 1983:82–83)

It has been argued that the primary way of achieving these goals is education and propaganda, but the Iranians are widely believed to supply financial, political, and military assistance to groups in various parts of the Muslim world. As with the Saudis, charges of Islamic revolutionary intrigue and influence often betray the exaggerated fears that many governments—in the West as well as the Muslim world—hold toward Iran. Yet there is no denying that Iran has provided logistical, training, and financial support to Hizbullah in Lebanon and, particularly since the Arab-Israeli peace process moved dramatically forward in 1993, to Hamas in the West Bank and Gaza. Iraqi Shi'i groups such as Hizb al-Da'wa al-Islamiyya and particularly al-Majlis al-A'la li-l-Thawra al-Islamiyya fi-l-'Iraq (the Supreme Assembly of the Islamic Revolution in Iraq) have also received significant amounts of Iranian assistance. Pasdaran or Revolutionary Guards have been despatched to the Biqa' Valley in Lebanon in support of Hizbullah and Islamic Jihad, and, putatively, to the Sudan where they are thought to bolster the Islamic-oriented military regime that seized power in 1985 (see Katzman 1993).

Calculated, state-sponsored efforts may prove counterproductive, however. In such circumstances, when the heavy hand of state manipulation becomes resented, a transnational movement like Tablighi Jama'at may acquire an advantage. Clearly, a movement which appears apolitical—even though in fact it may not be—and which advocates a kind of anti-institutional pan-Islam would have its attractions. This appeal would, in turn, allow the movement to manipulate the transnational ideology of "Islam" for its own purposes.

Indeed, although the Jama'at avers apoliticism (see Metcalf 1993: 593–96) and eschews confrontation with established authority, it inevitably participates in political activity as it propagates its message.[7] In light of what we have said about objectification, it would be surprising if politicization were avoided:

[T]he very radicalism of their faith and their models of reference are powerful elements in a critique of political systems, particularly those defining themselves as Islamic. Everything suggests that the Tablighis, far removed from power by virtue of their position in society, instead of attaching themselves to it engage in challenging its legitimacy. They go to the heart of the problem of power in "Muslim" countries without touching it (Dassetto 1988:162).

Even in societies such as Belgium, the self-conscious and standardized understanding of what Muslims regard as Islamic orthodoxy has telling effect. The Tablighis have used the law on associations to promote their group interests, and, in doing so, they have entered into competition with other Islamic *da'wa* or missionary groups such as the Rabita. The competition is rarely vitriolic, but it involves a pointed contest over who speaks for a morally transformative Islam.

Although the groups would deny it, the competition is over the right to manipulate the symbolic capital of Islam and, ultimately, territory: Who speaks for Islam *here*? To modify Appadurai's perspective, therefore, deterritorialization has its limits. Consistent with a worldview that interiorizes states of purity and unbelief but ends by a kind of exteriorization, the Tablighis view the Islamic realm (*dar al-Islam*) as the territory of the soul, but end by identifying it with the home, the local community, and only finally, the pan-Islamic community. Just as *kufr* (unbelief) or *bida'* (unacceptable innovations) are thought of as states of mind but dealt with on the level of social organization, *dar al-Islam*—sacred space—becomes externalized and identified with domestic and territorial space. This carries within it the seed of competition with other Muslim groups that espouse their own visions of Islamic community. The competitiveness and politicization of *da'wa* successively complicate the general transnational politics of Islam and render the search for pan-Islamic integration all the more difficult.

BLURRING OF BOUNDARIES BETWEEN INTERNAL AND EXTERNAL

As the prior discussion suggests, traditional dichotomizations of "inside/outside" and "internal/external" are unhelpful in understanding the dynamics of Muslim politics. The state is obviously permeable and "invites religious encroachment, precisely but not wholly because it is increasingly concerned with matters traditionally associated with the religious domain" (Robertson and Chirico 1985:225). One may, however, also point to structural factors, such as large-scale migration—the consequence of crises of the world capitalist system like mass un- or

under-employment and political repression (Gunatilleke 1986, 1991)—
and ideological fluidity as a result of both the global communications
network and the movement of peoples. One of the reasons why the
reaction to Rushdie's *Satanic Verses* in Britain was so vocal was that
Britain encompasses roughly 1.5 million Muslims, among whom
slightly more than half are of South Asian origin. Only a generation
removed from their peasant origins, they are, in one view, sensitive
to appeals framed in terms of defense of honor and tradition (Ruthven 1990).

But the process is complex. Given that, at least initially, they stand
apart from the traditional norms of British society and are compelled
to formulate their religious aspirations through the mediating language of English, they come to feel a certain form of solidarity as
against Christian British society. They "become" Muslim, rather than
Bangladeshi, Pakistani, Gujarati, or Pathan (compare Warner 1992:
32–33). Yet, at the same time, they remain open to the pulls of the
"homeland." British Muslims of South Asian origin are mainly
Barelwis, who follow *pirs* and are mystical in orientation but who are
not entirely averse to political activity. Their primary competitors are
the Deobandis, whose tendency is toward scripturalism in spiritual
matters and apoliticism in worldly matters. They have been especially
adept at disseminating their message of inner reform, owing largely to
the vigor and organizational skills of Tablighi Jama'at.

For the Tablighis, therefore, Muslimness is being affirmed on one
level of consciousness, while sectarianism on another is subtly invoked
and manipulated. Identifiably sectarian mosques and schools constitute fertile ground for the Tablighis, for they simultaneously provide
a bridge between the external world of South Asian, Deobandi Islam
and the internal world of British Islam, between the past of the family
homeland and the future of their new home. In many ways, as we
have seen throughout this work, the emergence of a transnational
Muslim civil society (see Peterson 1992: 376–88; Lipschutz 1992) has
constituted or reaffirmed local Muslim identities even as it may act
to subvert traditional hegemonic relations. To use inadequate but
evocative language, Islam out "there" is now "here," and the here of
contemporary Britain is intimately tied to and transformed by the
world out there.

In breaking down the barriers, therefore, transnational linkages may
both empower and endanger. On the one hand, the sense of the *umma*
grows more palpable in important respects and affirms to Muslims
that they are not alone in their struggles and aspirations. To use the
metaphor of Kalim Siddiqui, they feel increasingly able to plug into
the "global grid of the power of Islam" (Siddiqui 1990:7). Yet, on the

other hand, it is also clear that states and local identities may be reinforced, not undermined, by transnational interactions. Moreover, the electrical grid metaphor can be countered with the metaphor of the conveyor belt: political ideas and problems from elsewhere may be brought directly into one's society. As the Islamist hijacking of an Air France jet in late December 1994 indicates, the fear of the French authorities that the civil strife of Algeria would be imported to France is not without substance (Charpentier 1994; Sage 1994; Swain, Franchetti and Leppard 1995). As unpredictable as this intricate political geography is, it reveals a more subtle appreciation of Muslim politics than that afforded by an either-or frame of analysis.

The Civic Geography of Muslim Politics

In an earlier era, the interpretation of sacred texts throughout the Muslim world was predominately the domain of a religious elite. With the advent of mass education and mass communications, their reinterpretation has become more diffuse, engendering a heightened confrontation and bargaining over the often blurred boundaries of religion and politics. In one sense, this means a relativization in the interpretation of sacred texts. In his widely disseminated *al-Kitab wa-l-Qur'an: Qira'a Mu'asira* (The Book and the Qur'an: A contemporary reading), the Syrian civil engineer Muhammad Shahrur (1992) draws an analogy between the Copernican revolution and Qur'anic interpretation, which he says has been shackled by the conventions of medieval jurists:

> People believed for a long time that the sun revolved around the moon, but they were unable to explain some phenomena derived from this assumption until one person, human like themselves, said, 'The opposite is true: The earth revolves around the sun.'. . . After a quarter of a century of study and reflection, it dawned on me that we Muslims are shackled by prejudices (*musallimat*), some of which are completely opposite the [correct perspective] (1992:29).

On issues ranging from the role of women in society to rekindling a "creative interaction" with non-Muslim philosophies, Shahrur argues that Muslims should reinterpret sacred texts anew and apply them to contemporary social and moral issues: "If Islam is sound [*salih*] for all times and places," then we must not neglect historical developments and the interaction of different generations. We must act as if "the Prophet just . . . informed us of this Book" (Shahrur 1992:44; see also, Shahrur 1994).

In some respects, Shahrur's book is an intellectual equivalent in the Arab world to Allan Bloom's *The Closing of the American Mind* (1987), and in this respect he is not alone in attacking both conventional religious wisdom and the intolerant certainties of religious radicals and in arguing instead for a constant and open reinterpretation of how sacred texts apply to social and political life. A Kuwaiti bookseller argued in 1993 that Shahrur's book "is more dangerous than Rushdie's *Satanic Verses*, [because] Shahrur writes that he believes in the basic tenets of Islam like the rest of us" (cited in Eickelman 1993). Although most of the Arab mass media have avoided presenting the contents of his book, the attacks of the religious establishment against it have offered an indirect measure of its significance and inadvertently signaled its existence to new audiences. Like al-ʿAzm (1994) and Binsaʿid (1993), among others, Shahrur argues that a proper understanding of the principles of Islamic jurisprudence enjoins dialogue and a willingness to understand diverse opinions, and that this dialogue entails adaptation and the continual renewal of religious understandings within a framework of civility. Of course, such "frameworks of civility" remain fragile, as indicated by the censorship of the collected articles of Sadiq al-Nayhum (d. 1994) (1994) by Lebanon's highest Sunni religious authority, Dar al-Fatwa. The publisher, who had just relocated his business from London to Beirut, warned the Prime Minister that he would again leave Lebanon unless the censorship of this and other books was revoked. Over 120 Lebanese signed an open letter protesting the censorship (al-Rayyes 1995).

Such dialogue is not confined to the literati. Major innovations in the Muslim world have often come from the "edge" and the "periphery," notions that are highly fluid, as Bulliet (1994:201–7) reminds us. Today's innovators are more likely to be religiously minded engineers—such as Syria's Muhammad Shahrur—or Iran's late ʿAli Sharʿiati, a sociologist—than conventionally trained religious specialists. A second supposed "edge" is the explosively growing masses of urban poor throughout the post–World War II Muslim world. As Bulliet suggests, these recent migrants respond to leaders who emulate conventional forms of religious authority, but who also speak directly to them about things that matter, including "access to jobs, provision of social services, curbing of government neglect and corruption [and] morality in public behavior" (1994:202). As in the past, these transformations in religious sensibilities often come from the bottom up, rather than from established intellectual and political elites.

France is only one of many European states where there has been a major transformation in Muslim sensibilities. France, regarded through the 1970s as *dar al-harb* has become *dar al-Islam* for many believers, or—a somewhat intermediate position—*dar al-ʿahd*, or land of contractual peace, in which the state and religion reach a mutually satisfactory accommodation (Kepel 1994b:207). Thus, when Muslim militants speak about Islam *in* France, they implicitly claim that France and the state must adapt to Islam. Other Muslims act out a distinctly *French* Islam, suggesting that through education, socialization in French rather than in a Middle Eastern or South Asian language, and accommodation with non-Muslim neighbors, Islam as practiced and thought has taken a distinctly French form.

In France, as elsewhere, the state fails to manipulate Islam for its purposes, just as Muslims are unable to control fully the political and social environment in which Islam is practiced and expressed. In France, as in Germany, Britain, and the United States, Muslims are caught up in contexts in which they explicitly or indirectly contest and redefine the boundaries of Islam and politics. In so doing, often they challenge the boundaries of the state itself. Thus for France, the Algerian problem is not just a foreign concern, but a French one. As often as not, the Minister of the Interior takes the lead in defining French policy and in linking developments in France with those on the southern shore of the Mediterranean (see fig. 15).

Similarly, faxes sent to Saudi Arabia from outside the kingdom call into question the regime's religious credentials and authority, forcing it to recognize these challenges and respond to them through the media it controls or influences, condemning those who copy or distribute documents that slander the "legitimate rule" as guilty of a sin equal to that of those who create them (al-ʿUthaymayn 1994). Especially since the Gulf crisis of 1990–91, Saudi Arabia has witnessed an explosion of public discussion on the fundamental nature of its society and politics. Earlier attempts at such debate can certainly be found, such as Prince Talal ibn ʿAbd al-ʿAziz's unprecedented call for constitutional reform, *Risala ila muwatin* (Letter to a compatriot) (1985), originally written during the Nasserist-led challenges of the early 1960s. But the recent period is notable for the diversity and quantity of attacks on, and counterattacks from, a regime that prides itself on its paramount service to Islam. Cassettes of popular sermons, faxed indictments from individual dissidents, electronically mailed pronouncements of human rights groups, official *fatawa* and *bayan*s of the Committee of Grand ʿUlama, and publications of the Rabitat al-ʿAlam al-Islami (the Muslim World League) all compete for public support.

In this process, two trends are discernible. First, the Saudi government's attempt to manipulate religious discourse to bolster its legitimacy has produced an ironic countereffect: It has stimulated critics to

Fig. 15. "Good! Whew! In short, this isn't going to be easy." French Minister of the Interior explains to the police how to distinguish between "moderate Muslims" and "dangerous 'fundamentalists'."

seek in the printed formulation of their own views the most effective means to mount their protest. In a society in which considerable pride has been placed in the ability of individuals to seek direct redress of their grievances in regular *majlis* sessions with the king and other notables, attentive publics have increasingly turned to less personalized and more formal ways to express themselves. Thus, for example, government policies generate publicly critical memoranda *(nasihas)* that are responded to in official *fatawa*, which in turn encourage further unsolicited, and reproducible, "advice."

Second, among the disparate actors in Saudi society, a striking convergence of discourse is occurring. As we saw in Chapter 3, the Committee for the Defense of Legitimate Rights (Lajnat al-Difaᶜ ᶜan al-Huquq al-Sharᶜiyya)—consisting of lay and religiously trained individuals—in its very name evokes the language of both human rights and *shariᶜa*. This overlapping of discursive worlds is likely to strengthen the appeal of formalized criticism of the regime among the literate classes of society—however educated—and hence pose formidable challenges to ruling circles. The constitutional statement of March 1992, reaffirming the kingdom's Islamic destiny while articulating for the first time certain limitations on the power of government, indicates an official awareness, to some extent, of the need to be responsive. The boundaries of public life are being redrawn. Yet this reconfiguration—or, to change the metaphor, this opening of the Pandora's box of "print Islam"—is intensifying the fragmentation of authority. In the medium term, this may well generate an Islamic-tinged authoritarianism—in the kingdom as throughout the Muslim world—but over the long term it may well precipitate a civic pluralism.

If one is optimistic, the intensified confrontation and bargaining now apparent throughout the region can be seen as the incorporation, even if grudgingly, of voices previously excluded from the political arena. Even if the formal rhetoric of conservative states still stresses a trickle-down theory of development, in which all good flows from the top, large numbers of people now have the means to question authority and—thanks to a communications revolution that has undermined the efficacy of state censors—the ability to learn about a world independent of that offered by the state.

The issue of Islam's compatibility with democracy has been thoroughly explored for both the Middle East and other parts of the Muslim world (Hefner 1993; Madjid 1994; Norton 1993, 1995a, 1995b; Salamé 1994). Of signal importance is the strengthening of voluntary and nongovernmental organizations despite the fact that some terrain in the Muslim world may initially appear unpromising (compare Putnam 1993). Thus, it has been argued that Ottoman society lacked autonomous corporate bodies that could protect individuals against the arbitrary power of the state (see Ozbudun 1992:200–201). More recently, in a 1993 poll in Jordan, only 1.4 percent of respondents claimed affiliation with a political party and only 6.5 percent declared themselves prepared to do so in the future, in spite of an unprecedented wave of electoral activity—in 1993, Jordan had its second free parliamentary elections in four years (Brand 1995:148, 165). Yet politics pervaded the professional associations, labor unions, women's groups, sports clubs, and family and tribal associations that proliferated throughout Jordan. Through these associations, Jordanians could organize and express themselves and yet avoid a direct challenge to the state (Brand 1995:163–80).

Elsewhere, as in Morocco, recent municipal and parliamentary elections may appear indecisive, and certainly no triumph for organized political parties, but the numbers of people involved in registering, campaigning, arbitrating alleged irregularities, and voting have irreversibly heightened the general political consciousness (Eickelman 1994:269–70). Even though some people are disillusioned with existing political frameworks, most do not reject them outright. Some ruling elites undoubtedly cynically manipulate proclamations of adhesion to the "rule of law." Yet even in such cases, the act of claiming respect for such principles generates awareness among an increasingly sophisticated citizenry of what is needed to achieve a more just society.

In many Muslim majority countries, it can be argued that dynamic civil society can exist without formal political organizations because pervasive informal organizational structures often serve as the framework for effective political, social, and economic action. Over two decades ago, for example, James Bill suggested that an understanding of Iranian politics meant recognizing the significance of the *dawra*—an informal group of individuals who meet periodically. These circles could be formed through overlapping professional, religious, political, and economic ties, and networks of these interlocking coteries disseminated information and views and shaped forms of everyday resistance. Cumulatively, without an effective center or formal leadership for state authorities to co-opt, coerce, or suppress, such networks contributed to constraining the arbitrariness of the state and its exercise of authority. *Dawra*s fragmented and re-formed as the interests of their members changed, and many individuals belonged to multiple circles (Bill 1973). Most Iranians assumed that real access to authority was through informal channels, so direct personal ties of trust and obligation, more than declared ideological preferences, were integral to understanding political action.

One scholar has noted with irony that the small-scale monarchies of the Arab Gulf best replicate the attributes of "oligarchic republicanism" that prevailed in ancient Athens (Salamé 1994:100; see also Hicks and al-Najjar 1995). Although many residents of such oil-rich states are noncitizens and lack political rights, males with full citizenship participate vigorously in far-reaching debates. In Kuwait, some of these debates take place in the reconstituted parliament; others occur in the context of networks of interlocking *diwaniyya*s—it is tempting to gloss the term as "salon"—which function much like the Iranian *dawra*. As we noted in Chapter 4, *diwaniyya*s in Kuwait can be for men, for women, or, since the 1990s, for both men and women. Added to these institutions are the *jamaʿat taʿawuniyya*, neighborhood cooperative societies, which served as significant political arenas when Kuwait was deprived of its parliament and played a significant role in organizing daily life and resistance during the 1990–91 Iraqi occupation.

It might be argued that the Gulf states represent a special case of informal associations, but such ties are also crucial in larger political arenas. In Turkey, for example, the Islamic-oriented Welfare party (RP) won victories in the March 1994 local elections through a strategy that relied on building ties of interpersonal trust, taking "full advantage of neighborhood, regional, and other cultural bonds that tie people to one another in mutual assistance as well as its flip side: mutual obligation" (White 1995:11–12). In Algeria, the compact put forward by the FLN, in which citizens gave up political participation in exchange for economic security after Algeria's independence in 1962, gradually eroded in the face of mounting inefficiency and corruption. As a last resort, the FLN in the period before military rule in January 1992 offered another "grand bargain," this time a democratic one (Leca 1994:67–68)—granting new elites some access to authority in exchange for restored regime legitimacy and the prospects of future economic improvements and political liberalization. But it was too late for such a move to be convincing. Islamic associations, often existing on the margins of legality through the 1970s, gradually took over where state services had all but collapsed, building mosques, running schools and clinics, and providing services that the state was no longer willing or able to provide (Rouadjia 1990). The bonds of reciprocity and obligation created through these activities fostered a sense of moral and spiritual renewal and provided the necessary basis for Islamist organizations to create new political purpose and community and to achieve a significant victory in the 1990–91 Algerian elections (Vergès 1994:78–82). In some views, civil society has all but collapsed in Algeria and the Sudan, but underlying mutual ties of commitment, concealed from state authorities and outsiders out of necessity, often exist independent of the state or in defiance of it (Simone 1994:67). These networks of understanding and reciprocal obligation make a semblance of collective life possible where the state has failed.

From Morocco through Turkey and Indonesia, formal civic institutions have begun to reach a critical mass with associations of migrants, journalists, human rights organizations, doctors, lawyers, women's rights groups, and political parties. They are often built on the resilient framework of informal networks of trust and responsibility—informal associations—and the line between formal and informal associations is often exceedingly thin. Even in the Sultanate of Oman, seemingly removed from the vanguard of democratization and the development of civic associations, rising standards of education have created a citizenry that finds ways to breathe life into apolitical or moribund institutions. Discussions about fielding a sports team, improving hygiene in the market, or using a municipal budget to create a library or youth club rather than resurfacing a road or installing street lighting offer citizens an opportunity to express their views and learn to organize to get things done. Elsewhere, as in Morocco, the decision by a parents' group to refurbish and pay for a prayer room in a secondary school, to offer lodging to indigent university students, or to offer medical services to the needy may be formally framed as apolitical activities, but they offer citizens the opportunity to work together, independent of state initiatives, to achieve common goals.

An exclusive focus on election results or the assertion that democracy is categorically either present or absent deflects attention from major changes taking place beneath the surface. They suggest that a transition is being made to a less arbitrary, exclusive, and authoritarian rule, notwithstanding the conditions of rapid population growth, stagnating economies, rising unemployment, and a young citizenry that is more articulate than preceding generations and less patient with conventional political arrangements. Even if the "hidden transcript" often remains a better measure of political vitality than the "public" one (Bennani-Chraïbi 1994:283–93; compare Scott 1990), disillusion has not led inexorably to revolt or to religious and political radicalism. There may be disillusion with existing political frameworks, but this does not necessarily mean their outright rejection.

Of Paradigms and Policies

Lapidary formulas such as the "West versus Rest" (Huntington 1993) are deceptive in their Manichaean simplicity. This "essentializing" of civilizational traditions deflects attention from their internal and historical variations and from the vigorous internal debate among their adherents. Muslims, like other peoples, are themselves engaged in vigorous intellectual debates about the themes raised in this book. The upshot is Muslim "agency" in the sense that sociologist Anthony Giddens (1979:54, 256–57) uses the term—an individual's or group's capability to intervene, or to refrain from intervening, in a series of events so as to influence their course. Muslims increasingly perceive that Islam offers them agency, but not in the sense of a monolithic force. The new geography of Muslim politics also precludes a "West versus Rest" mentality because of the dissolution of prior notions of distance and frontier. A significant and continually growing Muslim voice is in the "West" itself. Muslim political voices are as likely to be heard in Washington as in Karachi, in Detroit as in Dhaka, and in Moscow as in Cairo. Because of permanent *hijra* (emigration), Western and Muslim societies are now on the threshhold of new understandings of one another.

Misleading in other respects, Huntington's provocative formula reintroduced the concept of culture—albeit a dated and deeply flawed one—to the study of foreign policy and international relations and underscored the notion that nation-states are no longer the sole source of identity in politics. Civilizations, however, do not act on the human stage; actors are shaped by civilizational traditions. Even in societies labeled as "traditional"—or, alternatively, as populist—there is diversity and internal debate over identifying key civilizational values, who is "authorized" to articulate them, and how they are implemented. As a result, civilizations, like cultures, are "contested, temporal, and emergent" (Clifford and Marcus 1986:18). Essentializing formulations such as Huntington's are pernicious because they deflect attention away from the cultural dynamics of political change.

Consistent with our argument throughout this book, Muslim politics is sufficiently complex that any attempt to reduce it to a single formula leads to mystification; rather than being monolithic, Muslim politics, while aspiring to *umma*-wide universals, derives its force and significance from the specific contexts, times, and localities in which it takes place. "Islam" cannot thus be a threat, any more than the "West" can be for Muslims, despite Khomeinist demonization of all Western policy as inherently malicious and antithetical to Muslim aspirations. Muslim politics have a transnational dimension, but this does not imply that one Muslim cultural unit has coalesced or that a transnational Islamic space has acquired dominance. Even Muslims who denounce Western values accept many Western borrowings, as brought home by one religious activist in the Arab Gulf. In a 1978 interview, he explained how democracy would never take hold in the Muslim world because it was a concept alien to *shura*, which was Qur'anic and Islamic. In 1990, however, he asserted that *al-dimuqratiyya* (democracy) was compatible with Islam. When reminded of what he said a decade earlier, he replied: "Now we know better. *Shura* is not a major concept in the Qur'an and its few usages there are ambiguous. Democracy can be adapted to Islamic ideals" (interview with Dale F. Eickelman, April 27, 1990).

There is a way to think about politics and policy that goes beyond simply replicating the structure of political wisdom that dominated the cold war years. Responding to critics of his proposal to replace the cold war foreign policy paradigm with one based on the clash of civilizations, Huntington (1993:86) argues that people think "abstractly" when they think "seriously." Although the cold war paradigm "could not account for everything that went on in world politics," it accounted for "more important phenomena than any of its rivals" and "shaped thinking about world politics for two generations." Huntington invokes Thomas Kuhn's *The Structure of Scientific Revolutions* (1962) to assert that scientific advances consist "of the displacement of one paradigm by another." By analogy, he claims that we need an equivalent "simple map of the post-Cold War world" (Huntington 1993:186–87).

A "simple map," however, may be precisely the problem, especially if it is based on dated and misleading assumptions. Historians of science no longer focus almost exclusively on "theory," as did Kuhn who, according to Peter Galison, invoked specific cases only to "confirm, refute, or generate theory" (1988:208). Galison, by way of comparison, proposes that those who seek to understand developments in science should avoid assuming that there is a fixed, hierarchical relation between theory, the instruments of perception, and experiment. There is no reason to assume that any one of these factors is inherently more important than the others. Similarly, a reliance on "simple" paradigms may inadvertently keep policymakers from envisioning alternative, more effective ways of thinking about other people's politics.

In the specific context of Muslim politics, deemphasizing paradigms and reimagining the challenges policymakers will face in the years ahead entail listening to the many Muslim voices, not merely those of a Westernized elite. The first step is to learn to elicit their cultural notions of legitimate authority and justice and to recognize that ideas of just rule, religious or otherwise, are not fixed, even if some claim that they are. These notions are debated, argued, fought about, and reformed in practice. But the challenge is not only to recognize that such debates are occurring, although that recognition in itself would be salutary. More important is the need to place these debates in their settings, to understand the obstacles, false starts, accommodations, interconnections, and decisive shifts that have emerged in Muslim political discourse and practice. In the end, such an understanding promises to undermine unreflective presumptions that Muslim relations with others are chiefly hostile, and that Muslim governance is almost inevitably arbitrary and authoritarian.

NOTES

1. Similar issues concerning the wearing of headscarves to cover women's hair and necks occurred in Great Britain at roughly the same time and were discussed in the popular press (for example, "School Backs Down in Scarf Battle" 1990).

2. Although the number of female students wearing the headscarf has continued to grow in France, just over 700 wore it in schools as of June 1994 (Jelen 1994:82), making them a small number of France's school-age Muslim population. Their reduced numbers reaffirm the power of the headscarf to instigate a major national debate. Note, however, ambiguities in official and unofficial estimates of "veiling" in schools. One anonymous expert estimated students with headscarves at 2,000 in June 1994, but only 860 at the beginning of the 1994–95 academic year. The Ministry of the Interior, however, estimated headscarves in schools at 15,000 in September 1994. Although some of this variation is politically inspired, it also can relate to whether "discreet" or "minimalist" headscarves are also counted (Stein 1994:24).

3. The citizen's decision to forego immediate and narrowly defined self-interest in the hope that others will do so for a mutually satisfactory solution—to sacrifice individual "rationality" for collective "rationality"—is a calculated gamble that theorists sometimes call the "prisoner's dilemma." Jon Elster goes so far as to say that "politics is the study of ways of transcending the Prisoner's Dilemma" (1976:249).

4. Visits to shrines elsewhere in the Muslim world have also acquired political significance. For example, the newly established revolutionary leadership in Egypt, including Muhammad Neguib and Gamal ʿAbdul Nasser, took part in the annual pilgrimage to the tomb of the founder of the Muslim Brotherhood, Hasan al-Banna, on February 13, 1953, the fourth anniversary of his assassination. Although Nasser and Neguib later split with the Brotherhood, they sought to acquire political legitimacy through association with this popular Muslim martyr (Mitchell 1969:111).

5. Of course, the transformation of religious pilgrimages into political events is not unique to Islam. In Israel, for example, national politicians often appear at pilgrimages to the shrines of leading saints (*saddiqim*) venerated by Israeli Jews of North African origin. During election campaigns, they hope to benefit from televised broadcasts of these visits (Weingrod 1990:231).

6. Throughout this book, we distinguish between ʿ*ulama*, Muslim intellectuals who have been trained in the *madrasa* (mosque school) to master the traditional religious texts under acknowledged authorities of an earlier generation, and "new" religious intellectuals, religious leaders who have been educated primarily in modern, state-supported educational institutions (see Kepel and Richard 1990). We include in this group those religious leaders who have experienced both styles of education. For example, in Iran during the 1960s and

1970s, the majority of students failed entrance examinations for secondary schools and universities. This is because Iran had been following the French model of rigorous admissions examinations. Many students who failed these state examinations, but who had significant prior experience of state schooling, pursued *madrasa* education. In Morocco, partially in response to the perceived threat of Islamic radicalism, Hassan II tried to recruit senior Ministry of the Interior officials trained in both traditions.

7. Salah al-Din al-ʿAyyubi (d. 1193), known in the West as Saladin, was a Kurdish general who took power in Egypt and Syria after overthrowing the Fatimid caliphate in 1169. In 1187, he recaptured Jerusalem from the Franks, but this conquest precipitated, in turn, the Third Crusade.

CHAPTER TWO

1. Khomeini's will, dated February 15, 1983, was made public upon his death in 1989.

2. Whereas Shlomo Eisenstadt's early work (for example, 1966) represents the school of thought that believed modernization would end in Western-style liberal democracy, Samuel Huntington (1968) pioneered the school of thought that preferred to speak of "order" rather than greater political participation as the end result.

3. The Iranian revolution, which occurred in 1978 and 1979, was a sufficient counterexample to persuade the authors of this text to abandon this claim. In Bill and Leiden (1974:53), Yemen and Afghanistan are cited as examples of "backward" communities in which Islamic influence and control remain strong; in Bill and Leiden (1979:69), Yemen and Oman provide the examples, with Afghanistan (following abolition of the monarchy in 1973) dropped. The argument is dropped altogether from Bill and Springborg (1990), the third edition of this text. A notable exception to such views was presented by Donald Smith (1974:7). Because Islam is an "historical religious system," which, unlike Hinduism and Buddhism, lives in time until it transcends time, it has proven to be adaptable throughout the centuries. Muslims, like Catholics, have a responsibility to bide their time as fairly and as comfortably as they can without adding to the misery of others; thus, waiting for the eschaton, they do their duty by promoting social justice and by coming to terms with the fluctuations of history.

4. For a reappraisal of Marxist-Leninist theories of development as they apply to Afghanistan, see Korgun (1993).

5. For detailed accounts of how Islamic law has been reformed in the twentieth century, see Anderson (1976) and Coulson (1964).

6. Modern Islamic political theory is developing the idea that the people constitute the *khalifa*. Ismaʿil al-Faruqi, for example, says that men are "perfect in form and endowed with all that is necessary to fulfill the divine will . . . even loaded with the grace of revelation" (al-Faruqi 1986/1406:10; compare Moussavi 1992). Although al-Faruqi does not specifically do so, other writers are developing this point as the basis for popular participation as essential to governance.

7. The Pakistani constitution of 1990 similarly displays the coexistence of contrasting notions of sovereignty. While reaffirming that "sovereignty over the entire Universe belongs to Almighty Allah alone," it also speaks in the name of the people of Pakistan. Following the injunction of Muhammad ʿAli Jinnah, the founder of the nation, it is the people's will that Pakistan be a "democratic state based on Islamic principles of justice." They are to be ruled by their elected representatives, but "in accordance with the teachings and requirements of Islam as set out in the Holy Quran and Sunnah" (Preamble) (Pakistan 1990).

8. Enayat (1982:69–83) provides an outstanding discussion of Rida's views on the Islamic state.

9. Madan (1987:749), however, takes a highly negative view of the rise of Hindu, Sikh, Buddhist, and Muslim activism—he uses the term "fundamentalist"—in the political sphere. By referring to contemporary activism as a "perversion of religion" because it has no precedent in "traditional" societies, he recognizes the objectification of religious tradition but goes too far in assuming that only "traditional" religious expression and practice are authentic.

10. Educational statistics for Egypt and Morocco are derived from the World Bank (1981–89) and for Oman from Oman (1979–89). These figures are necessarily approximate, as countries change their classification and reporting of educational institutions.

11. Although al-Ghannouchi uses the term *islamiyyun*, he uses other terms that seem virtually synonymous with it. Although he often refers to those Muslims committed to change the world as simply "the Muslims" (*al-muslimun*), it is clear that he means that they are distinguishable from the general community. This point is made apparent when he speaks of "the Islamic tendency" (*al-tiyyar al-islami*)—an implicit setting-off of the "tendency" from other religious-minded Muslims as well as secular ones, including the political elites which he opposes (for example, 1992:52, 164). Consider also his phrase, "we who are answerable as an Islamic movement" (*nahnu masʾulun ka-haraka islamiyya*)(Ghannushi 1992:47). All of these self-designations indicate a heightened awareness of Islam as an ideological system. In fact, Ghannouchi (1992:58) refers explicitly to "the source of Islamic thought or Islamic ideology" (*asl al-fikra al-islamiyya aw-idyulujiyya al-islamiyya*). His specific language is important because it indicates the implicit "objectification" of Islam. Although the term "Islamist" has only gained currency in the mid- to late–twentieth century, it first appeared in the medieval period in the work of Abu al-Hasan al-Ashʿari (d. 935), *Maqalat al-Islamiyyin* (The theses of the Islamists). His work influenced Ibn Taymiyya (d. 1328) (see al-Azm 1993a:99).

CHAPTER THREE

1. Although the term "Wahhabism" is a convenient shorthand expression, the Saudis resist it for fear that it implies that their ideas and practices constitute a separate sect of Islam. They argue, somewhat disingenuously, that they are simply "Muslims," but they accept the designation "unitarians" (*muwahhidun*), advocates of the absolute oneness of God.

2. In January 1988, a plan to impose income tax on foreign businesses and workers was canceled after protests (Ibrahim 1988a, 1988b).

3. Pharaonism has long been a controversial feature of Egyptian political thought. Muhammad Husayn Haykal (1888–1956) and Salama Musa (1887–1958), a Copt, found in Egypt's Pharaonic, pre-Islamic past the model for a postcolonial future of greatness. It at once connected Egyptians to a monotheistic past and disconnected them from a specifically Middle Eastern milieu. In this way, Egypt could be as "civilized" as Pharaonic Egypt—treating women equally with men, for example—and as modern as the European imperialists. Such pan-Islamic writers as Hafiz Ibrahim (1870–1932) and Ahmad Shawqi (1868–1932) also found some inspiration in the Pharaonic past (Gershoni and Jankowski 1986:166–70, 184–85, 270–71). However, Arab nationalists (for example, Yusif Haykal (1945:27), as well as more recent Islamists, have criticized such emphases as the result of a conscious policy of Westernization and de-Islamization (and, by extension, de-Arabization). The Islamic component has not been entirely absent in Pharaonic conceptualizations, but Muslim activists, in particular, have increasingly regarded the focus on Pharaonism as an intolerable celebration of the pre-Islamic *jahiliyya*.

4. As what we call a "new" intellectual, Siddiqui is concerned with showing the representative nature of the Muslim Parliament. His words are worth citing at length as an expression of the politics of inclusiveness, especially because many British Muslims attacked the parliament as unrepresentative and as promoting Iranian interests:

> Members have come from every part of Britain and from all Schools of Thought in Islam. What is more, Members of this Parliament are not drawn from any single section of British Muslim society. We are not all Arabic, Urdu, Punjabi, Farsi, Turkish, Bengali, Malay, or Hausa speakers. Those here today come from all linguistic and ethnic backgrounds of Muslims living in Britain. The only language common to all Members of the Muslim Parliament (MMPs) is English. Even more important is the fact that among us are men and women of a great variety of social and professional backgrounds. There are philosophers and academics, doctors and dentists, religious scholars and penitent Marxists, scientists and engineers, teachers and students, writers and journalists, and small businessmen and a few tycoons as well. But above all there are among us ordinary men and women whose only education has been through life's everyday hardships and the trials and tribulations of the first generation immigrant working classes. (Siddiqui 1992:6)

The literature of the parliament invites interested Muslims to join one of their "networks" of specialist and professional groups—educators, doctors, scientists, and businessmen (Muslim Parliament 1992).

5. But the state-controlled Muslim Spiritual Board of the North Caucasus, established under Soviet rule, issued a *fatwa* condemning the idea that women could be Sufis (Benningsen and Wimbush 1985:68).

CHAPTER FOUR

1. A certain conservative Islamic line of thought overlaps with Western criticisms of the public-private dichotomy. Abu-l A'la al-Mawdudi, for instance, spoke of Islam creating a benign kind of "Islamic totalitarianism" in which "no one can regard his affairs as personal or private" (cited in Esposito 1987:147).

2. A study in the late 1970s of 526 male and female heads of household in Kuwait indicates that 43 percent of households had relatives living in the immediate vicinity. Fully 80 percent visited their kin at least once a week. A significant number were in business with relatives and depended on members of their extended family for assistance in illness, child care, financial matters, the search for employment, and personal and business problems. Sibling help was most prominent, followed by assistance from parents (al-Thakeb 1985:576).

3. In a similar manner, Iranian officials have argued (like some Western feminists) that in the West, women's bodies are used as "commercial aids . . . to increase the sale of consumer goods," thereby contributing to "the disintegration of the family system" (FBIS, NES-94–239, December 13, 1994, p. 52).

4. Throughout the Muslim world, changes in the *shari'a* provisions on family law have been mooted over time and have met with varying degrees of success. Attempts to change the law in Egypt excited national controversy, and proposed reforms in 1943, 1945, 1960, 1966, and 1969 failed to be implemented. Law 44 of 1979—often called "Jehan's law" after President Sadat's wife—made significant changes and was supported by *'ulama* of the official establishment such as al-Azhar and judges of the *shari'a* courts. For example, it required the registration of a divorce with a notary public, thereby making it impossible for a husband to divorce his wife without her knowledge; second marriages were seen as injurious to the first wife; the mother was given priority in custodial matters; and divorced wives were entitled to compensaton if divorced without their consent or without just cause. The Muslim Brotherhood objected to the law, particularly its denial of the right to have multiple wives, and in 1985 the law was declared unconstitutional by the courts because it had been promulgated in an era of emergency rule. President Mubarak made crucial concessions to conservatives and secured the passage of Law 100 of July 1985. This version of the law said that second marriages were not necessarily injurious, and that a divorced wife is not automatically entitled to compensation.

The Tunisian Code of Personal Status of 1956 abolished polygamy and allowed women to initiate divorce. In 1968, women were granted the right to be employed outside the home without the permission of the husband. In 1981, the Code was amended, giving divorced women priority in the custody of their children; arranged marriages were outlawed; and the legal age for brides was set at eighteen (Fluehr-Lobban 1994:120–30; see also, Esposito 1982; Anderson 1976).

In the early 1970s, the Indonesian government proposed a new marriage law that departed significantly from traditional understandings of Islamic family law. The usually compliant ʿulama reacted strongly to the proposed reform (Katz and Katz 1975), forcing the government to rewrite the law to take their criticisms into account. Among other issues, they objected to the provisions that would have required formal registration of marriages and required a Muslim man to seek permission from a civil court before taking more than one wife. Both men and women would also have been required to seek permission from a civil court before divorcing their spouses. Objections were also raised to reforms in the status of adopted children, which some thought contravened the customary Islamic focus on blood relationships by placing adopted children on the same legal plane as natural children. Article 11(2) was particularly controversial because it maintained that religious differences were not obstacles to marriage, thereby in effect sanctioning intermarriage. In 1992, Indonesia's Minister of Religious Affairs precipitated further controversy when he suggested that, as a way to reduce the number of unmarried couples living together, interfaith marriages should be legalized. Dutch law, which allowed mixed marriages as a civil procedure, was finally abandoned in 1973–74 when the government responded to pressure from the ʿulama and entrusted them with control over marriage matters. But in 1986, a lacuna in the law, which had allowed separate civil ceremonies for mixed faith couples, was also eliminated, and bureaucrats in the Ministry of Religious Affairs often insist—contrary to a conventional interpretation of Muslim traditions—that a non-Muslim woman first convert before being allowed to marry a Muslim man. However, in 1989 the Supreme Court adopted a reformist position, ruling that a Muslim woman be allowed to marry her Christian fiancé. Since then, confusion and uncertainty have prevailed. Underlying this has been Muslim—especially ʿulama—fear of Christian missionary inroads into the Muslim community. By way of contrast, Abdurrahman Wahid of the Nahdatul Ulama has argued that mixed marriages are "imperfect" but permissible: "We can't just say that these people who marry non-Muslims are losing their right to be a Muslim" (M. Cohen 1992).

5. According to Abdurrahman Wahid, there are "hundreds" of women qadis in Indonesia. The first were appointed in the mid-1950s. Although this may seem to contradict al-Mawardi's argument that women cannot serve as judges, he argues, the practice of appointing women to shariʿa courts is justified on the grounds that, as Indonesia is not an Islamic state, al-Mawardi's stricture does not apply (Wahid 1995).

6. Personal communication, Carolyn Fluehr-Lobban, December 27, 1994.

7. The number of schools for girls run by resistance organizations was higher than those operated for the refugees by the Pakistani government. In 1985, there were eleven primary schools and six secondary schools for girls (compared with 248 primary schools for boys), and six secondary schools for girls (compared with thirteen for boys). In the Pakistani educational sector, there were sixty-eight secondary schools for boys, but none for girls (Majrooh 1989:92).

8. Such stage management is not confined to Muslim countries. When President Clinton met Salman Rushdie in November 1993, Clinton's words were

reported by the international press, but the White House did not allow photographs. In Britain, the opposite prevailed: Downing Street allowed a photograph of John Major's meeting with Rushdie but no report of the words exchanged.

9. Muhammad Husayn Fadlallah argues that a man must not indiscriminately discipline his wife but he may legitimately beat her if, without prior contractual arrangement, she refuses to have sexual relations with him. He argues that men have stronger sexual impulses than women, and, as these should be channeled through the sanctified institution of marriage, a wife's refusal of intercourse is "rebellion" that must be punished (Khudr 1994; see also Fadlallah 1993). Sisters in Islam (1991), a Malaysian women's group, presents a strongly contrary view of Islamic traditions.

10. The precise Al Saʿud genealogy is impossible to delineate because of shifting loyalties, affiliations, and leadership claims. As Andrew Shryock (in press) indicates in his account of oral history and textual authority in tribal Jordan, when ideas of a tribal past are primarily oral, claims of identity vary significantly with context and social position. Genealogical histories, "not meant to be universal," coexist awkwardly with one another when set down in writing. There is a search for "proper" sources, known to select individuals, and "constant allusion" to hidden, "accurate" versions of the past. For royalty of tribal origins, as for commoners, the structure of genealogical memory, like tribal society itself, is one of "power and pervasive inequality" (Shryock in press), in which subordinate persons and groups do not directly challenge the claims of the more powerful. Because the Masalikh tribal subdivision had declined in prominence in the prior three hundred years, King ʿAbd al-ʿAziz preferred to indicate his family's affiliation with a currently prominent group. He routinely referred to one of the heads of a major tribal grouping (the ʿAmarat) of the ʿAnayza confederation as his cousin, thus equating himself with the shaykh of the major tribe of a major group of the ʿAnayza, rather than to the subordinate grouping that the Masalikh had become. We are grateful to H. St. B. Armitage for explaining the intricacies of Al Saʿud genealogy (personal communication, July 4, 1994).

CHAPTER FIVE

1. For the purpose of examining demographic trends, Weeks excludes countries with "significant" Muslim minorities, such as China. With only 1.5 percent of its population Muslim (by 1988 figures), China's fifteen million Muslim minority nonetheless exceeds the total population of all but seven Muslim-majority countries. Likewise, India's estimated Muslim minority of over eighty-nine million in 1988 exceeded the total population of all Middle Eastern states and all but three Muslim-majority countries: Indonesia, Pakistan, and Bangladesh (Weeks 1988:8–9). Moreover, official Indian statistics indicate that the country's Muslim population is increasing at a significantly higher rate than non-Muslim populations. In 1951, 9.91 percent of India's population was Muslim; by 1991, 12.2 percent of Indians were Muslim (cited in Shahabuddin 1994).

2. In the 1992 elections at Birzeit University in the West Bank, Hamas took none of the nine student council seats. In the November 1993 Birzeit student elections—two months after the PLO-Israeli peace accord—Hamas participated for the first time in an electoral coalition with the anti-Arafat Popular Front for the Liberation of Palestine (PFLP) and the Democratic Front for the Liberation of Palestine. The coalition secured 52 percent of the vote, winning all nine of the council seats, of which Hamas took four. The victory was all the more significant because Birzeit is regarded as a Fatah stronghold. In the Islamic University in Gaza, Islamists have controlled the student council since the university was established in 1980. In 1992, Hamas obtained 89 percent of the vote, when Fatah did not participate in the elections. In December 1993, with formal Fatah involvement, Hamas won 81 percent of the vote and Islamic Jihad, 2 percent, while 11 percent went to Fatah and 2 percent to the PFLP ("Syria and Israel" 1993; Prusher 1993; "Radical Palestinian Groups" 1993). In June 1994, Hamas won only a single seat out of eleven in al-Najah University in Nablus; and in December 1994, at al-Azhar University in Gaza, Fatah received 76 percent of the votes, while Hamas and Islamic Jihad received 20 percent ("PLO Group" 1994; "Arafat's Fatah" 1994). At Najah University in Nablus, student politics has been dominated by competition between the pro-PLO Shabiba and the Islamic Bloc. The latter controlled the student council in 1979–80, but when not in office it has vigorously promoted an Islamist agenda through publications like the magazine *al-Muntalaq* (The starting point) (see Barghouti 1991:210–13).

3. In a 1992 speech, Ayatullah Khamene'i eulogized the power of the mosque and the Friday sermon: "You will yourselves recall the times of the revolution [of 1979], which began from the mosques. Today, too, mosques still act as centres whenever people do something or mobilise for political or military purposes." He recognizes the importance of the modern media in maximizing the mosque as a place to further the regime's goals: "I do not say that we should definitely use modern publicity equipment and instruments such as films and suchlike—except if, perhaps on some occasion or other, a prayer leader would want to" (cited in BBC SWB, ME/1322, A/3, March 6, 1992).

4. This invocation of foreign, non-Muslim sources is certainly not new. To give but one example, Muhammad ʿAbduh (1849–1905) cited the American writer on Islam, John William Draper (ʿAbduh 1954:15–16), as did the Indian intellectual, Ameer Ali (1922:221).

CHAPTER SIX

1. Hizb al-Tahrir has become a transnational movement, operating in the Palestinian territories, Jordan, the Arabian peninsula, the Maghrib, Britain, and possibly Malaysia and Indonesia, among other places. Since the 1980s, it has become particularly active on British university campuses, and it publishes a regular periodical, *al-Khilafah Magazine*, in London. The intention may be to recruit Muslim students in Britain who would then, in their home countries, propagate its message, including unmitigated hostility toward the Arab-Israeli peace process (Oliver 1994; Fisher 1994). "The International Muslim Khilafah

Conference" was held in August 1994 at Wembley Stadium, attracting a large number of Muslims and representatives of Muslim groups from around the world—and adverse reaction from the British and Western media, which viewed the conference as an international "fundamentalist" convocation at best, and as a possible cover for politically violent groups (Raufer 1994).

2. The postindependence government of Indonesia fought a war against an Islamic insurgency, the Dar ul-Islam movement in West Java (1948–62) that was militating for the establishment of an Islamic state. The official state ideology, *pançasila*, while acknowledging a divine being, does not go any further and the prevailing ideological ethos in Indonesia is secular. This reflects official sensitivities both to demands for a fully constituted Islamic state in the largest "Muslim" country in the world, and to the presence of a number of non-Muslim religions throughout the archipelago. Although formally part of the OIC, Indonesia has tended to downplay its membership—unlike neighboring and sometimes rival Malaysia, which empahsizes its role in the OIC network. In the case of Nigeria, membership in the OIC had long been considered, and resisted. But in January 1986, ostensibly because of the influence of important Nigerian Muslims, the government announced its adherence to the organization. However, the resulting backlash, from mainly Christian sources, has caused the government to refrain from any active participation in its activities.

3. This center produces a regular periodical entitled *Journal of Economic Cooperation among Islamic Countries*.

4. Since the 1980s, the King Fahd Complex for the Printing of the Qur'an in Medina has produced vast quantities of Qur'ans. Supervised by a committee of religious officials and employing over 1,600 persons, the institution produces 9.5 million copies each year, including 3 million in languages other than Arabic. The figures available are not precise, but the importance of exporting the Qur'an is clear from what has been reported. Of the approximately 70 million Qur'ans printed from the early 1980s to 1992, in keeping with King Fahd's directives, more than 50 million were sent outside of the kingdom: 45 million to Asia, 5 million to Africa, and 500,000 to Europe. Of the copies distributed inside Saudi Arabia, more than 5 million copies were given to pilgrims from various countries during the *hajj* (Complexe du Roi 1992).

5. Much of the information in this section has been drawn from material presented at a workshop on Tablighi Jamaʿat, sponsored by the Joint Committee for the Comparative Study of Muslim Societies of the Social Science Research Council and the American Council of Learned Societies. It was held in London, June 7–8, 1990 (Masud 1995).

6. In Singapore, to cite another example, the All Malayan Muslim Missionary Society (commonly known as Jamiyah) was founded in the 1930s by a "transnational guru," to use Peter van der Veer's evocative phrase. Born in India, Muhammad Abdul Alim Siddiqui completed his studies in Mecca and Medina and eventually joined the Qadiriyya, Naqshbandiyya, Chistiyya, and Suhrawardiyya Sufi orders. No doubt, such cosmopolitanism would not permit a simple-minded devotion to the Mecca and Medina of Wahhabi control. Arab and Indian merchant families in Singapore played an important financial

role from the beginning, and they seemed drawn to both Arabia and the Egypt of Salafiyya intellectual thought. Now strongly supported by the Muslim World League and reflecting its Saudi political agenda, the Jamiyah is predominantly Malay in membership while operating in an overhwhelmingly Chinese environment. The consequence is obvious: the sense of pull from Saudi Arabia, but also from Malaysia and Indonesia (Weyland 1990).

7. In France, some observers believe that Tablighi Jamaʿat, despite its stated unconcern for political matters, functions as a recruitment vehicle for the expressly political Muslim protest groups. The Tablighis are particularly successful in attracting young, unemployed men at such suburban mosques as the Bilal in Saint-Denis and the Sid Brahim el Khalil mosque in La Courneuve. Perhaps originally motivated by a desire to improve their faith, these individuals may be open to explicit political activity, such as that associated with Fraternité Algérienne en France, a group allied with FIS (de Villiers 1995:5–6).

GLOSSARY

A = Arabic; F = French; I = Bahasa Indonesian; M = Malay; ML = Malagasy; P = Persian; R = Russian; U = Urdu; T = Turkish. Many of the terms, especially Arabic ones with religious connotations, occur in more than one language. Variations are specified only when significantly different from the language of origin.

ʿalim; pl. *ʿulama* (A). — Learned man; in particular, one learned in Islamic legal and religious studies.

amir (A). — Prince or tribal chief.

amir al-muʾminin (A). — Commander of the faithful.

baraka (A). — Supernatural blessing; quality of divine grace; abundance.

bayʿa (A). — Pact, pledge.

bayan (A). — Decree, statement.

bidʿa; pl. *bidaʿ* (A). — Unworthy innovation.

daʿi; pl. *duʿa* (A). — One who invites; missionary.

dar al-ʿahd (A). — "Land of the covenant," i.e., under Muslim rule.

dar al-harb (A). — "Land of war"; against which war is religiously sanctioned.

dar al-Islam (A). — "Land of Islam."

dar al-kufr (A). — "Land of disbelief."

dar al-sulh (A). — "Land of settlement" or truce.

datu (M). — Honorary title granted by royalty.

daʿwa (A). — God's "call" to the true religion. Malay: *dakwah*.

al-dawla al-islamiyya (A). — Islamic state.

dawra (A, P). — "Circle"; discussion group.

dimuqratiyya (A). — Democracy.

din wa-dawla (A). — Religion and state.

diwaniyya (A). — Regular informal gathering of relatives, professionals, members of the same religious group or workmates (Arab Gulf).

faqih; pl. *fuqaha* (A). — Islamic legal scholar; jurist (fem. *faqiha*). West African variation: *faki*.

faqir (A). — Sufi mendicant (fem. *faqira*).

fatwa; pl. *fatawa* (A). — Legal opinion or decree issued by a recognized Muslim scholar.

fiqh (A). — Islamic jurisprudence.

fitna (A). — Rebellion or disorder against established authority.

fundi (ML). — Religious authority (Comoros Islands).

ghayba (A). — Occultation, concealment (esp. in Shiʿi theology).

hadith (A). — Reported saying of the Prophet Muhammad, based on the authority of a chain of reliable transmitters.

hajj (A). — Pilgrimage to Mecca.

halal (A). — Permitted food or activity.

haraka (A). — Movement.

hijab (A). — Veil or face covering.

hijra (A). — Migration.

hudud (A). — Prescribed Qur'anic punishments.

hukumat al-khilafa (A). — The government of the caliphate.

ihtijab (A). — Act of veiling.

ijtihad (A). — Independent judgment.

'ilm; pl. *'ulum* (A). — Knowledge, esp. the religious sciences.

imam (A). — Religious or prayer leader.

islamiyyun (A). — "Islamists."

isra' (A). — The Prophet's night journey.

jahil (A). — Ignorant (of Islam).

jahiliyya (A). — The pre-Islamic "time of ignorance."

jihad (A). — Religious struggle or endeavor; holy war.

kafir (A). — Unbeliever in the Islamic revelation.

khadim al-haramayn (A). — "Servant of the Two Holy Places," title of the Saudi monarch.

khalifa (A). — Caliph.

khatib (A). — Preacher (of Friday sermons).

khilafa (A). — The caliphate, the institution that inherited Muhammad's authority in all domains except prophecy.

khutba (A). — Friday sermon, lecture.

kufr (A). — Disbelief.

madhhab (A). — Established school of Islamic law.

madrasa (A). — Religious school, often associated with a mosque.

mahdi (A). — The expected, divinely guided leader.

majlis al-shura (A). — Consultative council.

marabout (F). — Sufi "saint." French term from Arabic: *murabit*. See *salih*.

marja'-i taqlid; *maraji'-i taqlid* (P). — Source of emulation; paramount Shi'i religious authority.

maslaha 'amma (A). — Public interest.

mevlûd (T). — A religious service commemorating Muhammad's birthday (from Arabic: *mawlid*).

minhaj (A). — System or program.

mi'raj (A). — Prophet's midnight ascension from Jerusalem to the seven heavens.

Mudawwana (A). — The 1958 *shari'a*-based legal code that is the basis for Moroccan laws regarding marriage, family, and inheritance.

mufti (A). — Jurisconsult; issuer of *fatawa*.

mujahidin; sing. *mujahid* (A). — Lit. "strivers," or those who struggle for the faith. Also used in a narrower sense to mean "freedom fighters," as in the Afghan *mujahidin*.

mukhabarat (A). — Security police; intelligence service.

mullah (P). — Preacher; prayer leader.

murid (A). — Sufi term for student or disciple.

murshid (A). — Sufi term for spiritual guide (fem. *murshida*).

nashid (A). — Chanted anthem.

nasiha (A). — Critical memorandum or report (Arab Gulf).

niqab (A). — Clothing that covers all of a woman's body including the face.

nizam (A). — Order, organization.

nomenklatura (R). — "Named" or elite persons.

pançasila (I). — Indonesia's secular national ideology.

pir (T, U). — Holy man, from a holy lineage; leader of a dervish order.

qadi (A). — Religious judge, magistrate (fem. *qadiya*).

qawm (A, P). — People or nation; kinship term in parts of Afghanistan.

quwwali (U, A). — Musical tradition in South Asia.

al-ra'is al-mu'min (A). — The "president-believer" (Egypt); term appropriated by Anwar al-Sadat.

salaf (A). — Ancestor, predecessor.

salafiyya (A). — Islamic reform movement founded at end of nineteenth century.

salih (A). — "Pious one," or saint; a person, living or dead, thought to have a special relation toward God that enables him or her to ask for God's grace on behalf of clients and to communicate it to them (North Africa).

sayyid (A). — Descendant of the Prophet (esp. Iraq and the Yemens).

shahada (A). — Declaration of faith in Islam; martyrdom.

shari'a (A). — The religious laws of Islam; "the straight path."

shaykh (A). — A tribal leader, scholar, or senior (fem. *shaykha*).

Shi'a (A). — Literally, "sect." Muslim minority community, principally located in Iran, southern Iraq, Lebanon, and Bahrain. Holds that legitimate succession to the Prophet is based on direct descent through his daughter, Fatima, and 'Ali, her husband and the Prophet's son-in-law.

shura (A). — Consultation.

sulta (A). — Political authority.

sunna (A). — Actions and sayings of the Prophet that constitute "orthodox" tradition for the Islamic community.

Sunni (A). — Muslim who belongs to the Muslim majority community; Sunnis accept the actions and authority of the early Muslim community and its caliphs.

sura (A). — Chapter of the Qur'an.

tabligh (A). — Propagation. Usually in the context of missionary activity. Related to *da'wa*.

tajdid (A). — Religious reform and renewal.

takfir (A). — The proclaiming of a fellow believer as an infidel.

taqlid (A). — Precedent.

tariqa (A). — Sufi brotherhood.

tawhid (A). — The oneness of God.

'ulama (A). — Muslim men of learning.

umma (A). — The Islamic community.

vilayat-i faqih (P). — Shi'i doctrine of the sovereignty of the jurist (Arabic: *wilayat al-faqih*.

waqf; pl. awqaf (A). — Pious endowment.

zakat (A). — Alms enjoined by the Qur'an.

ziyara (A). — Visit (to a saint's shrine).

ANNOTATED BIBLIOGRAPHY

A vast literature on Islam and politics exists and it would be impossible to provide an exhaustive review. Our intention, rather, is to highlight a number of works on several important themes that merit further examination and will serve as a point of departure for interested readers. Readers are also directed to other guides such as Burrell and Morgan (1989), Haddad, Voll, and Esposito (1991), and Brown (1992). The bibliographies that follow the relevant entries in the *Oxford Encyclopedia of the Modern Islamic World* (1995) are particularly helpful, while those in the second edition of the *Encyclopaedia of Islam*, begun in 1960 and still in progress, are usefully cross-referenced.

Both general and specific studies of the roles of Islam in politics have appeared with regularity since at least the advent of the Iranian revolution of 1978–79. Among others, Esposito (1980), Kramer (1980), Ayoob (1981), Dessouki (1982), Israeli (1982), Mortimer (1982), Piscatori (1983b), Dekmejian (1985), Carré and Dumont (1985), Carré (1987), and Hunter (1988) deal with the manifestations of the Islamic "revival" in a variety of countries in the Middle East, Africa, and Southeast Asia. Cole and Keddie (1986) and Kramer (1987) deal specifically with the mobilization of Shiʿi discontent and assess the significance of Shiʿi protest movements in Iran, Lebanon, the Gulf, and elsewhere. There are also many country- and region-specific studies of contemporary religious movements, such as Abdullah and Siddique (1986) on Southeast Asia, R. Tapper (1991) on Turkey, Nielsen (1992) on western Europe, Nakash (1994) on Iraq, and Villalón (1995) on Senegal.

Hussain (1984) compares and contrasts modernization, Marxist, nationalist, and "Islamic" perspectives on politics in the Muslim world, and Ismael and Ismael (1985) explain why Muslim politics is largely the search for legitimization by both governments and their critics. Esposito (1987) indicates the place of Islamic political movements in the modern history of Islam and explains the ideologies and programs of activists in diverse parts of the Muslim world. Organized both topically and geographically, Ayubi (1991) traces the development of political Islam from pre-Islamic Arabia to the present, focusing on what happened in the first centuries of Islam and on the ways this early period has figured in subsequent Islamic political thought and practice. Roy (1992, 1994) argues that the Islamist project is doomed to failure because of its inability to articulate a detailed political vision or to implement a strategy for governing. Muslim politics have also been illuminated in such comparative studies of religious "fundamentalism" as Antoun and Hegland (1987), Lawrence (1989), Sivan and Friedman (1990), the Fundamentalism Project of the American Academy of Arts and Sciences (for example, Marty and Appleby 1991, 1993, 1994), and Kepel (1994a).

Classical and modern Islamic political thought has been elaborated in a number of works by Muslim and non-Muslim scholars. Asad (1980) and el-Affendi (1991) present modernist interpretations which argue that Muslim political orders are built on consensus and consultation and essentially involve limitations on the rulers and the participation of the ruled. Khomeini (1981), building on but also significantly departing from Shiʿi traditions, provides the rationale for the governance of the ʿulama. Enayat (1983), Sachedina (1988), and Modarressi (1991), among others, explain the basis of this doctrine of vilayat-i faqih. Arkoun (1994) considers the relationship between "church" and state and between ethics and politics in the context of his distinctive reformulation of Islamic thought in general.

Watt (1980) puts the development of early Muslim political thought in the context of seventh-century Arabia and demonstrates the continuities and discontinuities in the community's ideological evolution. Lambton (1981) and Lewis (1988) provide further historical context, highlighting the medieval and early modern periods. Rosenthal (1965), Enayat (1982), Khadduri (1984), and Binder (1988) explain Muslim views on such modern themes as constitutionalism; democracy; socialism; legal, social, and political justice; and liberalism. Arjomand (1988) and Richard (1991) elaborate on Shiʿi political ideas, culture, and institutions. The variety of Muslim views on and formalized treatment of human rights is detailed in Mayer (1995).

Much attention has been devoted to specifically Islamist political ideas. Mitchell (1969) puts the thought of Hasan al-Banna in the context of the founding and early development of the Muslim Brotherhood, and Samman (1982) concentrates on al-Banna's ideological formation and contributions. Haddad (1983), Nettler (1987), Diyab (1989), and Moussalli (1992) explain the thought of Sayyid Qutb, while Kepel (1984), Sivan (1985), and Jansen (1986) elaborate on the thinking and programs of Islamist groups in Egypt and of such influential figures as Shaykh ʿAbd al-Hamad Kishk. Kepel and Richard (1990) indicate the range of ideas offered by the "new" intellectuals and activists in the Muslim world, including the influential Iranian ʿAli Shariʿati (for example, 1971; also see Richard 1991). Munson (1991, 1998) and Shahin (1994), explicate the thinking of the Moroccan Abd Assalam Yassine, and Hassan (1982) addresses the thinking of the Indonesian intellectual Nurcholish Madjid as well as others associated with the influential Muslim student movement in Indonesia.

One view of Islam and politics has long held that states are authoritarian, and perhaps "strong," because of the absence of countervailing institutions. P. Springborg (1992) argues that this view is a classic Orientalist contrivance. Moore (1974) and Ozbudun (1992) attribute the unrestrained power of government in part to the nature of Islamic law and social traditions which, they argue, do not recognize corporate bodies and institutions that mediate between the individual and the state, while Gellner argues that "Islam . . . exemplifies a social order which seems to lack much capacity to provide political countervailing institutions or associations" (1994:29). Sadowski (1993) notes that, as oil revenues declined in the Middle East, scholars came to regard states in the Muslim world as "weak," or at least that civil societies were stronger than anticipated (for example, Migdal 1988). Standing the conventional view on its head, Sivan (1990b) argues that, if we accept that Islamist groups and movements are autonomous of the state, civil society possesses such potency that it "strikes back."

Two studies bring the issue of Islam and civil society into focus. Norton (1995a, 1995b), based on a major Ford Foundation–sponsored project, gathers both comprehensive conceptual essays and country- and region-specific studies that assess not only scholarly writings on the topic but also recent developments in the Arab Middle East, Iran, and Turkey. Salamé (1994) focuses principally on the Arab Middle East, and is particularly strong on the Arab Gulf, Egypt, and North Africa. The compatibility of Muslim politics with civil society has also figured prominently in European political debates on the assimilation of Muslim immigrants, notably, although not exclusively, in France (Kepel 1994b; Lewis and Schnapper 1994). Polonskaya and Malashenko (1994) explain the ways in which Muslim groups and social practices in Central Asia persisted in spite of official Soviet antipathy and, since the collapse of the Soviet state, how they condition national and regional politics; Allworth (1994) highlights the role of ethnicity and nationalism in the reconstitution of Muslim and political identities in Central Asia and the former Yugoslavia. Hefner (1993) places the development of the Association of Muslim Intellectuals (ICMI) in the broader picture of Indonesian politics and explores the possibilities of "civic pluralism," while Othman (1994), noting the Malaysian situation in particular, discusses civil society in the context of the national role of the *shariᶜa*. Brenner (1993) brings together a number of studies that explore the "politicization of public life" in sub-Saharan Muslim societies, with special attention devoted to Muslim interest groups.

Particular focus has been placed on the question of Islam's compatibility with democracy. Lewis (1990, 1993), Kedourie (1992), and Kramer (1993) stress the obstacles that Islamic political ideas or structures pose to the process of democratization, whereas Hudson (1991), Krämer (1992, 1993), and Ayubi (1993) find in evolving social, economic, and intellectual trends the possibility, though by no means the certainty, of greater political participation and pluralism. Intellectuals in the Muslim world have turned to the matter of Islam's democratic potential (for example, Markaz Ibn Khaldun (1992). Al-Mahdi (1990) argues that Islam is essentially democratic, whereas some Algerian Islamist intellectuals stress that democracy leads to the imposition of the will of the majority rather than to what is morally right (see al-Ahnaf, Botiveau, and Frégosi 1991). Esposito and Piscatori (1991) survey the various Muslim intellectual responses to this question.

Key studies of the role of women in Muslim politics include Kandiyoti (1991), who explores the ambiguities of the relationship between women as citizens and subjects, and the state, and Keddie and Baron (1991), whose contributors, like L. Ahmed (1992), encompass Middle Eastern Islamic history in general. Among key country-specific studies, Taarji (1991) deals principally with Egypt and North Africa, Afkhami and Friedl (1994) focus on postrevolutionary Iran, and Altorki (1986) investigates elite women in Saudi Arabia, while Doumato (1992) looks at Saudi women in the political process and as political symbols. C. Eickelman (1988) deals with women's politics in an Omani oasis, and Göle (1993) bases her discussion of the interaction between secularists and women Islamists on the case of Turkey. Mumtaz and Shaheed (1987) and Shaheed and Mumtaz (1992), associated with the transnational group Women Living under Muslim Laws (see Shaheed 1994), chart the changing positions of women in Pakistani society, and Coulon (1988) examines the gender dimensions of Sufism and finds that, in societies of West Africa, women have possessed *baraka* and have assumed leading roles in the *tariqas*.

The writing on Islam and international relations has been preoccupied with the question of Islam's compatibility with nationalism. Vatikiotis (1987) emphasizes the problems associated with nationalism, whereas Piscatori (1986) finds that territorial pluralism has long been entrenched, and accepted, in the Muslim world. Yavuz (1993) describes how Muslim intellectuals contributed to the construction of Turkish nationalism. Khadduri (1955) and Abu-Sulayman (1987) explain that classical Islamic sources allow Muslims to engage in conventional international relations, and Hamidullah (1961) demonstrates that modern Muslim diplomacy builds on the example of the Prophet and the early Muslim community. The history of the pan-Islamic idea and of plans to implement it is found in Narayan (1982), Kramer (1986), and Landau (1990), while Dawisha (1983) shows that foreign policies are not doctrinally prescribed but that Islamic values and concerns often enter into the determination of national interests and policies. Rajaee (1983) places the international-relations thought of Ayatullah Khomeini into perspective by examining his larger political thought and focusing on his ideas of territorial nationalism, the export of the revolution, and the international destiny of Iran.

The Muslim interstate Organization of the Islamic Conference is treated in Moinuddin (1987) and Ahsan (1988), and Schulze (1990) shows how the Rabitat al-ʿAlam al-Islami (Muslim World League) functions as an international *daʿwa* organization at the same time as it advances a Saudi political and religious agenda. Von der Mehden (1993) explores the international and transnational linkages between two parts of the broader *umma*, Southeast Asia and the Middle East, and Gladney (1992b) considers the impact of transnational Muslim issues on Uighur national identity in China. Ahmed and Donnan (1994) investigate the implications that globalization has for Muslim societies and self-understandings, and Beyer (1994) specifically looks at the Iranian revolution in the course of a general consideration of globalized communications, cultural values, and religious movements.

The policy implications of Muslim politics have increasingly occupied the attention of Western scholars, journalists, and political officials. Lewis (1990) and Miller (1993) are concerned that elements within Muslim movements may be uncompromisingly hostile to Western interests, but Hadar (1993) and Esposito (1992) regard fears of an "Islamic threat" or "green peril" as exaggerated and emphasize that only a minority of Muslim activists—let alone Muslims—resort to violence in the pursuit of their goals. Fuller and Lesser (1995) advocate a nuanced approach, which avoids stereotyping Muslim critics of Western policy as "fundamentalist" and ascribing all political conduct to specifically religious motivations.

REFERENCES

ʿAbd al-Hadi, Muhammad. 1983. "Wa madha ʿan hizb al-daʿwa al-islamiyya" [What about the Islamic Daʿwa Party?]. *al-Mujtamaʿa*, no. 650 (December 20): 18–19.

ʿAbd al-Raziq, ʿAli. 1925. *al-Islam wa-usul al-hukm* [Islam and the roots of government]. 2d ed. Cairo: Matbaʿat Misr.

ʿAbduh, Muhammad. 1954. *al-Islam wa-l-Nasraniyya maʿa-l-ʿilm wa-l-madaniyya* [Islam and Christianity with knowledge and civilization]. Cairo: Maktabat Muhammad ʿAli Shaykh.

———. [1925] 1978. *Rissalat al-Tawhid: Exposé de la Religion Musulman*. Translated by B. Michel and Moustapha Abdel Razik. Paris: Librairie Orientaliste Paul Geuthner.

ʿAbduh, ʿUmar. 1990. *Al Saʿud: shariʿat al-saqitayn* [The Al Saʿud: The path of the disreputable]. London: Sharikat al-Hayat al-Janibiyya.

Abdullah, Taufiq, and Sharon Siddique, eds. 1986. *Islam and Society in Southeast Asia*. Brookfield, Vt.: Gower.

Abduvakhitov, Abdujabar. 1993. "Islamic Revivalism in Uzbekistan." In *Muslim Politics and Societies: Russian, Central Asian, and Western Perspectives*, edited by Dale F. Eickelman, pp. 79–97. Bloomington: Indiana University Press.

Abu-Amr, Ziad. 1994. *Islamic Fundamentalism in the West Bank and Gaza*. Bloomington: Indiana University Press.

Abun-Nasr, Jamil M. 1965. *The Tijaniya: A Sufi Order in the Modern World*. London: Oxford University Press.

Abu-Sulayman, Abdul Hamid A. 1987. *The Islamic Theory of International Relations: New Directions for Islamic Methodology and Thought*. Herndon, Va.: International Institute of Islamic Thought.

Abu Zayd, Nasr Hamid. 1992. *Naqd al-khitab al-dini* [A critique of religious discourse]. Cairo: Sina li-l-Nashr.

el-Affendi, Abdelwahab. 1991. *Who Needs an Islamic State?* London: Grey Seal.

———. 1992. *Turabi's Revolution: Islam and Power in Sudan*. London: Grey Seal.

Afkhami, Mahnaz, and Erika Friedl, eds. 1994. *In the Eye of the Storm: Women in Post-Revolutionary Islam*. Syracuse: Syracuse University Press.

Ahmad, Aijazuddin. 1993. *Muslims in India: Their Educational, Demographic, and Socio-Economic Status with Comparative Indicators for Hindus, Sikhs, Christians, and Other Communities, Based on a Singular and Systematic Field Survey, 1990–1993. Vol. 1, Bihar*. New Delhi: Inter-India Publications.

———. 1994. *Muslims in India: Their Educational, Demographic, and Socio-Economic Status with Inter-Community Comparisons, Based on Field Survey Conducted in 1991. Vol. 2, Rajasthan*. New Delhi: Inter-India Publications.

Ahmad, Ashfaq. 1981. "The Muslim World Seen from Economic Angle." *Islamic Herald* (Kuala Lumpur) 5, nos. 1 and 2: 27–29.

Ahmad, Khurshid. 1976. "Islam: Basic Principles and Characteristics." In *Islam:*

Its Meaning and Message, 2d ed., edited by Khurshid Ahmad, pp. 27–44. Leicester: Islamic Foundation.

Ahmad, Mumtaz. 1991. "The Politics of War: Islamic Fundamentalisms in Pakistan." In *Islamic Fundamentalisms and the Gulf Crisis*, edited by James Piscatori, pp. 155–85. Chicago: Fundamentalism Project of the American Academy of Arts and Sciences.

Ahmad, Rifʿat Sayyid. 1991. *al-Nabiy al-musallah: al-Rafidun* [The Armed prophet: The rejectionists]. London: Riad el-Rayyes Booksellers.

Ahmed, Akbar S., and Hastings Donnan. 1994. *Islam, Globalization, and Postmodernity*. London and New York: Routledge.

Ahmed, Eqbal. 1985. "Islam and Politics." In *Islam: Politics and the State; The Pakistan Experience*, pp. 13–30. London: Zed Books.

Ahmed, Leila. 1992. *Women and Gender in Islam: Historical Roots of a Modern Debate*. New Haven: Yale University Press.

Ahmed, Rafiuddin. [1981] 1988. *The Bengal Muslims, 1871–1906*. 2d ed. Delhi: Oxford University Press.

al-Ahnaf, M., Bernard Botiveau, and Franck Frégosi, eds. 1991. *L'Algérie par ses islamistes*. Paris: Éditions Karthala.

al-Ahsan, ʿAbdallah. 1988. *The Organization of the Islamic Conference: An Introduction to an Islamic Political Institution*. Herndon, Va.: International Institute of Islamic Thought.

Ajami, Fouad. 1986. *The Vanished Imam: Musa al-Sadr and the Shia of Lebanon*. Ithaca: Cornell University Press.

———. [1982] 1992. *The Arab Predicament: Arab Political Thought and Practice since 1967*. Updated ed. New York: Cambridge University Press.

———. 1994. "In Europe's Shadows." *New Republic*, November 24, pp. 29–37.

Akinci, Uğur. 1994. "Welfare Party's Political Rise: A Re-evaluation." *Turkish Daily News*, September 16.

Alavi, Hamza. 1986. "Ethnicity, Muslim Society, and the Pakistan Ideology." In *Islamic Reassertion in Pakistan: The Application of Islamic Laws in a Modern State*, edited by Anita M. Weiss, pp. 21–47. Syracuse: Syracuse University Press.

Albin, Michael W. 1990. "Moroccan-American Bibliography." In *The Atlantic Connection: 200 Years of Moroccan-American Relations, 1786–1986*, edited by J. Bookin-Weiner and M. el-Mansour, pp. 5–18. Rabat: EDINO.

Ali, Ameer. 1922. *The Spirit of Islam: A History of the Evolution and Ideals of Islam, with a Life of the Prophet*. Rev. ed. London: Christopher's Ltd.

Allworth, Edward, ed. 1994. *Muslim Communities Reemerge: Historical Perspectives on Nationality, Politics, and Opposition in the Former Soviet Union and Yugoslavia*. Durham and London: Duke University Press.

Almond, G. A., and G. B. Powell. 1966. *Comparative Politics: A Developmental Approach*. Boston: Little, Brown.

Altorki, Soraya. 1986. *Women in Saudi Arabia: Ideology and Behavior among the Elite*. New York: Columbia University Press.

American Muslim Council. 1992. Announcement of Second Annual Leadership Conference, February 21–23. New York: American Muslim Council. Leaflet.

Amin, Samir. 1990. *Delinking: Towards a Polycentric World.* London: Zed Books.

Anderson, Benedict. 1983. *Imagined Communities: Reflections on the Origins and Spread of Nationalism.* London: Verso. (2d ed., 1991).

Anderson, J. N. D. 1976. *Law Reform in the Muslim World.* London: Athlone Press.

Anderson, Jon, ed. 1994. *On-Line Research and Teaching Resources for Middle East Studies.* Tucson: Middle East Studies Association.

Aniba, Mokhtar. 1991. "L'Islam et les droits de la femme." In *L'Algérie par ses islamistes,* edited by M. al-Ahnaf, Bernard Botiveau, and Franck Frégosi, pp. 251–58. Paris: Éditions Karthala.

"Les Antennes paraboliques." 1994. *Al Bayane* (Casablanca), April 3.

Antoun, Richard T., and Mary Elaine Hegland, eds. 1987. *Religious Resurgence: Contemporary Cases in Islam, Christianity, and Judaism.* Syracuse: Syracuse University Press.

Anwar, Zainah. 1987. *Islamic Revivalism in Malaysia: Dakwah among the Students.* Petalingjaya, Malaysia: Pelanduk Publications.

Appadurai, Arjun. 1990. "Disjuncture and Difference in the Global Cultural Economy." *Public Culture* 2, no. 2 (spring): 1–24.

"Arafat's Fatah Wins Gaza University Election." 1994. Reuters World Service, December 20.

Arendt, Hannah. [1969] 1986. "Communicative Power." In *Power,* edited by Steven Lukes, pp. 59–74. Oxford: Blackwell.

Arjomand, Said, ed. 1988. *Authority and Political Culture in Shiism.* Albany: State University of New York Press.

Arkoun, Mohammed. 1994. *Rethinking Islam: Common Questions, Uncommon Answers.* Translated and edited by Robert D. Lee. Boulder: Westview.

Asad, Muhammad. [1961] 1980. *The Principles of State and Government in Islam.* Gibraltar: Dar al-Andalus.

al-Ashmawi, Muhammad Sa'id. 1987. *al-Islam al-siyasi* [Political Islam]. Cairo: Sinan li-l-Nashr.

———. 1990. *al-Khilafa al-Islamiyya* [The Islamic caliphate]. Cairo: Sinan li-l-Nashr.

Associated Press. 1985. "Kuwait Won't Budge—No Vote for Women." *San Francisco Chronicle,* July 23, p. 11.

Auda, Gehad. 1994a. "The 'Normalization' of the Islamic Movement in Egypt from the 1970s to the Early 1990s." In *Accounting for Fundamentalisms,* edited by Martin E. Marty and R. Scott Appleby, pp. 374–412. Chicago: University of Chicago Press.

———. 1994b. Personal communications to James Piscatori, New York, December 18–19.

A'usht. ca. 1982. *Dirasat Islamiyya fi-l-usul al-Ibadiyya* [Islamic studies in Ibadi sources]. Algiers: n.p.

Ayalon, Ami. 1987. *Language and Change in the Arab Middle East: The Evolution of Modern Political Discourse.* New York: Oxford University Press.

Aykan, Mahmut B. 1994. *Turkey's Role in the Organization of the Islamic Conference, 1960–1992: The Nature of Deviation from the Kemalist Heritage.* New York: Vantage Press.

Ayoob, Mohammad, ed. 1981. *The Politics of Islamic Reassertion.* London: Croom Helm.

Ayubi, Nazih N. 1991. *Political Islam: Religion and Politics in the Arab World.* London: Routledge.

———. 1993. "Is Democracy Possible in the Middle East?" Paper delivered at the European Consortium for Political Research Joint Sessions, Leiden, April.

al-ʿAzm, Sadiq J. 1968. *Al-naqd al-dhati baʿd al-hazima* [Self-criticism after the defeat]. Beirut: Dar al-Taliʿa.

———. 1982. *Naqd al-fikr al-dini* [A critique of religious thought]. Beirut: Sina li-l-Nashr.

———. 1993a. "Islamic Fundamentalism Reconsidered: A Critical Outline of Problems, Ideas, and Approaches, Part I." *South Asian Bulletin* 13, no. 1: 93–121.

———. 1993b. "Islamic Fundamentalism Reconsidered: A Critical Outline of Problems, Ideas, and Approaches, Part II." *South Asian Bulletin* 13, no. 2: 73–98.

———. 1994. *Dhihniyya al-tahrim: Salman Rushdi wa-haqiqat al-adab* [The tabooing mentality: Salman Rushdie and the truth of literature]. 2d ed. Nicosia: Center for Socialist Studies and Research in the Arab World.

al-Azmeh, Aziz. 1993. *Islams and Modernities.* New York: Verso.

Backmann, René. 1990. "Islam: Les Financiers de l'intégrisme." *Le Nouvel Observateur,* July 19–24, pp. 4–8.

Bakhash, Shaul. 1985. "Islam and Social Justice." Paper delivered at the annual meeting of the American Historical Association, New York, December.

———. 1990. "The Politics of Land, Law, and Social Justice in Iran." In *Iran's Revolution: The Search for Consensus,* edited by R. K. Ramazani, pp. 27–47. Bloomington: Indiana University Press.

Bakhtin, M. M. 1981. *The Dialogic Imagination: Four Essays.* Edited by Michael Holquist. Austin: University of Texas Press.

Baktiari, Bahman. In press. *Parliamentary Politics in Revolutionary Iran, 1980–1992.* Gainesville: University Presses of Florida.

Bannerman, Patrick. 1988. *Islam in Perspective: A Guide to Islamic Society, Politics, and Law.* London: Routledge for the Royal Institute of International Affairs.

Banuazizi, Ali, and Myron Weiner. 1986. "Introduction." In their *The State, Religion, and Ethnic Politics: Afghanistan, Iran, and Pakistan,* pp. 1–20. Syracuse: Syracuse University Press.

Baram, Amatzia. 1991. "From Radicalism to Radical Pragmatism: The Shiʿite Fundamentalist Opposition Movements of Iraq." In *Islamic Fundamentalisms and the Gulf Crisis,* edited by James Piscatori, pp. 28–51. Chicago: Fundamentalism Project of the American Academy of Arts and Sciences.

———. 1994. "Two Roads to Revolutionary Shiite Fundamentalism in Iraq." In *Accounting for Fundamentalisms: The Dynamic Character of Movements,* edited by Martin E. Marty and R. Scott Appleby, pp. 531–88. Chicago and London: University of Chicago Press.

Baran, Paul. 1957. *The Political Economy of Growth.* New York: Monthly Review Press.

Barghouti, Iyad. 1991. "Religion and Politics among the Students at Najah National University." *Middle Eastern Studies* 27 (April): 203–18.

Barthes, Roland. 1957. *Mythologies*. Paris: Éditions du Seuil.

Batatu, Hanna. 1982. "Syria's Muslim Brethren." *Merip Reports*, no. 110 (November–December): 12–20, 34, 36.

Bayart, Jean-François. 1991. "Finishing with the Idea of the Third World: The Concept of the Political Trajectory." In *Rethinking World Politics*, edited by James Manor, pp. 51–71. London: Longman.

Bayrou, François. 1994. "Plus de voile à l'école" (interview). *Le Point*, September 10, pp. 86–87.

Bazargan, Mehdi. 1979. *The Inevitable Victory*. 2d ed. Translated by Mohammad Yusefi. Houston: Free Islamic Literatures.

Belhadj, ʿAli. 1991. "Un coup de massue porté au dogme démocratique." In *L'Algérie par ses islamistes*, edited by M. al-Ahnaf, Bernard Botiveau, and Franck Frégosi, pp. 87–94. Paris: Éditions Karthala.

Bennani-Chraïbi, Mounia. 1994. *Soumis et rebelles: Les Jeunes au Maroc*. Paris: CNRS Éditions.

Benningsen, Alexander, and S. Enders Wimbush. 1985. *Mystics and Commissars: Sufism in the Soviet Union*. London: C. Hurst and Company.

Berger, Morroe. 1964. *The Arab World Today*. Garden City: Doubleday.

———. 1970. "Economic and Social Change." In *The Cambridge History of Islam*, edited by P. M. Holt, Ann K. S. Lambton, and Bernard Lewis, 1:698–730. Cambridge: Cambridge University Press.

Berman, Bruce, and John Lonsdale. 1992. *Unhappy Valley: Conflict in Kenya and Africa*. London: James Currey.

Beyer, Peter. 1994. *Religion and Globalization*. London: Sage.

Bill, James A. 1973. "The Plasticity of Informal Politics: The Case of Iran." *Middle East Journal* 27, no. 2 (spring): 131–51.

Bill, James A., and Carl Leiden. 1974. *The Middle East: Politics and Power*. Boston: Allyn and Bacon.

———. 1979. *Politics in the Middle East*. Boston: Little, Brown.

———. 1984. *Politics in the Middle East*. 2d ed. Boston: Little, Brown.

Bill, James A., and Robert Springborg. 1990. *Politics in the Middle East*. 3d ed. Glenview: Scott, Foresman/Little Brown Higher Education.

Binder, Leonard. 1986. "The Natural History of Development Theory." *Comparative Studies in Society and History* 28, no. 1 (January): 3–33.

———. 1988. *Islamic Liberalism: A Critique of Development Ideologies*. Chicago: University of Chicago Press.

Binsaʿid, Said. 1993. "al-Hiwar wa-l-fahm la al-qaflʿiyya wa-l-jahl" [Dialogue and understanding, not alienation and ignorance]. *al-Sharq al-Awsat* (London), July 7, p. 10.

Birge, John Kingsley. 1937. *The Bektashi Order of Dervishes*. London: Luzac and Company.

Birtek, Faruk, and Binnaz Toprak. 1993. "The Conflictual Agendas of Neo-Liberal Reconstruction and the Rise of Islamic Politics in Turkey: The Hazards of Rewriting Modernity." *Praxis International* 13, no. 2 (July): 192–212.

Black, C. E. 1966. *The Dynamics of Modernization: A Study in Comparative History.* New York: Harper and Row.

Black, Ian, Deborah Pugh, Simon Tisdall, Kathy Evans, and Leslie Plommer. 1992. "Militant Islam's Saudi Paymasters." *Guardian*, February 29, p. 9.

Bloom, Allan. 1987. *The Closing of the American Mind.* New York: Simon and Schuster.

Bott, Elizabeth. [1957] 1971. *Family and Social Networks.* 2d ed. London: Tavistock Publications.

Boudjedra, Rachid. 1992. *FIS de la haine.* Paris: Éditions Denoël.

Boularès, Habib. 1990. *Islam: Fear and Hope.* London: Zed Books.

Bourdieu, Pierre. 1976. "Marriage Strategies as Strategies for Social Reproduction." In *Family and Society: Selections from the Annales,* edited by Robert Forster and Orest Ranum, translated by Elborg Forster and Patricia M. Ranum, pp. 117–44. Baltimore and London: Johns Hopkins University Press.

———. 1988. *Homo Academicus.* Translated by Peter Collier. Stanford: Stanford University Press.

———. 1989. *La noblesse d'état.* Paris: Les Éditions de Minuit.

Brand, Laurie. 1995. "'In the Beginning was the State . . .': The Quest for Civil Society in Jordan." In *Civil Society in the Middle East,* edited by Augustus Richard Norton, 1:148–85. Leiden: Brill.

Brenner, Louis. 1988. "Concepts of *Tariqa* in West Africa: The Case of the Qadiriyya." In *Charisma and Brotherhood in African Islam,* edited by Donal B. Cruise O'Brien and Christian Coulon, pp. 33–52. Oxford: Clarendon Press.

———, ed. 1993. *Muslim Identity and Social Change in Sub-Saharan Africa.* Bloomington: Indiana University Press.

Brinkley, Joel. 1990. "Palestinians Give Passionate Support to Hussein as a Hero and a Liberator." *New York Times,* August 12, p. 14.

British Broadcasting Corporation. *Summary of World Broadcasts* (BBC SWB), Part 4: The Middle East.

Brooke, James. 1988. "For Women in Politics, the Microphone is Dead." *New York Times,* August 22.

Brown, L. Carl. 1984. *International Politics in the Middle East: Old Rules, Dangerous Game.* Princeton: Princeton University Press.

———. 1992. "Bibliographic Essay." In *Modernization in the Middle East: The Ottoman Empire and Its Afro-Asian Successors,* edited by Cyril E. Black and L. Carl Brown, pp. 335–56. Princeton: Darwin Press.

Brown, Yasmin Alibhai. 1994. "No Simple Heretic, Taslima Nasrin." *Independent,* August 1, p. 15.

Buccianti, Alexandre, and Patrice Claude. 1992. "Bouillonnement islamiste en Haute-Egypte." *Le Monde,* July 30, pp. 1, 3.

al-Bukhari, Abu ʿAbdallah Muhammad ibn Ismaʿil (810–70). n.d. *al-Sahih,* vol. 4, edited by al-Sindi. Cairo: Dar al-Ihyaʾ al-Kutub al-ʿArabiyya.

Bulliet, Richard W. 1994. *Islam: The View from the Edge.* New York: Columbia University Press.

Burrell, R. M., and D. O. Morgan. 1989. "A Guide to Further Reading." In *Islamic Fundamentalism,* edited by R. M. Burrell, pp. 75–86. London: Royal Asiatic Society.

Canard, M. 1965. "Da'wa." In *Encyclopaedia of Islam*, new ed., 2:168–70. Leiden: E. J. Brill.

Canfield, Robert L. 1986. "Ethnic, Regional, and Sectarian Alignments in Afghanistan." In *The State, Religion, and Ethnic Politics: Afghanistan, Iran, and Pakistan*, edited by Ali Banuazizi and Myron Weiner, pp. 75–103. Syracuse: Syracuse University Press.

———. 1989. "Afghanistan: The Trajectory of Internal Alignments." *Middle East Journal* 43, no. 4 (autumn): 636–48.

Carr, Raymond. 1985. "Protecting the Enterprise," review of *Notable Family Networks in Latin America*, by Diana Balmori, Stuart F. Voss, and Miles Wortman. *Times Literary Supplement*, May 10, p. 515.

Carré, Olivier. 1987. *Islam and the State in the World Today*. New Delhi: Manohar Publishers.

Carré, Olivier, and Paul Dumont, eds. 1985. *Radicalismes islamiques*. Paris: Harmattan.

Cash Crew. 1994. "Looking for Allah in Britain." BBC1 "Everyman," broadcast May 1. Produced by Double E/Amy Hardie.

Caton, Steven C. 1987. "Power, Persuasion, and Language: A Critique of the Segmentary Model in the Middle East." *International Journal of Middle East Studies* 19, no. 1 (February): 77–102.

CEDEFS (Centre d'Études et de Documentations Économiques, Financières, et Sociales). 1967. *The Law of Income Tax and Zakat in the Kingdom of Saudi Arabia*. Beirut: Centre d'Études et de Documentations Économiques, Financières, et Sociales.

"Censoring the History of Kashmir." 1994. *Islamic World Journal*, Issue 940609, June 9, Internet.

Cerny, Philip G. 1990. *The Changing Architecture of Politics: Structure, Agency, and the Future of the State*. London: Sage Publications.

Charpentier, Benoit. 1994. "Les Ramifications du FIS en France." *Le Figaro*, April 7, p. 36.

Che Man, W. K. 1990. *Muslim Separatism: The Moros of Southern Philippines and the Malays of Southern Thailand*. Singapore: Oxford University Press.

Cherkaoui, Mohamed. 1976. "Socialisation et conflit: Les Systèmes educatifs et leur histoire selon Durkheim." *Revue française de sociologie* 17: 197–212.

Chipaux, Françoise. 1988. "L'Image obsédante de l'Iran." *Le Monde*, May 24, pp. 1–3.

Chirac, Jacques. 1995. "Le Maroc occupe une place à part dans le coeur des Européens" [Text of Chirac's speech at Moroccan state dinner in his honor, July 21, 1995]. *Le Matin du Sahara et du Maghreb* (Casablanca), July 22, p. 3.

Clarke, Peter B. 1988. "Charismatic Authority and the Creation of a New Order: The Case of the Mahdiyyat Movement in South-Western Nigeria." In *Charisma and Brotherhood in African Islam*, edited by Donal B. Cruise O'Brien and Christian Coulon, pp. 157–82. Oxford: Clarendon Press.

Clifford, James, and George E. Marcus. 1986. *Writing Culture: The Poetics and Politics of Ethnography*. Berkeley and Los Angeles: University of California Press.

Cockburn, Patrick. 1992. "Shia Shrines Still Bear Scars of a Painful Past." *Independent*, May 6, p. 13.

Cody, Edward. 1989. "France Rules on Moslem Scarf Issue." *Washington Post*, November 28.

Cohen, Amnon. 1982. "The Beginnings of Egypt's Involvement in the Palestine Question: Some European Perspectives." *Asian and African Studies* 16:137–45.

Cohen, Margot. 1992. "To Mecca with Love." *Far Eastern Economic Review*, April 9, pp. 28–29.

Cole, Donald Powell. 1975. *Nomads of the Nomads: The Al Murrah Bedouin of the Empty Quarter.* Chicago: Aldine.

Cole, Juan R. I., and Nikki R. Keddie, eds. 1986. *Shiʿism and Social Protest.* New Haven: Yale University Press.

Combs-Schilling, M. E. 1989. *Sacred Performances: Islam, Sexuality, and Sacrifices.* New York: Columbia University Press.

"Le Complexe du Roi Fahd pour L'Impression du Coran." 1992. *Arabies* (Paris), no. 66 (June): 64–65.

Cottam, Richard W. 1993, "United States Military Policy in the Cold War Era." In *Russia's Muslim Frontiers: New Directions in Cross-Cultural Analysis*, edited by Dale F. Eickelman, pp. 19–37. Bloomington: Indiana University Press.

Coulon, Christian. 1988. "Women, Islam, and *Baraka*." In *Charisma and Brotherhood in African Islam*, edited by Donal B. Cruise O'Brien and Christian Coulon, pp. 113–33. Oxford: Clarendon Press.

Coulson, Noel James. 1959. *Islamic Law in the Modern World.* New York: New York University Press.

———. 1964. *A History of Islamic Law.* Edinburgh: University Press.

Cuau, Yves. 1994. "Algérie: Le Jeu secret de la France." *L'Express*, August 11–17, pp. 10–14.

Cudsi, Alexander S. 1983. "Islam and Politics in the Sudan." In *Islam in the Political Process*, edited by James P. Piscatori, pp. 36–55. Cambridge: Cambridge University Press.

Curtius, Mary. 1993. "Iran, Other Muslim Nations Offer Troops to UN to Protect 'Safe Havens' in Bosnia." *Boston Globe*, July 14, pp. 1, 4.

Daoud, Zakya. 1991. "La Frustration des classes moyennes au Maghreb." *Le Monde Diplomatique*, November 6, p. 6.

Dassetto, Felice. 1988. "The Tabligh Organization in Belgium." In *The New Islamic Presence in Western Europe*, edited by Tomas Gerholm and Yngve Georg Lithman, pp. 159–73. London and New York: Mansell Publishing.

David, Renée. 1992. "Foulards islamiques: L'École crispée." *Le Monde de l'Éducation*, no. 193 (May): 22–24.

Davis, Eric. 1984. "Ideology, Social Class, and Islamic Radicalism in Modern Egypt." In *From Nationalism to Revolutionary Islam*, edited by Said Amir Arjomand, pp. 134–57. Albany: State University of New York Press.

Davis, John. 1987. *Libyan Politics: Tribe and Revolution.* Berkeley and Los Angeles: University of California Press.

Dawisha, Adeed. 1983. *Islam and Foreign Policy.* Cambridge: Cambridge University Press.

Dekmejian, R. Hrair. 1985. *Islam in Revolution: Fundamentalism in the Arab World*. Syracuse: Syracuse University Press.

Della Cava, Ralph. 1991. "'Financing the Faith': The Case of Roman Catholicism." *Journal of Church and State* 35, no. 1 (winter): 37–59.

———. 1993. "Thinking about Current Vatican Policy in Central and East Europe and the Utility of the 'Brazilian Paradigm.'" *Journal of Latin American Studies* 25: 257–81.

Delval, Raymond, ed. 1984. *A Map of the Muslims in the World*. Leiden: E. J. Brill.

Demko, George J., and William B. Wood. 1994. "International Relations through the Prism of Geography." In *Reordering the World: Geopolitical Perspectives on the Twenty-first Century*, edited by George J. Demko and William B. Wood, pp. 3–13. Boulder: Westview Press.

Denoeux, Guilain. 1993. *Urban Unrest in the Middle East: A Comparative Study of Informal Networks in Egypt, Iran, and Lebanon*. Albany: State University of New York Press.

Depont, Octave, and Xavier Coppolani. 1897. *Les confréries religieuses musulmanes*. Algiers: A. Jourdan.

Derrida, Jacques. 1974. *Of Grammatology*. Baltimore: Johns Hopkins University Press.

Dessouki, A. E. Hillal, ed. 1982. *Islamic Resurgence in the Arab World*. New York: Praeger.

Deutsch, Karl W. 1966. *The Nerves of Government: Models of Political Communication and Control*. New York: Free Press.

de Villiers, Gérard. 1995. "La France sous la menace Islamique." *Paris Match*, February 23, pp. 3–6.

Dhaher, Ahmad J. 1981. "Culture and Politics in the Arab Gulf States." *Journal of South Asian and Middle Eastern Studies* 4, no. 4 (summer): 21–36.

Diyab, Muhammad Hafiz. 1989. *Sayyid Qutb: al-Khitab wa-l-idiyulujiyya* [Sayyid Qutb: The discourse and the ideology]. Cairo: Dar al-Thaqafa al-Jadida.

Doi, 'Abdur Rahman I. 1989. *Women in Shariʿah*. 2d ed., rev. London: Ta-Ha Publishers.

Doumato, Eleanor A. 1992. "Gender, Monarchy, and National Identity in Saudi Arabia." *British Journal of Middle Eastern Studies* 19, no. 1: 31–47.

Drayf, Muhammad. 1992. *al-Islam al-siyasi fi-l-Maghrib: Muraqaba wathaqiya* [Political Islam in North Africa: A documentary survey]. Casablanca: Nasharat al-majalla al-Maghribiya li-ʿilm al-ijtimaʿ al-siysasi.

Dresch, Paul, and Bernard Heikal. 1994. "Islamists and Tribesfolk in Yemen: A Study of Styles and Stereotypes." Unpublished manuscript.

Dreyer, June Teufel. 1982–1983. "The Islamic Community of China." *Central Asian Survey* 1, nos. 2–3 (October-January): 31–60.

Duben, Alan, and Cem Behar. 1991. *Istanbul Households: Marriage, Family, and Fertility, 1880–1940*. Cambridge and New York: Cambridge University Press.

Durkheim, Émile. 1977. *The Evolution of Educational Thought*. Translated by Peter Collins. London: Routledge and Kegan Paul.

Early, Evelyn A. 1993. *Baladi Women of Cairo*. Boulder: Lynne Rienner Publishers.

Easton, David. 1965. *A Framework for Political Analysis*. Englewood Cliffs: Prentice-Hall.

Edelman, Murray. 1984. "The Political Language of the Helping Professions." In *Language and Politics*, edited by Michael J. Shapiro, pp. 44–60. New York: New York University Press.

Edwards, David. 1993. "Summoning Muslims: Print, Politics, and Religious Ideology in Afghanistan." *Journal of Asian Studies* 52, no. 3 (August): 609–28.

———. 1995. "Print Islam: Media and Mass Revolution in Afghanistan." *Anthropological Quarterly*, 68, no. 3 (July): 171–84.

Egypt. 1925. *Journal Officiel* 92 (September 28), enclosed in Cairo Dispatch to London, October 15, 1925 (J 3143/2350/16), FO 371/109–13.

Eickelman, Christine. 1984. *Women and Community in Oman*. New York: New York University Press.

———. 1988. "Women and Politics in an Arabian Oasis." In *A Way Prepared: Essays on Islamic Culture in Honor of Richard Bayly Winder*, edited by Farhad Kazemi and R. D. McChesney, pp. 199–215. New York: New York University Press.

Eickelman, Dale F. 1985. *Knowledge and Power in Morocco: The Education of a Twentieth-Century Notable*. Princeton: Princeton University Press.

———. 1989a. *The Middle East: An Anthropological Approach*. 2d ed. Englewood Cliffs: Prentice-Hall.

———. 1989b. "National Identity and Religious Discourse in Contemporary Oman." *International Journal of Islamic and Arabic Studies* 6:1–20.

———. 1991. "Counting and Surveying an 'Inner' Omani Community: Hamra al-ʿAbriyin." In *Tribe and State: Essays in Honour of David Montgomery Hart*, edited by E.G.H. Joffé and C. R. Pennell, pp. 253–77. Wisbech, England: MENAS Press.

———. 1992. "Mass Higher Education and the Religious Imagination in Contemporary Arab Societies." *American Ethnologist* 19, no. 4 (November): 1–13.

———. 1993. "Islamic Liberalism Strikes Back." *Middle East Studies Association Bulletin* 27, no. 2 (December): 163–68.

———. 1994. "Re-Imagining Religion and Politics: Moroccan Elections in the 1990s." In *Islam and Secularism in North Africa*, edited by John Reudy, pp. 253–73. New York: St. Martin's Press.

Eickelman, Dale F., and Kamran Pasha. 1991. "Muslim Societies and Politics: Soviet and U.S. Approaches—A Conference Report." *Middle East Journal* 45, no. 4 (autumn): 630–47.

Eickelman, Dale F., and James Piscatori. 1990. "Social Theory in the Study of Muslim Societies." In *Muslim Travellers: Pilgrimage, Migration, and the Religious Imagination*, edited by Dale F. Eickelman and James Piscatori, pp. 1–25. London: Routledge; Berkeley: University of California Press.

"Eighth Session of the Muslim Parliament." 1994. *Q News* (London), May 13–20, pp. 6–7.

Eisenstadt, S. N. 1966. *Protest and Change*. Englewood Cliffs: Prentice-Hall.

———. 1986. *A Sociological Approach to Comparative Civilizations: The Development and Directions of a Research Program*. Jerusalem: Harry S. Truman Research Institute for the Advancement of Peace.

Elias, Jamal J. 1988. "Female and Feminine in Islamic Mysticism." *Muslim World* 78, nos. 3–4 (July–October): 209–24.

Elmandjra, Mahdi. 1992. *Première guerre civilisationelle.* Casablanca: Les Éditions Toubkal.

Elster, Jon. 1976. "Some Conceptual Problems in Political Theory." In *Power and Political Theory: Some European Perspectives,* edited by Brian Barry, pp. 245–70. London: John Wiley.

Enayat, Hamid. 1982. *Modern Islamic Political Thought.* Austin: University of Texas Press.

———. 1983. "Iran: Khumayni's Concept of the 'Guardianship of the Jurisconsult.'" In *Islam in the Political Process,* edited by James P. Piscatori, pp. 160–80. Cambridge: Cambridge University Press.

Encyclopaedia of Islam. 1960–. 2d ed. Edited by C. E. Bosworth, E. van Donzel, and W. P. Heinrichs. Leiden: E. J. Brill.

Endress, Gerhard. 1988. *An Introduction to Islam.* Translated by Carole Hillenbrand. New York: Columbia University Press.

Esposito, John L., ed. 1980. *Islam and Development: Religion and Socio-Political Change.* Syracuse: Syracuse University Press.

———. 1982. *Women in Muslim Family Law.* Syracuse: Syracuse University Press.

———. 1983. "Muhammad Iqbal and the Islamic State." In his *Voices of Resurgent Islam,* pp. 175–90. New York: Oxford University Press.

———. 1987. *Islam and Politics.* 2d ed. New York: Syracuse University Press.

———. 1992. *The Islamic Threat: Myth or Reality?* New York: Oxford University Press.

Esposito, John L., and James P. Piscatori. 1991. "Democratization and Islam." *Middle East Journal* 45, no. 3 (summer): 427–40.

"Express politique." 1994. *L'Express,* November 3, p. 6.

Fadlallah, Muhammad Husayn. 1985. "Nanazar mazidan min ʿamaliyat al-tafajir wa-l-ightiyal" [We expect an abundance of bombing and assassination operations] (interview). *al-Ittihad* (Abu Dhabi), June 7.

———. 1986. *al-Islam wa-mantiq al-quwa* [Islam and the logic of force]. 3d ed. Beirut: al-Idara al-Islamiyya.

———. 1990. *al-Haraka al-Islamiyya: Humum wa-qadiyya* [The Islamic movement: Concerns and issues]. Beirut: Dar al-Malak.

———. 1993. *Taʾamulat Islamiyya hawl al-maraʾ* [Islamic considerations about women]. Beirut: Dar al-Kalima.

Fahd ibn ʿAbd al-ʾAziz. 1983. "Inaugural Address at the Constituent Conference of the Islamic Jurisprudence Academy, 7–9 June 1983." Jidda: Organization of the Islamic Conference.

———. 1992. "Al Anzima al-Saʿudiyya al-Jadida" [The new Saudi system]. Address to the nation, published in *Al-Sharq al-Awsat,* March 2, p. 3.

al-Faruqi, Ismaʿil R. 1986/A.H. 1406. *Islamic Daʿwah: Its Nature and Demands.* Indianapolis: American Trust Publications.

Findley, Carter Vaughn. 1992. "Knowledge and Education." In *Modernization in the Middle East: The Ottoman Empire and Its Afro-Asian Successors,* edited by Cyril E. Black and L. Carl Brown, pp. 121–49. Princeton: Darwin Press.

Fischer, Michael M. J. 1980. *Iran: From Religious Dispute to Revolution.* Cambridge: Harvard University Press.

Fischer, Michael M. J., and Mehdi Abedi. 1990. *Debating Muslims: Cultural Dialogues in Postmodernity and Tradition.* Madison: University of Wisconsin Press.

Fisher, Ruth. 1994. "Hitler's Heirs Incite Islamic Students." *Sunday Times* (London), March 13, p. 25.

Fluehr-Lobban, Carolyn. 1987. *Islamic Law and Society in the Sudan.* London: Frank Cass.

———. 1990. "Islamization in Sudan: A Critical Assessment." *Middle East Journal* 44, no. 4 (autumn): 610–23.

———. 1994. *Islamic Society in Practice.* Gainesville: University Press of Florida.

"Focus on Bosnia." 1994. *British Muslims: Monthly Survey* 2, no. 5 (June 20): 1–2.

Foreign Broadcast Information Service (FBIS), Near East and South Asia Daily Report.

Fortes, Meyer, and E. E. Evans-Pritchard. 1940. "Introduction." In *African Political Systems,* edited by M. Fortes and E. E. Evans-Pritchard, pp. 1–23. Oxford: Oxford University Press for the International African Institute.

"Frenzy of Grief at Khomeini's Shrine." 1990. *Times* (London), June 5.

Friedman, Menachem. 1994. "Habad as Messianic Fundamentalism: From Local Particularism to Universal Jewish Mission." In *Accounting for Fundamentalisms: The Dynamic Character of Movements,* edited by Martin E. Marty and R. Scott Appleby, pp. 328–57. Chicago and London: University of Chicago Press.

Fuller, Graham E., and Ian O. Lesser. 1995. *A Sense of Siege: The Geopolitics of Islam and the West.* Boulder: Westview.

"The Future of the Marja'iyya." 1994. *Dialogue* (Public Affairs Committee for Shia Muslims, London), January, p. 1.

Gaffney, Patrick D. 1994. *The Prophet's Pulpit: Islamic Preaching in Contemporary Egypt.* Berkeley and Los Angeles: University of California Press.

Galison, Peter. 1988. "History, Philosophy, and the Central Metaphor." *Science in Context* 2, no. 1 (1988): 197–212.

Gambari, Ibrahim. 1990. "Islamic Revivalism in Nigeria: Homegrown or Externally Induced?" In *The Iranian Revolution: Its Global Impact,* edited by John L. Esposito, pp. 302–16. Miami: Florida International University Press.

Geertz, Clifford. 1973. *The Interpretation of Cultures.* New York: Basic Books.

———. 1979. "Suq: The Bazaar Economy in Sefrou." In *Meaning and Order in Moroccan Society,* by Clifford Geertz, Hildred Geertz, and Lawrence Rosen, pp. 123–313. New York: Cambridge University Press.

Gelb, Leslie H. 1992. "Hear, O Islam." *New York Times,* June 22, A17.

Gellner, Ernest. 1992. *Postmodernism, Reason, and Religion.* London and New York: Routledge.

———. 1994. *Conditions of Liberty: Civil Society and Its Rivals.* London: Hamish Hamilton.

Gershoni, Israel, and James P. Jankowski. 1986. *Egypt, Islam, and the Arabs: The Search for Egyptian Nationhood, 1900–1930.* New York: Oxford University Press.

al-Ghannouchi [al-Ghannushi], Rashid. 1992. *Hiwarat* [Dialogues], with Qusayy Salah al-Darwish. London: Khalil Media Service.

———. 1993. "The Participation of Islamists in a Non-Islamic Government." In *Power-Sharing Islam*, edited by Azzam Tamimi, pp. 51–64. London: Liberty for Muslim World Publications.

al-Ghazali, Abu Hamid Muhammad. (d. 1111). n.d. *al-Munqidh min al-dalal* [Deliverer from error]. Cairo: Maktabat al-Jandi.

al-Ghazali, Shaykh Muhammad. 1989. "al-Shaykh al-Ghazali yasharh madmun wa-asbab bayyan al-Azhar" [Shaykh al-Ghazali comments on the meaning and reasons for the al-Azhar statement]. *Ai-Sha'b* (Cairo), January 10, pp. 1–2.

al-Ghazali, Zaynab. 1992. *Ayyam min hayati* [Days of my life]. 13th ed. Cairo: Dar al-Shuruq.

Ghazi, Katayon. 1994. "Iran Offers an Islamic Way to Improve the Lot of Women." *New York Times*, December 21, p. A11.

"Le GIA annonce la formation d'un gouvernement islamique." 1994. *Le Monde*, August 28–29, p. 3.

Gibbins, John R. 1989. "Contemporary Political Culture: An Introduction." In *Contemporary Political Culture: Politics in a Postmodern World*, edited by John R. Gibbins, pp. 1–30. London: Sage Publications.

Giddens, Anthony. 1979. *Central Problems in Social Theory: Action, Structure, and Contradiction in Social Analysis.* London: Macmillan.

Gladney, Dru C. 1991. *Muslim Chinese: Ethnic Nationalism in the People's Republic.* Cambridge: Harvard University Press for the Council on East Asian Studies, Harvard University.

———. 1992a. "The Hui, Islam, and the State: A Sufi Community in China's Northwest Corner." In *Muslims in Central Asia: Expressions of Identity and Change*, edited by Jo-Ann Gross, pp. 89–111. Durham and London: Duke University Press.

———. 1992b. "Transnational Islam and Uighur National Identity: Salman Rushdie, Sino-Muslim Missile Deals, and the Trans-Eurasian Railway." *Central Asian Survey* 11, no. 3: 1–18.

———. 1994a. "Salman Rushdie in China: Religion, Ethnicity, and State Definition in the People's Republic." In *Asian Visions of Authority: Religion and the Modern States of East and Southeast Asia*, edited by Helen Hardacre, Laura Kendall, and Charles Keyes, pp. 255–78. Honolulu: University of Hawaii Press.

———. 1994b. "Sino-Middle Eastern Perspectives and Relations since the Gulf War: Views from Below." *International Journal of Middle East Studies* 26, no. 4 (November): 677–91.

———. 1994c. "Ethnic Identity in China: The New Politics of Difference." *China Briefing, 1994*, edited by William A. Joseph, pp. 171–92. Boulder: Westview Press.

Goldberg, Ellis. 1992. "Smashing Idols and the State: The Protestant Ethic and Egyptian Sunni Radicalism." In *Comparing Muslim Societies: Knowledge and the State in a World Civilization*, edited by Juan R. I. Cole, pp. 195–236. Ann Arbor: University of Michigan Press.

Göle, Nilüfer. 1993. *Musulmanes et modernes: Voile et civilisation en Turquie.* Paris: Éditions la Decouverte.

Gonzalez-Quijano, Yves. 1989. "Le Livre arabe et l'édition en Egypte." Special issue of *Bulletin du CEDEJ*, no. 25. Cairo: Centre d'Études et de Documentation Économiques, Juridiques, et Sociales.

———. 1994. "Les Gens du livre: Champ intellectuel et edition dans l'Egypte republicaine (1952-1993)." Ph.D diss., l'Institut d'Études Politiques de Paris, Mention Sciences Politiques.

Goody, Jack, ed. 1968. *Literacy in Traditional Societies.* Cambridge: Cambridge: University Press.

———. 1977. *The Domestication of the Savage Mind.* New York: Cambridge University Press.

———. 1986. *The Logic of Writing and the Organization of Society.* New York: Cambridge University Press.

Goytisolo, Juan. 1994. *Argelia, en el vendeval.* Madrid: Ediciones El País/ Aguilar.

Grillo, Ralph. 1989. "Anthropology, Language, Politics." In *Social Anthropology and the Politics of Language*, edited by Ralph Grillo, pp. 1–24. Sociological Review Monograph, no. 36. London: Routledge.

Guigon, Laurent. 1993. "L'Imam turc de Nantua a été expulsé." *Le Monde*, November 12, p. 3.

El Guindi, Fadwa. 1981. "Veiling *Infitah* with Muslim Ethic: Egypt's Contemporary Islamic Movement." *Social Problems* 28, no. 4 (April): 465–83.

Gunatilleke, Godfrey, ed. 1986. *Migration of Asian Workers to the Arab World.* Tokyo: United Nations University Press.

———. 1991. *Migration to the Arab World: Experience of Returning Migrants.* Tokyo: United Nations University Press.

Habermas, Jürgen. 1981. *The Theory of Communicative Action.* Vol. 1, *Reason and the Socialization of Society.* Translated by Thomas McCarthy. Boston: Beacon Press.

Hadar, Leon T. 1993. "What Green Peril?" *Foreign Affairs* 72, no. 2 (spring): 27–42.

Haddad, Yvonne. 1983. "Sayyid Qutb: Ideologue of Islamic Revival." In *Voices of Resurgent Islam*, edited by John L. Esposito, pp. 67–98. New York: Oxford University Press.

Haddad, Yvonne, John Obert Voll, and John L. Esposito. 1991. *The Contemporary Islamic Revival: A Critical Survey and Bibliography.* New York and Westport: Greenwood Press.

Haeri, Safa. 1991. "Saudi Arabian Clerics Call on King Fahd to Reshape Society." *Independent* (London), May 25, p. 12.

Halm, Heinz. 1991. *Shiism.* Edinburgh: Edinburgh University Press.

Halpern, Manfred. 1963. *The Politics of Social Change in the Middle East and North Africa.* Princeton: Princeton University Press.

Hamidullah, Muhammad. 1959. *Introduction to Islam.* New ed. Publications of the Centre Culturel Islamique, Paris, no. 1. Paris: Centre Culturel Islamique.

———. 1961. *Muslim Conduct of State.* 4th rev. ed. Lahore: Sh. Muhammad Ashraf.

Hannerz, Ulf. 1989. "Notes on the Global Ecumene." *Public Culture* 1, no. 2 (spring): 66–75.

Hardacre, Helen. 1993. "The Impact of Fundamentalisms on Women, the Family, and Interpersonal Relations." In *Fundamentalism and Society: Reclaiming the Sciences, the Family, and Education*, edited by Martin E. Marty and R. Scott Appleby, pp. 129–50. Chicago and London: University of Chicago Press.

Haron, Muhammed. 1993. "The 'Muslim News' (1960–1986): Expression of an Islamic Identity in South Africa." In *Muslim Identity and Social Change in Sub-Saharan Africa*, edited by Louis Brenner, pp. 210–25. Bloomington: Indiana University Press.

Hassan, Muhammad Kamal. 1982. *Muslim Intellectual Responses to "New Order" Modernization in Indonesia*. Kuala Lumpur: Dewan Bahasa dan Pustaka, Kementerian Pelajaran Malaysia.

Hassan, Sharifah Zaleha Syed. 1993. "The Life and Work of a Malaysian Kadhi." *NIASnytt* (Nordic Newsletter of Asian Studies), no. 1 (February): 20–24.

Hassan II. 1984. *Discours et Interviews*. Rabat: Ministry of Information.

———. 1993. "al-Maghrib wa-l-Hasan al-Thani . . ." [Morocco and Hassan II . . .] (interview). *Al Sharq al-Awsat* (London), January 13, pp. 7–9.

al-Hawali, Safar. 1991. *Kashf al-ghumma ʿan ʿulama al-umma; risala min al-Shaykh Safar al-Hawali ila al-Shaykh ʿAbd al-ʿAziz ibn Baz* [The unveiling of distress about the ʿulama; A letter from Shaykh Safar al-Hawali to Shaykh ʿAbd al-ʿAziz ibn Baz]. N.p.: Dar al-Hikma.

Haykal, Yusif. 1945. *Nahwa al-Wahda al-ʿArabiyya* [Toward Arab unity]. Cairo: Dar al-Maʿarif.

Hedges, Chris. 1993. "Egypt Cracking Down on Islamic Student Groups." *New York Times*, November 28, p. 16.

Hefner, Robert W. 1985. *Hindu Javanese: Tengger Tradition and Islam*. Princeton: Princeton University Press.

———. 1987. "The Political Economy of Islamic Conversion in Modern East Java." In *Islam and the Political Economy of Meaning*, edited by William R. Roff, pp. 53–78. London: Croom Helm.

———. 1993. "Islam, State, and Civil Society: ICMI and the Struggle for the Indonesian Middle Class." *Indonesia* 56 (October): 1–35.

Hegland, Mary. 1991. "Political Roles of Aliabad Women: The Public-Private Dichotomy Transcended." In *Women in Middle Eastern History: Shifting Boundaries in Sex and Gender*, edited by Nikki R. Keddie and Beth Baron, pp. 215–30. New Haven: Yale University Press.

Henderson, Neville. 1925. Acting High Commissioner, Cairo, Confidential Report to Foreign Secretary, August 24 (J 2461/2350/16), FO 371/10913.

Heritage Foundation. 1984. "Fundamentalist Muslims and U.S. Policy." International Briefing, no. 13. August 10.

Hicks, Neil, and Ghanim al-Najjar. 1995. "The Utility of Tradition: Civil Society in Kuwait." In *Civil Society in the Middle East*, 1:186–213. Leiden: E. J. Brill.

Higgott, Richard A. 1983. *Political Development Theory: The Contemporary Debate*. London: Croom Helm.

Hijab, Nadia. 1988. *Womanpower: The Arab Debate on Women at Work*. Cambridge: Cambridge University Press.

Hitti, Philip K. 1953. *History of the Arabs: From the Earliest Times to the Present*. 5th ed., rev. New York: St. Martin's Press.

"Hizbullah: Haraka ʿaskariyya am siyasiyya am diniyya?" [Hizbullah: Military, political, or religious movement?]. 1986. *al-Shiraʿ*, March 17, pp. 14–21.

Hizb ut-Tahrir. n.d. *The Khilafah*. London: Al-Khilafah Publications.

Hobsbawm, Eric. 1983. "Introduction: Inventing Traditions." In *The Invention of Tradition*, edited by Eric Hobsbawm and Terence Ranger, pp. 1–14. Cambridge: Cambridge University Press.

Hoffman, Valerie J. 1985. "An Islamic Activist: Zaynab al-Ghazali." In *Women and the Family in the Middle East: New Voices of Change*, edited by Elizabeth W. Fernea, pp. 233–54. Austin: University of Texas Press.

Hoffman-Ladd, Valerie J. 1987. "Polemics on the Modesty and Segregation of Women in Contemporary Egypt." *International Journal of Middle East Studies* 19, no. 1 (February): 23–50.

Horikoshi, Hioko. 1975. "The Dar-ul Islam Movement in West Java (1948–62): An Experience in Historical Process." *Indonesia* 20 (October): 59–86.

Horvatich, Patricia. 1993. "The Politics of Identity in the Southern Philippines." Paper delivered at the conference, "Islam and the Social Construction of Identities: Comparative Perspectives on Southeast Asian Muslims," Center for Southeast Asian Studies, University of Hawaii at Manoa, August 4–6.

Hourani, Albert. 1970. *Arabic Thought in the Liberal Age, 1798–1939*. London: Oxford University Press.

Hourcade, Bernard. 1987. *Téhéran au dessous du volcan*, edited by Bernard Hourcade and Yann Richard. Paris: Autrement.

Hudson, Michael C. 1980. "Islam and Political Development." In *Islam and Development: Religion and Socio-Political Change*, edited by John L. Esposito, pp. 1–24. Syracuse: Syracuse University Press.

———. 1991. "After the Gulf War: Prospects for Democratization in the Arab World." *Middle East Journal* 45, no. 3 (summer): 407–26.

Hunter, Shireen T., ed. 1988. *The Politics of Islamic Revivalism: Diversity and Unity*. Bloomington: Indiana University Press.

Huntington, Samuel. 1968. *Political Order in Changing Societies*. New Haven: Yale University Press.

———. 1993. "The Clash of Civilizations?" *Foreign Affairs* 72, no. 3 (summer): 22–49.

Huq, Maimuna. 1994. "Old Fetters, New Frontiers: Women's Islamic Activism in Bangladesh." Senior Fellow Thesis, Dartmouth College, June.

Hussain, Asaf. 1984. *Political Perspectives on the Muslim World*. New York: St. Martin's Press.

Hussain, Zahid. 1992. "Scandals Plague Pakistan." *Times* (London), January 10.

IANA [Islamic Association of North America]. 1995. "IANA: Fatwa Center." Internet message, April 9.

Ibn Khaldûn (d. 1406). 1967. *The Muqaddimah: An Introduction to History*. 2d ed. Translated by Franz Rosenthal. Princeton: Princeton University Press.

Ibrahim, Saad Eddin. 1980. "Anatomy of Egypt's Militant Islamic Groups: Methodological Note and Preliminary Findings." *International Journal of Middle East Studies* 12, no. 4 (December): 423–53.

Ibrahim, Youssef M. 1988a. "Taxes Imposed on Foreigners in Saudi Arabia." *New York Times*, January 5, pp. A1, D5.

———. 1988b. "Saudis Cancel Tax after Complaints." *New York Times*, January 6, pp. A1, D6.

Idris, Nor Azizan. 1991. "Family and Kinship in Malaysian Politics." Paper delivered at the International Conference on Asian Studies, Centre for Asian Studies, University of Waikato, Hamilton, New Zealand, August 23–26.

Inalcik, Halil. 1970. "The Rise of the Ottoman Empire." In *Cambridge History of Islam*, edited by P. M. Holt, Ann K. S. Lambton, and Bernard Lewis, 1:295–323. Cambridge: Cambridge University Press.

"L'interdiction des antennes paraboliques jugés inconstitutionnelle en Iran." 1995. *Libération*, January 12, p. 16.

Iran, Islamic Republic of. 1980. "Constitution of the Islamic Republic of Iran" (ratified December 2–3, 1979). *Middle East Journal* 34, no. 2 (spring): 181–204.

"Iran Prohibits Satellite Dishes to Bar U.S. TV." 1994. *New York Times*, December 27, p. A6.

"*al-Irhabi*" [The Terrorist], #2018. 1994. Distributed in the United States and Canada by Diana Nour International Films.

'Isa, Ibrahim. 1992. "Shra'it al-tatarruf 'ala al-rasif: Jins wa-fitna wa-tahrid" [Extremist cassettes on the sidewalk: Sex, rebellion, and incitement]. *al-Ishtiraki* (Casablanca), June 21, pp. 2–3.

Islam, Mahmuda. 1991. *Woman Heads of Household in Rural Bangladesh: Struggle for Survival*. n.p.: Narigrantha Prabartana.

Islam, Yusuf (Cat Stevens). n.d. *Nasyid Afghanistan*. Nasyid an-Nadwah, no. 3. Distributed by Pustaka An-Nadwah. Terengganu, Malaysia.

Ismael, Tareq Y., and Jacqueline S. Ismael. 1985. *Government and Politics in Islam*. New York: St. Martin's Press.

Israeli, Rafael, ed. 1982. *Crescent in the East: Islam in Asia Major*. London: Curzon Press.

Jadhakhan, Haroon M., ed. 1992. *The Thieves of Riyadh: Lives and Crimes of the Al Sauds and the Al Nahyans*. 2d. ed. London: Muslim Chronicle.

Jalil, A.M.M. Abdul. 1981. *The Palestine Issue and the Muslim World*. 2d ed. Dhaka: Islamic Research Centre.

Jameelah, Maryam. 1980. *The Resurgence of Islam and Our Liberation from the Colonial Yoke*. Lahore: Muhammad Yusuf Khan and Sons.

———. [1969] 1982a. *Correspondence between Maulana Maudoodi and Maryam Jameelah*. Delhi: Taj Company.

———. 1982b. *The Great Islamic Movements in the Arab World of the Recent Past: The Movement of Shaikh Muhammad bin Abdul Wahab, the Sanussi Movement, the Mahdi of the Sudan*. Delhi: Taj Company.

———. 1982c. *Is Western Civilization Universal?* Delhi: Taj Company.

Jansen, Johannes J. J. 1986. *The Neglected Duty: The Creed of Sadat's Assassins and Islamic Resurgence in the Middle East*. New York: Macmillan.

Jelen, Christian. 1994. "L'Intégrisme à l'assaut de l'école." *Le Point*, September 10, pp. 82–87.

Jubran, Michel, and Laura Drake. 1993. "Fundamentalism, West Bank, and Gaza." *Middle East Policy* 2, no. 2: 1–15.

Kamm, Henry. 1994. "Battle among the Bhuttos: From Politics to Gunfire." *New York Times*, January 6, p. A3.

Kandiyoti, Deniz. 1991. "Introduction." In *Women, Islam, and the State*, edited by Deniz Kandiyoti, pp. 1–21. Philadelphia: Temple University Press.

Kane, Ousmane. 1992. "Some Considerations on Sufi Transnationalism in Africa with Particular Reference to the Niassene Tijaniyya." Paper delivered at the Social Science Research Council workshop on Transnational Religious Regimes, Chicago, April 24–26.

———. 1994. "Izala: The Rise of Muslim Reformism in Northern Nigeria." In *Accounting for Fundamentalisms*, edited by Martin E. Marty and R. Scott Appleby, pp. 488–510. Chicago: University of Chicago Press.

Karp, Jonathon. 1994. "Allah's Bounty: al-Arqam Sect Draws Strength from Business Empire." *Far Eastern Economic Review*, September 1, p. 78.

Karrar, Ali Salih. 1992. *Sufi Brotherhoods in the Sudan*. Evanston: Northwestern University Press.

al-Karsani, Awad al-Sid. 1993. "Beyond Sufism: The Case of Millennial Islam in the Sudan." In *Muslim Identity and Social Change in Sub-Saharan Africa*, edited by Louis Brenner, pp. 135–53. Bloomington and Indianapolis: Indiana University Press.

Katz, June S., and Ronald S. Katz. 1975. "The New Indonesian Marriage Law: A Mirror of Indonesia's Political, Cultural, and Legal System." *American Journal of Comparative Law* 23, no. 4 (fall): 653–81.

Katzman, Kenneth. 1993. *The Warriors of Islam: Iran's Revolutionary Guard*. Boulder: Westview.

Keddie, Nikki R. 1981. *Roots of Revolution: An Interpretive History of Modern Iran*. New Haven: Yale University Press.

Keddie, Nikki R., and Beth Baron, eds. 1991. *Women in Middle Eastern History: Shifting Boundaries in Sex and Gender*. New Haven: Yale University Press.

Kedourie, Elie. 1992. *Democracy and Arab Political Culture*. Washington, D.C.: Institute for Near East Policy.

Kellner, Peter. 1988. "Forging a New Political Vocabulary." *Independent* (London), October 17, p. 20.

Kennan, George F. 1994. "The Failure in Our Success." *New York Times*, March 14, p. A17.

Kepel, Gilles. 1984. *Le Prophète et pharaon: Les mouvements islamistes dans l'Egypte contemporaine*. Paris: La Decouverte.

———. 1985. *Muslim Extremism in Europe: The Prophet and the Pharaoh*. Translated by Jon Rothschild. Berkeley and Los Angeles: University of California Press.

———. 1987. *Les banlieues de l'Islam*. Paris: Éditions du Seuil.

———. 1994a. *The Revenge of God: The Resurgence of Islam, Christianity, and Judaism in the Modern World*. Translated by Alan Braley. University Park: Pennsylvania State University Press.

———. 1994b. *À l'Ouest d'Allah.* Paris: Éditions du Seuil.

Kepel, Gilles, and Yann Richard, eds. 1990. *Intellectuels et militants de l'Islam contemporaine.* Paris: Éditions du Seuil.

Kessler, Clive S. 1978. *Islam and Politics in a Malay State: Kelantan, 1838–1969.* Ithaca: Cornell University Press.

———. 1990. "New Directions in the Study of Islam: Remarks on Some Trends and Prospects." *Jurnal Antropologi Dan Sosiologi* 18: 3–22.

Khadduri, Majid. 1955. *War and Peace in the Law of Islam.* Baltimore: Johns Hopkins Press.

———. 1984. *The Islamic Conception of Justice.* Baltimore: Johns Hopkins University Press.

Khalaf, Roula. 1994. "Saudi Businessmen Reach for the Media Stars." *Financial Times,* November 16, p. 6.

Khalid, Adeeb. 1992. "Muslim Printers in Tsarist Central Asia: A Research Note." *Central Asian Survey* 11:113–18.

al-Khalil, Samir. 1991. *The Monument: Art, Vulgarity, and Responsibility in Iraq.* Berkeley and Los Angeles: University of California Press.

al-Khalili, Ahmad bin Hamad. 1988. *Who Are the Ibadhis?* Translated by A. H. Al-Maamiry. Zanzibar: al-Khaiyirah Press.

Khan, Farush, and Juhaidi Yean Abdullah. 1993. "PM Backed for Criticising Western Failure in Bosnia." *New Straits Times* (Kuala Lumpur), August 11, p. 2.

Khan, Qamaruddin. 1982. *Political Concepts in the Quran.* Lahore: Islamic Book Foundation.

el-Khazen, Farid, and Paul Salem. 1993. *Al-intikhabat al-awali fi Lubnan ma ba'd al-harb* (The first elections in Lebanon after the war). Beirut: al-markaz al-Lubnani li-l-Dirasat.

Khomeini, Ayatullah Ruhollah. 1981. *Islam and Revolution: Writings and Declarations of Imam Khomeini.* Edited and translated by Hamid Algar. Berkeley: Mizan Press.

———. [1983] n.d. "Imam Khomeini's Last Will and Testament." Washington: Embassy of the Democratic and Popular Republic of Algeria, Interests Section of the Islamic Republic of Iran.

———. 1988. "Excerpts from Imam Khomeini's Message on the Occasion of Women's Day." *Mahjubah* 8, no. 61 (May).

Khudr, Adele. 1994. "An Islamic Discourse with Sayyed Mohammed Hussein Fadlallah" (interview). *Al Raida* [Institute for Women's Studies in the Arab World] 11, nos. 65/66 (spring-summer): 30–31.

Khuri, Fuad I. 1975. *From Village to Suburb: Order and Change in Greater Beirut.* Chicago: University of Chicago Press.

Korgun, Victor G. 1993. "The Afghan Revolution: A Failed Experiment." In *Russia's Muslim Frontiers: New Directions in Cross-Cultural Analysis,* edited by Dale F. Eickelman, pp. 101–13. Bloomington and Indianapolis: Indiana University Press.

Krämer, Gudrun. 1992. "Liberalization and Democracy in the Arab World." *Middle East Report* 22, no. 1 (January-February): 22–25, 35.

Krämer, Gudrun. 1993. "Islamist Notions of Democracy." *Middle East Report* 23, no. 4 (July-August): 2–8.

Kramer, Martin. 1980. *Political Islam.* Beverly Hills: Sage.

———. 1986. *Islam Assembled: The Advent of the Muslim Congresses.* New York: Columbia University Press.

———, ed. 1987. *Shiism, Resistance, and Revolution.* Boulder: Westview.

———. 1993. "Islam vs. Democracy." *Commentary* 95, no. 1 (January): 35–42.

Kuhn, Thomas S. 1962. *The Structure of Scientific Revolutions.* Chicago: University of Chicago Press.

Labat, Séverine. 1994. "Islamismes et islamistes en Algérie: Un Nouveau militantisme." In *Exils et royaumes: Les Appartenances au monde arabo-musulman aujourd'hui,* edited by Gilles Kepel, pp. 41–67. Paris: Presses de la Fondation Nationale des Sciences Politiques.

"Lajnat al-Difaᶜ ᶜan al-huquq al-sharᶜiyya" [Committee for the Defense of Legitimate Rights]. 1993. *al-Jazira al-ᶜArabiyya* [The Arabian peninsula] 3, no. 29 (June): 5–28.

Lambek, Michael. 1990. "Certain Knowledge, Contestable Authority: Power and Practice in the Islamic Periphery." *American Ethnologist* 17, no. 1 (February): 23–40.

Lambton, Ann K. S. 1981. *State and Government in Medieval Islam: An Introduction to the Study of Islamic Political Theory.* Oxford: Oxford University Press.

Lancaster, William. 1981. *The Rwala Bedouin Today.* New York and Cambridge: Cambridge University Press.

Landau, Jacob M. 1990. *The Politics of Pan-Islam: Ideology and Organization.* Oxford: Clarendon Press.

Lapidus, Ira M. 1975. "The Separation of State and Religion in the Development of Early Islamic Society." *International Journal of Middle East Studies* 6, no. 4 (October): 363–85.

Laslett, Peter. 1984. "The Family as a Knot of Individual Interests." In *Households: Comparative and Historical Studies of the Domestic Group,* edited by Robert McC. Netting, Richard R. Wilk, and Eric J. Arnould, pp. 353–79. Berkeley and Los Angeles: University of California Press.

Lasswell, Harold D. [1935] 1965. *World Politics and Personal Insecurity.* New York: Free Press.

Launay, Robert. 1992. *Beyond the Stream: Islam and Society in a West African Town.* Berkeley and Los Angeles: University of California Press.

Lawrence, Bruce. 1989. *Defenders of God: The Fundamentalist Revolt against the Modern Age.* New York: Harper and Row.

Layne, Linda L. 1994. *Home and Homeland: The Dialogics of Tribal and National Identities in Jordan.* Princeton: Princeton University Press.

Leca, Jean. 1994. "Democratization in the Arab World: Uncertainty, Vulnerability, and Legitimacy: A Tentative Conceptualization and Some Hypotheses." In *Democracy without Democrats? The Renewal of Politics in the Muslim World,* edited by Ghassan Salamé, pp. 48–83. London and New York: I. B. Tauris.

Legrain, Jean-François. 1990. "Les Elections étudiantes en Cisjordanie (1978–1987)." *Egypte/Monde Arabe* 4, no. 4: 87–116.

———. 1991. "A Defining Moment: Palestinian Islamic Fundamentalism." In *Islamic Fundamentalisms and the Gulf Crisis*, edited by James Piscatori, pp. 70–87. Chicago: Fundamentalism Project of the American Academy of Arts and Sciences.

Lembaga Konsultasi & Bantuan Hukum Untuk Wanita & Keluarga [LKBHUWK]. n.d. *An Introduction to the Institute for Consultation and Legal Aid for Women and Families.* Jakarta: LKBHUWK.

Lemu, B. Aisha. 1978. "Woman in Islam." In *Women in Islam*, edited by B. Aisha Lemu and Fatima Heeren, pp. 13–30. Leicester: Islamic Council of Europe.

Lerner, Daniel. [1958] 1964. *The Passing of Traditional Society: Modernizing the Middle East.* New York: Free Press.

Lesieur, Jean. 1994. "Paris-Washington: Des Divergences de Fond." *L'Express*, August 11–17, pp. 12–13.

Lewis, Bernard. 1961. *The Emergence of Modern Turkey.* London: Oxford University Press for the Royal Institute of International Affairs.

———. 1979. "Politics and War." In *The Legacy of Islam*, 2d ed., edited by Joseph Schacht and C. E. Bosworth, pp. 156–209. Oxford: Oxford University Press.

———. 1988. *The Political Language of Islam.* Chicago: University of Chicago Press.

———. 1990. "The Roots of Muslim Rage." *Atlantic* 266 (September): 47–54, 56, 59–60.

———. 1993. "Islam and Liberal Democracy." *Atlantic*, 271 (February): 89–94.

Lewis, Bernard, and Dominique Schnapper, eds. 1994. *Muslims in Europe.* London: Pinter Publishers.

Lienhard, Marc. 1989. "Luther in Europe." In *The Reformation*, edited by Pierre Chaunu, pp. 82–109. London: Guild Publishing.

Lipschutz, Ronnie D. 1992. "Reconstructing World Politics: The Emergence of Global Civil Society." *Millennium: Journal of International Studies* 21, no. 3 (winter): 389–420.

Lockwood, William G. 1975. *European Muslims: Economy and Ethnicity in Western Bosnia.* New York: Academic Press.

Lubeck, Paul. 1987. "Structural Determinants of Urban Protest in Northern Nigeria." In *Islam and the Political Economy of Meaning: Comparative Studies of Muslim Discourse*, edited by William R. Roff, pp. 79–107. Berkeley and Los Angeles: University of California Press.

Lukes, Steven. 1986. "Introduction." In *Power*, edited by Steven Lukes, pp. 1–18. Oxford: Blackwell.

McCloud, Aminah Beverly. 1995. *African American Islam.* New York and London: Routlege.

McKenna, Thomas. 1993. "Uncovering Islam in the Muslim Philippines." Paper delivered at the conference, "Islam and the Social Construction of Identities: Comparative Perspectives on Southeast Asian Muslims," Center for Southeast Asian Studies, University of Hawaii at Manoa, August 4–6.

MacLeod, Arlene Elowe. 1991. *Accommodating Protest: Working Women, the New Veiling, and Change in Cairo.* New York: Columbia University Press.

Madan, T. N. 1987. "Secularism in Its Place." *Journal of Asian Studies* 6: 747–59.

Madjid, Nurcholish. 1994. "Islamic Roots of Modern Pluralism: Indonesian Experiences." *Studia Islamika: Indonesian Journal for Islamic Studies* 1, no. 1 (April-June): 54–77.

———. 1995. Interview with James Piscatori, Bellagio, Italy, March 23.

al-Mahdi, Sadiq. 1990. *Tahaddiyat al-Tis'iniyat* [The challenges of the 1990s]. Cairo: Sharikat al-Nil li-l-Sahafa wa-l-Tiba'a wa-l-Nashr.

Majrooh, Parwin. 1989. "Afghan Women between Marxism and Islamic Fundamentalism." *Central Asian Survey* 8, no. 3: 87–98.

"Malaysia's Stand on the Bosnian Issue." 1992. *Al-Nahdah* 12, nos. 3–4 (3d and 4th quarters): 11–14.

Malik, S. Jamal. 1990. "*Waqf* in Pakistan: Change in Traditional Institutions." *Die Welt des Islams* 30: 63–97.

Mann, Michael. 1986. *The Sources of Social Power*. Vol. 1, *A History of Power from the Beginning to* A.D. *1760*. Cambridge: Cambridge University Press.

Mardin, Şerif. 1983. "Religion and Politics in Modern Turkey." In *Islam in the Political Process*, edited by James P. Piscatori, pp. 138–59. Cambridge: Cambridge University Press.

———. 1989. *Religion and Social Change in Modern Turkey: The Case of Bediüzzaman Saïd Nursi*. Albany: State University of New York Press.

Markaz Ibn Khaldun. 1992. *al-Mujtama'a al-Madani wa-l-tahawwul al-dimuqrati fi-l-watan al-'arabi* [Civil society and the democratic transition in the Arab nation]. Cairo: Dar Su'ad al-Sabah.

Marlowe, Lara. 1992. "The New Saudi Press Barons." *Time*, June 22, pp. 49–50.

Marty, Martin E., and R. Scott Appleby, eds. 1991. *Fundamentalisms Observed*. Chicago and London: University of Chicago Press.

———. 1993. *Fundamentalism and Society: Reclaiming the Sciences, the Family, and Education*. Chicago and London: University of Chicago Press.

———. 1994. *Accounting for Fundamentalisms; The Dynamic Character of Movements*. Chicago: University of Chicago Press.

Masud, Khalid. 1990. "The Obligation to Migrate: The Doctrine of *Hijra* in Islamic Law." In *Muslim Travellers: Pilgrimage, Migration, and the Religious Imagination*, edited by Dale F. Eickelman and James Piscatori, pp. 29–49. London: Routledge; Berkeley and Los Angeles: University of California Press.

———, ed. 1995. "Travellers in Faith: Studies of Tablighi Jama'at as an International Movement." Unpublished manuscript.

al-Mawardi, Abu-l-Hasan. 1960. *Kitab al-ahkam al-sultaniyya* [Book of the principles of governance]. Cairo: n.p.

al-Mawdudi, Abu-l A'la. 1976. *Political Theory of Islam*. Lahore: Islamic Publications.

———. 1982. *Birth Control: Its Social, Political, Economic, Moral, and Religious Aspects*. 6th ed. Translated and edited by Khurshid Ahmad and Mis Bahul Islam Faruqi. Lahore: Islamic Publications.

———. 1983. *First Principles of the Islamic State*. 6th ed. rev. Translated and edited by Khurshid Ahmad. Lahore: Islamic Publications.

———. 1986. *Islamic State: Political Writings of Malauna Sayyid Abul 'Ala Maudoodi*. Compiled and translated by Mazheruddin Siddiqi. Karachi: Islamic Research Academy.

Mayer, Ann Elizabeth. 1993. "Moroccans—Citizens or Subjects? A People at the Crossroads." *New York University Journal of International Law and Politics* 26, no. 1 (fall): 63–105.

———. 1995. *Islam and Human Rights: Tradition and Politics.* 2d ed. Boulder: Westview.

Meenai, S. J. 1990. *The Islamic Development Bank: A Study of Islamic Cooperation.* London: Routledge.

Mernissi, Fatima. 1990. *Sultanes oubliées: Femmes chefs d'État en Islam.* Paris: Albin Michel.

Messick, Brinkley. 1993. *The Calligraphic State: Textual Domination and History in a Muslim Society.* Berkeley and Los Angeles: University of California Press.

Metcalf, Barbara D. 1990. "The Pilgrimage Remembered: South Asian Accounts of the *hajj.*" in *Muslim Travellers: Pilgrimage, Migration, and the Religious Imagination,* edited by Dale F. Eickelman and James Piscatori, pp. 85–107. London: Routledge; Berkeley and Los Angeles: University of California Press.

———. 1993. "Living Hadith in the Tablighi Jamaʿat." *Journal of Asian Studies* 52, no. 3 (August): 584–608.

Migdal, Joel S. 1988. *Strong Societies and Weak States: State-Society Relations and State Capabilities in the Third World.* Princeton: Princeton University Press.

Miller, Judith. 1993. "The Challenge of Radical Islam." *Foreign Affairs* 72, no. 2 (spring): 43–56.

Milton-Edwards, Beverley. 1991a. "The Rise of the Islamic Movement in the West Bank and Gaza since 1967." Ph.D. diss., University of Exeter, Department of Politics.

———. 1991b. "A Temporary Alliance with the Crown: The Islamic Response in Jordan," In *Islamic Fundamentalisms and the Gulf Crisis,* edited by James Piscatori, pp. 88–108. Chicago: Fundamentalism Project of the American Academy of Arts and Sciences.

Mirsky, Jonathan. 1990. "Muslims Ordered to Worship Mao in China's Wild West." *Observer* (London), November 11, p. 17.

Mitchell, C. R. 1981. *The Structure of International Conflict.* Basingstoke and London: Macmillan.

Mitchell, Richard P. 1969. *The Society of the Muslim Brothers.* London: Oxford University Press.

Modarressi, Hossein. 1991. "The Just Ruler." *Journal of the American Oriental Society* 3, no. 3: 549–62.

Moghadam, Val. 1991. "The Neopatriarchal State in the Middle East: Development, Authoritarianism, and Crisis." In *The Gulf War and the New World Order,* edited by Haim Bresheeth and Nira Uyval-Davis, pp. 199–210. London: Zed Books.

Moinuddin, Hasan. 1987. *The Charter of the Islamic Conference: The Legal and Economic Framework.* Oxford: Clarendon Press.

Moore, Clement Henry. 1974. "Authoritarian Politics in Unincorporated Society: The Case of Nasser's Egypt." *Comparative Politics* 6, no. 2 (January): 193–218.

Morgenthau, Hans J. 1961. *Politics among Nations: The Struggle for Power and Peace*. 3d ed. New York: Alfred A. Knopf.

Mortimer, Edward. 1982. *Faith and Power: The Politics of Islam*. London: Faber and Faber.

Mottahedeh, Roy. 1985. *The Mantle of the Prophet: Religion and Politics in Iran*. New York: Simon and Schuster.

Moussalli, Ahmad S. 1992. *Radical Islamic Fundamentalism: The Ideological and Political Discourse of Sayyid Qutb*. Beirut: American University of Beirut.

Moussavi, Ahmad Kazemi. 1992. "A New Interpretation of the Theory of Vilayat-i Faqih." *Middle Eastern Studies* 28, no. 1 (January): 101–7.

Moynihan, Daniel Patrick. 1993. *Pandaemonium: Ethnicity in International Politics*. New York and Oxford: Oxford University Press.

Mumtaz, Khawar, and Farida Shaheed. 1987. *Women of Pakistan: Two Steps Forward, One Step Back?* Lahore: Vanguard Books.

Munson, Henry, Jr. 1991. "Morocco's Fundamentalists." *Government and Opposition* 26, no. 3 (summer): 331–44.

———. 1993. *Religion and Politics in Morocco*. New Haven and London: Yale University Press.

Muslim Parliament of Great Britain. 1992. "Inauguration, 4 January 1992." London: Steering Committee, Muslim Parliament. Leaflet.

Muslim World League Journal. 1994. 21, no. 11 (May).

Mutalib, Hussin. 1990. *Islam and Ethnicity in Malay Politics*. Singapore: Oxford University Press.

al-Nabahani, Taqi al-Din. 1953a. *Mafahim Hizb al-Tahrir* [Concepts of the Liberation Party]. 3d ed. Jerusalem: Hizb al-Tahrir al-Islami.

———. 1953b. *Nizam al-Islam* [The Order of Islam]. 6th ed. Jerusalem: Hizb al-Tahrir.

"Nadwat al-Islam fi wasaʾil al-iʿlam al-gharbi; taʾkud al-hiwar li-tashih al-mafahim al-khatiʾa [Colloquium on "Islam in the Western Media" urges dialogue for the correction of the notions of the sinner]. 1995. *Al-Sharq al-Awsat*, January 20.

al-Nafiʿ, ʿAbdallah. 1993. *Safah al-Saʿudiyya* [The bloodletter of Saudi Arabia]. [London?]: Dar al-Qasim.

Nakash, Yitzhak. 1994. *The Shiʿis of Iraq*. Princeton: Princeton University Press.

Narayan, B. K. 1982. *Pan-Islamism: Background and Prospects*. New Delhi: S. Chand.

Nasr, Seyyed Vali Reza. 1992. "Students, Islam, and Politics: Islami Jamiat-i Tulaba in Pakistan." *Middle East Journal* 46, no. 1 (winter): 59–76.

———. 1994. *The Vanguard of the Islamic Revolution; The Jamaʿ at-i Islami of Pakistan*. Berkeley and Los Angeles: University of California Press.

"Nasyid Ikhwanul Muslimin (Arab)." n.d. Nasyid an-Nadwah, no. 5. Distributed by Pustaka An-Nadwah. Terengganu, Malaysia.

"Nasyid Iran." n.d. Nasyid an-Nadwah, no. 2. Distributed by Pustaka An-Nadwah. Terengganu, Malaysia.

al-Nayhum, Sadiq. 1994. *al-Islam didd al-Islam* [Islam against Islam]. London and Beirut: Riyad El-Rayyes Books.

"Nearer, my God, to Theocracy." 1992. *Economist*, September 5–11, pp. 38, 43.

Nettler, Ronald L. 1987. *Past Trials and Present Tribulations: A Muslim Funda-mentalist's View of the Jews.* Oxford and New York: Pergamon Press.

"New Saudi Rights Panel Sparks ICHR-GAP Drive." 1993. *Arabia Monitor* 2, no. 6 (June): 1.

Nicholson, Linda J. 1992. "Feminist Theory: The Private and the Public." In *Defining Women: Social Institutions and Gender Divisions,* edited by Linda McDowell and Rosemary Pringle, pp. 36–43. Cambridge: Polity Press.

Nielsen, Jörgen. 1992. *Muslims in Western Europe.* Edinburgh: Edinburgh University Press.

Nigeria, Federal Government of. 1981. *Report of Tribunal of Inquiry on Kano Disturbances.* Lagos: Federal Government Press.

Norris, H. T. 1993. *Islam in the Balkans: Religion and Society between Europe and the Arab World.* London: Hurst and Company.

Norton, Augustus Richard. 1987. *Amal and the Shiʿa: Struggle for the Soul of Lebanon.* Austin: University of Texas Press.

——. 1993. "The Future of Civil Society in the Middle East." *Middle East Journal* 47, no. 2 (spring): 205–16.

——, ed. 1995a. *Civil Society in the Middle East.* Vol. 1. Leiden: E. J. Brill.

——, ed. 1995b. *Civil Society in the Middle East.* Vol. 2. Leiden: E. J. Brill.

Novossyolov, Dimitri B. 1993. "The Islamization of Welfare in Pakistan." In *Russia's Muslim Frontiers: New Directions in Cross-Cultural Analysis,* edited by Dale F. Eickelman, pp. 160–74. Bloomington: Indiana University Press.

Nurcî, Saîd. 1985a. *The Miracles of Muhammad.* Translated from the Turkish by Ümit Şimşek. Istanbul: Yeni Asya Yanınları.

——. 1985b. *Belief and Man.* Translated from the Turkish by Ümit Şimşek. Istanbul: Yeni Asya Yanınları.

——. 1985c. *Resurrection and the Hereafter.* Translated from the Turkish by Hamid Algar. Istanbul: Yeni Asya Yanınları.

——. 1985d. *Nature: Cause or Effect?* Translated from the Turkish by Ümit Şimşek. Istanbul: Yeni Asya Yanınları.

Nuri, Shaykh Fadlullah. 1982. "Refutation of the Idea of Constitutionalism." In *Islam in Transition: Muslim Perspectives,* edited by John J. Donohue and John L. Esposito, pp. 292–96. New York: Oxford University Press.

O'Brien, Donal B. Cruise. 1971. *The Mourides of Senegal.* Oxford: Clarendon Press.

——. 1975. *Saints and Politicians: Essays in the Organization of a Senegalese Peasant Society.* London: Cambridge University Press.

——. 1988. "Charisma Comes to Town: Mouride Urbanization, 1945–1986." In *Charisma and Brotherhood in African Islam,* edited by Donal B. Cruise O'Brien and Christian Coulon, pp. 135–55. Oxford: Clarendon Press.

Oliver, Ben. 1994. "Fundamental Questions of Hate." *The Times Higher Education Supplement* (London), February 25, p. 8.

Oman, Sultanate of; Development Council, Technical Secretariat. 1979–89. *Statistical Year Books, 1979–1989.* Muscat: Directorate General of National Statistics.

Omran, Abdel R., and Farzaneh Roudi. 1993. "The Middle East Population Puzzle," *Population Bulletin* 48, no. 1 (July): 2–40.

Ong, Aihwa. 1990. "State versus Islam: Malay Families, Women's Bodies, and the Body Politic in Malaysia." *American Ethnologist* 17, no. 2 (May): 258–76.

Organization of the Islamic Conference. 1981. *Declarations and Resolutions of Heads of State and Ministers of Foreign Affairs Conferences, 1969–1981.* Jidda: Organization of the Islamic Conference.

Ossman, Susan. 1994. *Picturing Casablanca: Portraits of Power in a Moroccan City.* Berkeley and Los Angeles: University of California Press.

Othman, Norani, ed. 1994. *Shari'a Law and the Modern Nation-State: A Malaysian Symposium.* Kuala Lumpur: Sisters in Islam.

Oxford Encyclopedia of the Modern Islamic World. 1995. Edited by John L. Esposito. New York: Oxford University Press.

Ozbudun, Ergün. 1992. "Political Structure." In *Modernization in the Middle East: The Ottoman Empire and Its Afro-Asian Successors,* edited by Cyril E. Black and L. Carl Brown, pp. 199–218. Princeton: Darwin Press.

Pakistan, Islamic Republic of. 1990. *The Constitution of the Islamic Republic of Pakistan.* Islamabad: Federal Judiciary Board.

Parsons, Talcott. [1963] 1986. "Power and the Social System." In *Power,* edited by Steven Lukes, pp. 94–143. Oxford: Blackwell.

Parsons, Talcott, and Robert F. Bales. 1955. *Family, Socialization, and Interaction Process.* Glencoe: Free Press.

Patel, Rashida. 1986. *Islamisation of Laws in Pakistan.* Karachi: Faiza Publishers.

Peirce, Leslie P. 1993. *The Imperial Harem: Women and Sovereignty in the Ottoman Empire.* New York and Oxford: Oxford University Press.

Pekonen, Kyösti. 1989. "Symbols and Politics as Culture in the Modern Situation: The Problem and Prospects of the 'New.'" In *Contemporary Political Culture: Politics in a Postmodern World,* edited by John R. Gibbins, pp. 127–43. London: Sage Publications.

Peterson, M. J. 1992. "Transnational Activity, International Society, and World Politics." *Millennium: Journal of International Studies* 21, no. 3 (winter): 371–88.

Philip, Bruno. 1993. "Taslima Nasreen, romancière maudite du Bangladesh." *Le Monde,* December 30, pp. 1, 4.

Philips, Anne. 1991. *Engendering Democracy.* Cambridge: Polity Press.

Piscatori, James P. 1983a. "Ideological Politics in Sa'udi Arabia." In *Islam in the Political Process,* edited by James P. Piscatori, pp. 56–72. Cambridge: Cambridge University Press.

———, ed. 1983b. *Islam in the Political Process.* Cambridge: Cambridge University Press.

———. 1986. *Islam in a World of Nation-States.* Cambridge: Cambridge University Press.

———. 1987. "Asian Islam: International Linkages and Their Impact on International Relations." In *Islam in Asia: Religion, Politics, and Society,* edited by John L. Esposito, pp. 230–61. New York: Oxford University Press.

———. 1989. "The Shia of Lebanon and Hizbullah, the Party of God." In *Politics of the Future: The Role of Social Movements,* edited by Christine Jennett and Randal G. Stewart, pp. 292–320. Melbourne: Macmillan.

———. 1990. "The Rushdie Affair and the Politics of Ambiguity." *International Affairs* 66, no. 4 (fall): 767–89.

Pitchford, Ruth. 1991. "Pakistan Tribal Hunt for Rapists." *Independent* (London), December 21, p. 11.

"PLO Group Wins Student Elections in West Bank." 1994. Reuters World Service, June 8.

Polonskaya, Ludmilla, and Alexei Malashenko. 1994. *Islam in Central Asia.* Reading: Ithaca Press.

Pope, Hugh. 1993. "Turks Call for Arms from Islamic Nations." *Independent* (London), January 12, p. 8.

Popovic, Alexandre. 1986. *L'Islam balkanique: Les Musulmans du sud-est européen dans la période post-Ottomane.* Vol. 11. Berlin: Osteuropa Institut an der Freien Universität Balkanologische Veröffentlichungen.

Population Reference Bureau. 1993. *World Population Data Sheet, 1993.* Washington, D.C.: Population Reference Bureau.

Prusher, Ilene. 1993. "Palestinian Student Polls Considered as Referendum." United Press International, November 24.

Public Enemy. 1988. "It Takes a Nation of Millions to Hold Us Back." New York: CBS. Audiocassette.

Putnam, Robert D. 1993. *Making Democracy Work: Civic Traditions in Modern Italy.* Princeton: Princeton University Press.

al-Qadhdhafi, Muʿammar. 1985. Interview, *al-Safir* (Beirut), March 21, pp. 8–9. In *FBIS-MEA*, March 29, p. Q3.

Qurashi, M. M. 1989. "The Tabligh Movement: Some Observations." *Islamic Studies* 28, no. 3 (autumn): 237–48.

Qutb, Sayyid. 1981. *Maʿalim fi-l-tariq* [Signposts]. Cairo: Dar al-Shuruq.

———. 1985. *Fi-Zilal al-Qurʾan* [In the shade of the Qurʾan]. Vol. 3. Beirut: Dar al-Shuruq.

Rabinovitch, Dina. 1992. "Lifting the Veil from Islamic Britain." *Independent* (London), January 7.

"Radical Palestinian Groups Hail Election Results." 1993. Reuter Library Report, November 25.

Rahman, Fazlur. 1982. *Islam and Modernity: Transformation of an Intellectual Tradition.* Chicago: University of Chicago Press.

Rajaee, Farhang. 1983. *Islamic Values and World View: Khomeyni on Man, the State, and International Politics.* Lanham, Md.: University Press of America.

Ramadan, Wafik. 1993. "Toujane al-Fayçal: La Modernité face à l'obscurantisme." *Arabies*, no. 84 (December): 7.

Rashid, Ahmad. 1991a. "Rape Scandal Rocks Pakistan." *Independent* (London), December 29, p. 14.

———. 1991b. "Backward Tajikistan Moves toward Islamic Future." *Independent* (London), December 30, p. 8.

Raufer, Xavier. 1994. "Islamisme, Capital Londres." *L'Express*, August 11–17, pp. 18–19.

al-Rayyes, Riad. 1995. "The Islamic 'Inquisition' Comes to Lebanon." *Mideast Mirror*, January 30, pp. 15–20.

Reagan, Ronald. 1990. *An American Life.* New York: Simon and Schuster.

"Recevant des deleguées d'associations feminines." 1993. *Al Bayane* (Casablanca), May 3, p. 9.

Reichmuth, Stefan. 1993. "Islamic Learning and Its Interaction with 'Western' Education in Ilorin, Nigeria." In *Muslim Identity and Social Change in Sub-Saharan Africa*, edited by Louis Brenner, pp. 179–97. Bloomington and Indianapolis: Indiana University Press.

"A Religious Backlash: Conservative Clerics Target Women and NGOs." 1994. *Asiaweek* 20, no. 43 (October 26): 30.

Rezette, Robert. 1955. *Les partis politiques marocains*. Paris: Librairie Armand Colin.

Richard, Yann. 1991. *L'Islam chiʿite: Croyances et idéologies*. Paris: Fayard.

Rida, Muhammad Rashid. 1934/A.H. 1352. *Al-Khilafa aw al-Imama al-Uzma* [The caliphate or the great imamate]. Cairo: Matbaʿat al-Manar bi-Misr.

Robertson, Roland, and JoAnn Chirico. 1985. "Humanity, Globalization, and Worldwide Religious Resurgence: A Theoretical Exploration." *Sociological Analysis* 46, no. 3: 219–42.

Robinson, Francis. 1993. "Technology and Religious Change: Islam and the Impact of Print." *Modern Asian Studies* 27, no. 1: 229–51.

Rogers, Susan Carol. 1975. "Female Forms of Power and the Myth of Male Dominance." *American Ethnologist* 2, no. 4 (November) 727–56.

Rosario, Santi. 1992. *Purity and Communal Boundaries: Women and Social Change in a Bangladesh Village*. London: Zed Books.

Rosenthal, Erwin I. J. 1965. *Islam in the Modern National State*. Cambridge: Cambridge University Press.

Rouadjia, Ahmed. 1990. *Les frères et la mosquée: Enquête sur le mouvement islamiste en Algérie*. Paris: Karthala.

Roy, Olivier. [1985] 1990. *Islam and Resistance in Afghanistan*. 2d ed. New York: Cambridge University Press.

———. 1992. *L'Échec de l'Islam politique*. Paris: Éditions du Seuil.

———. 1994. *The Failure of Political Islam*. Translated by Carol Volk. Cambridge: Harvard University Press.

Royal Mail International. 1993. *RMI International Service Guide*. London: Royal Mail International.

Rubin, Barnett R. 1995. *The Fragmentation of Afghanistan: State Formation and Collapse in the International System*. New Haven: Yale University Press.

Ruthven, Malise. 1990. *A Satanic Affair: Salman Rushdie and the Rage of Islam*. London: Chatto and Windus.

Sabat, Khalil. 1989. "Le Livre imprimé en Égypte." In *Le livre arabe et l'édition en Égypte*, edited by Yves Gonzalez-Quijano. *Bulletin du CEDEJ*, no. 25 (1st semester): 13–20.

Sachedina, A. A. 1988. *The Just Ruler in Shiʿite Islam: The Comprehensive Authority of the Jurist in Imamate Jurisprudence*. New York and Oxford: Oxford University Press.

el-Sadat, Anwar. 1957. *Revolt on the Nile*. Translated by Thomas Graham. London: Allan Wingate.

Sadowski, Yahya. 1993. "The New Orientalism and the Democracy Debate." *Middle East Report*, 23, no. 4 (July-August): 14–21, 40.

Sage, Adam. 1994. "Arms Shipments Put France on Islamic Hit List." *Times* (London), December 26, p. 8.

Sakamoto, Yoshikazu. 1975. "Toward Global Identity." In *On the Creation of a Just World Order: Preferred Worlds for the 1990s,* edited by Saul H. Mendlovitz. New York: Free Press.

Salamé, Ghassan, ed. 1994. *Democracy without Democrats? The Renewal of Politics in the Muslim World.* New York: I. B. Tauris.

Sammam, Muhammad. 1982. *Hasan al-Banna: al-Rajul wa-l-fikra* [Hasan al-Banna: The man and the thought]. Tunis: Dar Bu Salama.

Samuel, Raphael, and Paul Thompson. 1990. "Introduction." In *The Myths We Live By,* edited by Raphael Samuel and Paul Thompson, pp. 1–22. London: Routledge.

"Saudi Arabia Bans All Satellite Dishes." 1994. *Independent* (London), June 29, p. 12.

Saudi Arabia, Kingdom of. 1992. "Nusus al-anzima al-jadida li-"hukm" wa-l-"shura" wa-l-"manatiq" fi-l-saʿudiyya" [Texts of the new system of "governance," "consultation," and "regions" in Saudi Arabia]. *Al-Sharq al-Awsat,* March 2, pp. 4–6.

Scarritt, James R. 1972. *Political Development and Culture Change Theory.* Beverly Hills: Sage.

Schatzberg, Michael. 1988. *The Dialectics of Oppression in Zaire.* Bloomington and London: Indiana University Press.

Schimmel, Annemarie. 1975. *Mystical Dimensions of Islam.* Chapel Hill: University of North Carolina Press.

Schirazi, Asghar. 1993. *Islamic Development Policy: The Agrarian Question in Iran.* Translated by P. J. Ziess-Lawrence. Boulder: Lynne Rienner.

Schneider, David M., and Raymond T. Smith. 1973. *Class Differences and Sex Roles in American Kinship and Family Structure.* Englewood Cliffs: Prentice-Hall.

Scholte, Jan Aart. 1993. *International Relations of Social Change.* Buckingham: Open University Press.

"School Backs Down in Scarf Battle." 1990. *Today* (London), January 24, pp. 1, 12–13.

Schulze, Reinhard. 1990. *Islamischer Internationalismus im 20, Jahrundert Untersuchungen zur Geschichte der Islamischen Weltliga.* Leiden: E. J. Brill.

Schwarz, Adam. 1992a. "Islam and Democracy: Muslim Leader Warns Curbs May Backfire." *Far Eastern Economic Review,* March 19, p. 32.

———. 1992b. "Charismatic Enigma: Foes Call Muslim Leader Wahid 'Zionist' and 'Christian.'" *Far Eastern Economic Review,* November 12, pp. 34–36.

Scott, James C. 1985. *Weapons of the Weak: Everyday Forms of Peasant Resistance.* New Haven: Yale University Press.

———. 1990. *Domination and the Arts of Resistance: Hidden Transcripts.* New Haven: Yale University Press.

———. 1992. "Domination, Acting, and Fantasy." In *The Paths to Domination, Resistance, and Terror,* edited by Carolyn Nordstrom and JoAnn Martin, pp. 55–84. Berkeley and Los Angeles: University of California Press.

"al-Saʿudiyya ʿadad al-mawqufin 110 akshkhas wa-la tahawun maʿ ay ikhlal aw ʿabath bi-l-aman" [Saudi Arabia: 110 Persons Arrested; Neither Neglect of Any Transgression nor Trifling with Security] 1994. *al-Hayat* (London), September 27, pp. 1, 4.

Seale, Patrick. 1990. *Asad: The Struggle for the Middle East*. Berkeley and Los Angeles: University of California Press.

"Secretary-General's Letter." 1994. *Muslim World* 31, no. 47: 1.

Shahabuddin, Syed. 1994. "Population of India in Percentage from the Year 1881 to 1991, Religion-wise, According to Census Reports." *Muslim India*, no. 140 (August): 358.

Shaheed, Farida. 1994. "Controlled or Autonomous: Identity and the Experience of the Network, Women Living under Muslim Laws." *Signs* 19, no. 4 (summer): 997–1012.

Shaheed, Farida, and Khawar Mumtaz. 1992. *Women's Economic Participation in Pakistan: A Status Report*. Islamabad: UNICEF Pakistan.

Shahin, Emad Eldin. 1994. "Secularism and Nationalism: The Political Discourse of ʿAbd al-Salam Yassin." In *Islam and Secularism in North Africa*, edited by John Reudy, pp. 167–86. New York: St. Martin's Press.

Shahrur, Muhammad. 1992. *al-Kitab wa-l-Qurʾan: qiraʾa muʿasira* [The Book and the Qurʾan: A contemporary reading]. Beirut: Sharikat al-Matbuʿat li-l-Tawziʿ wa-l-Nashr.

———. 1994. *Dirasat al-Islamiyya al-muʿasira fi-l-dawla wa-l-mujtamaʿa* [Contemporary Islamic studies on the state and society]. Damascus: al-Ahali li-l-Tabaʿa wa-l-Nashr wa-l-Tawziʿ.

Shapiro, Michael J., ed. 1984. *Language and Politics*. New York: New York University Press.

Sharabi, Hisham. 1988. *Neopatriarchy: A Theory of Distorted Change in Arab Society*. New York: Oxford University Press.

Shaʿrawi, Muhammad Mutawalli. n.d. *Ma yahum al-marʾa al-Muslima* [Concerning Muslim women]. Cairo: Dar al-Risala.

Shariʿati, Ali. 1979. *On the Sociology of Islam*. Translated from the Persian by Hamid Algar. Berkeley: Mizan Press.

al-Sharif, Muhamad Shakir. 1992/A.H.1412. *Haqiqat al-dimuqratiyya* [The truth about democracy]. Riyadh: Dar al-Watan li-l-Nashr.

Shils, Edward. 1981. *Tradition*. Chicago and London: University of Chicago Press.

al-Shiraʿ. [1984] n.d. *al-Harakat al-Islamiyya fi-Lubnan* [The Islamic movements in Lebanon]. Beirut: Dar al-Sanin.

Shryock, Andrew J. 1994. In press. *Nationalism and the Genealogical Imagination: Oral History and Textual Authority in Tribal Jordan*. Berkeley and Los Angeles: University of California Press.

Siddiqui, Kalim. 1990. "Generating Power without Politics." Speech delivered at the conference on "The Future of Muslims in Britain," London, July 14.

———. 1992. "The Muslim Parliament of Great Britain: Political Innovation and Adaptation" (Inaugural address, January 4). London: Muslim Parliament of Great Britain.

———. 1993. "The Leader's Report: The First Year of the Muslim Parliament" (January 9). London: Muslim Parliament of Great Britain.

Simone, T. Abdou Maliqalim. 1994. *In Whose Image? Political Islam and Urban Practices in Sudan*. Chicago: University of Chicago Press.

Singerman, Diane. 1994. *Avenues of Participation: Family, Politics, and Networks in Urban Quarters of Cairo*. Princeton: Princeton University Press.

Sisters in Islam. 1991. "Are Muslim Men Allowed to Beat Their Wives?" Selangor: United Selangor Press.

Sivan, Emmanuel. 1985. *Radical Islam: Medieval Theology and Modern Politics*. New Haven and London: Yale University Press.

———. 1990a. "Symboles et rituels arabes." *Annales ESC* 45, no. 4 (July-August): 1005–17.

———. 1990b. "The Islamic Resurgence: Civil Society Strikes Back." *Journal of Contemporary History* 25, no. 3 (May-June): 353–64.

Sivan, Emmanuel, and Menachem Friedman, eds. 1990. *Religious Radicalism and Politics in the Middle East*. Albany: State University of New York Press.

Smith, Donald E. 1974. "Religion and Political Modernization: Comparative Perpsectives." In *Religion and Political Development*, edited by Donald E. Smith, pp. 3–28. New Haven: Yale University Press.

Smith, Wilfred Cantwell. 1963. *The Meaning and End of Religion: A New Approach to the Religious Traditions of Mankind*. New York: Macmillan.

So, Alvin Y. 1990. *Social Change and Development*. Newbury Park, Calif.: Sage.

Sorabji, Cornelia. 1988. "Islamic Revival and Marriage in Bosnia." *Journal [of the] Institute of Muslim Minority Affairs* 9, no. 2 (July): 331–37.

———. 1993. "Ethnic War in Bosnia?" *Radical Philosophy*, no. 63 (spring): 33–35.

Southall, Aidan. 1970. "The Illusion of Tribe." *Journal of Asian and African Studies* 5, nos. 1–2 (January-April): 28–50.

Soymen, Mehmet. 1979. *Concise Islamic Catechism*. Translated by Ihsan Ekmeleddin. Ankara: Directorate of Religious Affairs.

Soysal, Yasemin Nuhoğlu. 1994. *Limits of Citizenship: Migrants and Postnational Membership in Europe*. Chicago and London: University of Chicago Press.

Spellberg, Denise A. 1991. "Political Action and Public Example: ʿAʾisha and the Battle of the Camel." In *Women in Middle Eastern History: Shifting Boundaries in Sex and Gender*, edited by Nikki R. Keddie and Beth Baron, pp. 45–57. New Haven: Yale University Press.

Springborg, Patricia. 1992. *Western Republicanism and the Oriental Prince*. Austin: University of Texas Press.

Springborg, Robert. 1982. *Family, Power, and Poli.ics in Egypt: Sayed Bey Marei—His Clan, Clients, and Cohorts*. Philadelphia: University of Pennsylvania Press.

Sreberny-Mohammadi, Annabelle, and Ali Mohammadi. 1994. *Small Media, Big Revolution: Communication, Culture, and the Iranian Revolution*. Minneapolis: University of Minnesota Press.

Starrett, Gregory Steven. 1991. "Our Children and Our Youth: Religious Education and Political Authority in Mubarak's Egypt." Ph.D. diss., Stanford University, Department of Anthropology.

Stein, Arthur A. 1990. *Why Nations Cooperate: Circumstance and Chance in International Relations*. Ithaca: Cornell University Press.

Stein, Sylvanie. 1994. "Le Complot," *L'Express*, November 24, pp. 22–26.

"Structure, Aims of Muslim Brotherhood Detailed." 1992. *al-Musawwar*, April 3, p. 5. Reported in Foreign Broadcast Information Service, NES-92–069 (April 9, 1992), p. 9.

Subhi, Karim. 1993. "Masani' siriyya li-l-silah . . . wa-l-tujjar taht al-ard." *Rose El Yussef*, June 14, pp. 42–45.

Sulaiman, Ibraheem. 1991. *The Islamic State and the Challenge of History: Ideals, Policies, and Operation of the Sokoto Caliphate*. London: Mansell Publishing.

Sullivan, Denis J. 1994. *Private Voluntary Organizations in Egypt: Islamic Development, Private Initiative, and State Control*. Gainesville: University Press of Florida.

"Supplement: The International Muslim Khilafah Conference." 1994. *Khilafah Magazine*, August 7.

Swain, Jon, Mark Franchetti, and David Leppard. 1995. "Holy War Hijack." *Sunday Times* (London), January 1, p. 13.

"Syria and Israel: Waiting for Thursday." 1993. *Mideast Mirror*, December 6.

Taarji, Hinde. 1991. *Les voilées de l'Islam*. 2d ed. Casablanca: Éditions Eddif.

Tabandeh, Sultanhussein. 1970. *A Muslim Commentary on the Universal Declaration on Human Rights*. London: F. T. Goulding.

Tabatabai, Sassan. 1993. "Frustration with UN Response Leads Some Islamic Nations to Aid Bosnians." *Christian Science Monitor*, May 11, Internet.

Tahir, Ibrahim A. 1975. "Scholars, Sufis, Saints, and Capitalists in Kano, 1904–1974: The Pattern of Bourgeois Revolution in an Islamic Society." Ph.D. diss., University of Cambridge.

Talal ibn 'Abd al-'Aziz. [1960s] 1985. *Risala ila muwatin* [Letter to a compatriot]. Beirut: Ansar al-Dimuqratiyya fi "al-Sa'udia" [Democratic Companions in "Saudi"].

"Tales of Love for a President." 1993. *Independent* (London), December 7, p. 11.

Tapper, Nancy. 1991. *Bartered Brides: Politics, Gender, and Marriage in an Afghan Tribal Society*. Cambridge: Cambridge University Press.

Tapper, Nancy, and Richard Tapper. 1987. "The Birth of the Prophet: Ritual and Gender in Turkish Islam." *Man*, n.s., 22, no. 1 (March): 69–92.

Tapper, Richard, ed. 1991. *Islam in Modern Turkey: Religion, Politics, and Literature in a Secular State*. London: I. B. Tauris.

"Le Terrorisme intellectuel au nom de l'Islam." 1994. *Al-Bayane* (Casablanca), January 9, p. 1.

Tétreault, Mary Ann. 1993. "Civil Society in Kuwait: Protected Spaces and Women's Rights." *Middle East Journal* 47, no. 2 (spring): 275–91.

al-Thakeb, Fahed T. 1985. "The Arab Family and Modernity: Evidence from Kuwait." *Current Anthropology* 26, no. 3 (December): 575–80.

al-Turabi, Hasan. 1983. "The Islamic State." In *Voices of Resurgent Islam*, edited by John L. Esposito, pp. 241–51. New York: Oxford University Press.

―――. 1987. *Tajdid al-fikr al-Islami* [The renewal of Islamic thought]. Jidda: al-Dar al-Sa'udiyya.

―――. 1992. "Islam, Democracy, the State, and the West." *Middle East Policy* 1, no. 3: 49–61.

al-ʿUthaymayn, Muhammad ibn Salih. 1994. "al-Shaykh Muhammad al-ʿUthaymayn fi hadith ʿan nasharat al-masʿari" [Shaykh Muhammad ibn Salih al-ʿUthaymayn in a discussion about inflammatory publications]. *al-Sharq al-Awsat* (London), November 20.

van Bruinessen, Martin. 1992a. "Kurdish Society, Ethnicity, Nationalism, and Refugee Problems." In *The Kurds: A Contemporary Overview*, edited by Philip G. Kreyenbroek and Stefan Sperl, pp. 33–67. London: Routledge.

———. 1992b. *Agha, Shaikh, and State: The Social and Political Structures of Kurdistan.* London: Zed Books.

Van Dam, Nikolaos. 1981. *The Struggle for Power in Syria: Sectarianism, Regionalism, and Tribalism in Politics, 1961–1980.* London: Croom Helm.

Vatikiotis, P. J. 1987. *Islam and State.* London and New York: Croom Helm.

Vatin, Jean-Claude. 1982. "Revival in the Maghrib: Islam as an Alternative Political Language." In *Islamic Resurgence in the Arab World*, edited by Ali Hilal Dessouki, pp. 221–50. New York: Praeger.

Vergès, Meriem. 1994. "La Casbah d'Alger: Chronique de survie dans un quartier en sursis." In *Exils et royaumes: Les Appartenances au monde arabo-musulman aujourd'hui*, edited by Gilles Kepel, pp. 69–88. Paris: Presses de la Fondation Nationale des Sciences Politiques.

Villalón, Leonardo A. 1995. *Islamic Society and State Power in Senegal: Disciples and Citizens in Fatick.* Cambridge: Cambridge University Press.

von der Mehden, Fred R. 1993. *Two Worlds of Islam: Interaction between Southeast Asia and the Middle East.* Gainesville: University Press of Florida.

"WABIL Warns Muslim Immigrants of the Dangers of Western Society." 1994. *Ahlul-Bayt*, no. 18 (April): 8.

Wadud-Muhsin, Amina. 1992. *Qurʾan and Woman.* Kuala Lumpur: Penerbit Fajar Bakti Sdn. Bhd.

Wahid, Abdurrahman. 1995. Interview with James Piscatori, New York, April 19.

Walker, Christopher. 1992. "Muslims Attack Pyramid Power." *Times* (London), August 20.

———. 1993. "Saudi Human Rights Group Suppressed." *Times* (London), May 14, p. 9.

Wallerstein, Immanuel. 1983. "Crises: The World-Economy, the Movements, and the Ideologies." In *Crises in the World-System*, edited by Albert Bergesen, pp. 21–36. Beverly Hills: Sage Publications.

———. 1991. *Geopolitics and Geoculture: Essays on the Changing World System.* Cambridge: Cambridge University Press.

Walzer, Michael. 1974. *The Revolution of the Saints.* New York: Atheneum.

———. 1983. *Spheres of Justice: A Defense of Pluralism and Equality.* New York: Basic Books.

———. 1984. "Liberalism and the Art of Separation." *Political Theory* 12, no. 3 (August): 315–30.

Wang, Jianping. 1992. "Islam in Yunnan." *Journal [of the] Institute of Muslim Minority Affairs* 13, no. 2 (July): 364–74.

Warner, R. Stephen. 1992. "Work in Progress: Toward a New Paradigm for the Sociological Study of Religion in the United States." Paper delivered at the fall 1992 symposium of the Center for the Study of American Religion, Princeton.

Watt, W. Montgomery. [1968] 1980. *Islamic Political Thought: The Basic Concepts*. Islamic Surveys, no. 6. Edinburgh: Edinburgh University Press.

Waugh, Earle H. 1989. *The Munshidin of Egypt: Their Word and Their Song*. Columbia: University of South Carolina Press.

Weber, Max. 1968. *Economy and Society*. Edited by Guenther Roth and Claus Wittich. New York: Bedminster Press.

Weeks, John R. 1988. "The Demography of Islamic Nations." *Population Bulletin* 43, no. 4 (July): 4–54.

Weiner, Myron, and Samuel P. Huntington. 1987. *Understanding Political Development: An Analytic Study*. New York: HarperCollins.

Weingrod, Alex. 1990. "Saints and Shrines, Politics, and Culture: A Morocco-Israel Comparison." In *Muslim Travellers: Pilgrimage, Migration, and the Religious Imagination*, edited by Dale F. Eickelman and James Piscatori, pp. 217–35. London: Routledge; Berkeley and Los Angeles: University of California Press.

Weiss, Anita M. 1986. "Implications of the Islamization Program for Women." In *Islamic Reassertion in Pakistan: The Application of Islamic Laws in a Modern State*, edited by Anita M. Weiss, pp. 97–113. Syracuse: Syracuse University Press.

Wells, Steven. 1990. "100 Per Cent Prof" [interview with Professor Griff of Public Enemy]. *New Musical Express* 31 (March): 11, 43.

Wenner, Manfred M. 1993. "National Integration and National Security: The Case of Yemen." In *The Many Faces of National Security in the Arab World*, edited by Bahgat Korany, Paul Noble, and Rex Brynen, pp. 169–84. New York: St. Martin's Press.

"Western Women 'Are Puppets of Males.'" 1992. *Independent* (London), January 6.

Weyland, Peter. 1990. "International Muslim Networks and Islam in Singapore." *Sojourn (Social Issues in Southeast Asia)* 5, no. 2 (August): 219–54.

Wheatley, Paul. 1976. "Levels of Spatial Awareness in the Traditional Islamic City." *Ekistics* 42, no. 253 (December): 354–66.

White, Jenny B. 1995. "Islam and Democracy: The Turkish Experience." *Current History* 94, no. 1 (January): 7–12.

"al-Wihdat al-Tunisiya Newspaper Reveals the Criminal Behaviour of the Muslim Brothers' Gang against the Arab Nation." 1984. *Rissalat al-Jihad*, no. 21, June, p. 30.

"Williamson County, Texas Says No to the Apple Co. and Homosexuals." 1993. *Islamic Information and News Service* 4, no. 24-TX (December 2), Internet.

Wilson, Rodney. 1995. "Islamic Development Bank." In *Oxford Encyclopedia of the Modern Islamic World*, edited by John L. Esposito, 2:307–9. New York: Oxford University Press.

Wong, Siu-Lun. 1988. *Emigrant Entrepreneurs: Shanghai Industrialists in Hong Kong*. Hong Kong: Oxford University Press.

World Bank. 1981–89. *World Development Reports, 1981–1989*. New York: Oxford University Press.

Yamin, Nani. 1984. "The Role of the Women/Moslem Women in Indonesia." Jakarta: Lembaga Konsultasi & Bantuan Hukum Untuk Wanita & Keluarga.

Yassine, Abd Assalam. 1981. *La Révolution à l'heure de l'Islam*. Gignac-La-Nerthe: Imprimerie Borel et Feraud.

Yavuz, M. Hakan. 1993. "Nationalism and Islam: Yusuf Akçura and Üç Tarz-ı Siyaset." *Journal of Islamic Studies* 4, no. 2 (July): 175–207.

Yilmaz, Sinan. 1994. "Aczmendis Reject All Types of Armed Actions." *Turkish Daily News*, June 2, p. B1.

Yusif, Ahmad ibn. ca. 1989. *Ahmad Yasin*. Worth, Ill.: ICRS.

INDEX